THE SOUTH CHINA SEA DISPUTES

Historical, Geopolitical and Legal Studies

Series on Contemporary China

(ISSN: 1793-0847)

This series will include books on state-of-the-art developments in computational and experimental methods in structures, and as such it will comprise several volumes covering the latest developments. Each volume will consist of single-authored work or several chapters written by the leading researchers in the field. The aim will be to provide the fundamental concepts of experimental and computational methods as well as their relevance to real world problems.

The scope of the series covers the entire spectrum of structures in engineering. As such it will cover both classical topics in mechanics, as well as emerging scientific and engineering disciplines, such as: smart structures, nanoscience and nanotechnology; NEMS and MEMS; micro- and nano-device modelling; functional and smart material systems.

*Published**

Vol. 42 *The South China Sea Disputes: Historical, Geopolitical and Legal Studies*
edited by Tsu-Sung Hsieh

Vol. 41 *Moralization of China*
by Xin Liu

Vol. 40 *Social Construction in Contemporary China*
edited by Xueyi Lu

Vol. 39 *China's Economic Statecraft: Co-optation, Cooperation, and Coercion*
edited by Mingjiang Li

Vol. 38 *The Domestic Dynamics of China's Energy Diplomacy*
by Chi Zhang

Vol. 37 *Understanding Chinese Society: Changes and Transformations*
by Eileen Yuk-ha Tsang

Vol. 36 *Health Policy Reform in China: A Comparative Perspective*
by Jiwei Qian & Åke Blomqvist

Vol. 35 *Township Governance and Institutionalization in China*
by Shukai Zhao

Vol. 34 *The World Turned Upside Down:*
The Complex Partnership between China and Latin America
by Alfredo Toro Hardy

*To view the complete list of the published volumes in the series, please visit:
http://www.worldscientific.com/series/scc

Series on Contemporary China – Vol. 42

THE SOUTH CHINA SEA DISPUTES

Historical, Geopolitical and Legal Studies

Editor

Tsu-Sung Hsieh

Ming Chuan University, Taiwan

World Scientific

NEW JERSEY • LONDON • SINGAPORE • BEIJING • SHANGHAI • HONG KONG • TAIPEI • CHENNAI • TOKYO

Published by

World Scientific Publishing Co. Pte. Ltd.
5 Toh Tuck Link, Singapore 596224
USA office: 27 Warren Street, Suite 401-402, Hackensack, NJ 07601
UK office: 57 Shelton Street, Covent Garden, London WC2H 9HE

Library of Congress Cataloging-in-Publication Data
Names: Hsieh, Tsu-Sung.
Title: The South China Sea disputes : historical, geopolitical and legal studies /
edited by Tsu-Sung Hsieh (Ming Chuan University, Taiwan).
Description: New Jersey : World Scientific, 2018. | Series: Contemporary China ; Volume 42 |
Includes bibliographical references.
Identifiers: LCCN 2017053359 | ISBN 9789813234888 (hc : alk. paper)
Subjects: LCSH: South China Sea--International status. | Taiwan--Foreign relations.
Classification: LCC KZA1692 .S674 2018 | DDC 341.4/20959--dc23
LC record available at https://lccn.loc.gov/2017053359

British Library Cataloguing-in-Publication Data
A catalogue record for this book is available from the British Library.

For any available supplementary material, please visit
http://www.worldscientific.com/worldscibooks/10.1142/10845#t=suppl

Desk Editors: Chandrima Maitra/Dong Lixi

Typeset by Stallion Press
Email: enquiries@stallionpress.com

Preface

The South China Sea Disputes — Historical, Geopolitical, and Legal Studies is a book covering various issues from different perspectives regarding the currently controversial theme of the South China Sea (SCS) disputes. This book contains chapters from scholars who participated in the "2017 South China Sea Conference," organized by Ming Chuan University, Republic of China (Taiwan), at Taipei on June 1, 2017.

Scholars in that conference are mostly from Taiwan, but there also scholars from Peoples' Republic of China (mainland China), the Philippines, Australia, and the US. They provided wonderful insights through panel presentations and roundtable discussion. This is one of the few conferences where the opinions of SCS issues can be heard from the perspective of Taiwan and also jointly and separately from the other side of the Taiwan Strait and the other parts of the world. Owing to its diversity, this book is divided into three sections: the historical, the geopolitical, and the legal one.

Part I contains four chapters. Professor Lin illustrates certain important but currently neglected treaties for SCS, e.g., San Francisco Peace Treaty, Taipei Treaty, and Cairo Declaration, and suggests that the Taipei Treaty could be a more effective legal basis to deal with issues related to SCS. Professor Chen points out that there are solid grounds in history and international law for Chinese sovereignty over the islands in the SCS, and in particular, facts are provided to reveal the

Nationalist government's efforts to recover the Chinese sovereignty over the islands in SCS after the end of World War II. After conducting archival researches in the national archives of Taiwan, the UK, the US, and Japan, Professor Forbes reveals materials with potential for enhancing territorial and sovereignty claims. And, Professor Batongbacal traces US diplomatic correspondence and the contours of US policy on the SCS disputes in relation to the Philippine claim to the Kalayaan Island Group.

The geopolitical study section contains two chapters. Professor Kao specifically addresses the state practice to SCS by Taiwan and suggests that, in order to safeguard the national interests, Taiwan should seek to participate in regional negotiation and collaboration with claimant countries in the future. From another perspective, Professor Liu addresses Taiwan's evolving attitudes from thoughtful planning to perfunctory policy thereof, while the circumstances of US–China rivalry in the SCS are also discussed.

The legal study section has one chapter. I provide this chapter to include an explanation of the arbitral award of the SCS, wherein I argue that the arbitration is a non-justiciable dispute resolution. I further challenge the validity of the arbitration on the grounds that the tribunal had failed to satisfy its duty due to, *inter alia*, determining the Taiping Island (Itu Aba) as a rock based solely on indirect evidences.

I appreciate the participating of these scholars in this conference. Without their excellent contributions, this conference would not have been held and this book not published.

Tsu-sung Hsieh
Professor, School of Law, Ming Chuan University
Shilin District, Taipei, Taiwan

About the Authors

Man-houng Lin received her education mainly in Taiwan and obtained her Ph.D. in History and East Asian Languages from Harvard University in 1989. Lin has been a Senior Research Fellow at the Institute of Modern History, Academia Sinica since 1990 and Professor at the Department of History, National Taiwan Normal University since 1991. Lin's main area of research focuses on treaty ports and modern China, native opium of late Qing China, currency crisis and early 19th-century China, and Taiwanese merchants' overseas economic networks in 1895–1945. She has published 4 books and about 80 papers in Chinese, English, Japanese and Korean in the abovementioned areas. Her book, *China Upside Down: Currency, Society and Ideologies, 1808–1856* (Harvard East Asian Series, 2006) links China's topsy-turvy change from the center of the East Asian order to its modern tragedy with the Latin American Independence Movement. From May 20, 2008 to December 16, 2010, she served as the President of the Republic of China's Academia Historica (State History Academy). Then, she returned to Academia Sinica to finish her project on *Pacificbound: The Rise of the Taiwanese Merchants in the Asia-Pacific Commercial Network, 1895–1945.* It was during the research of this project that Lin encountered the Taipei Treaty signed in 1952 and appreciated its significance.

Jay L. Batongbacal is a lawyer from the Philippines with a master's degree in Marine Management and a doctorate in Science of Law, both from Dalhousie University in Canada. Since 1997, he has done diverse work in maritime affairs, including community-based fisheries management, coastal resource management, marine environment protection, maritime boundaries, high seas fishing, offshore energy, seafaring, and shipping. He was a legal advisor to the Philippine delegation that successfully pursued the Philippines' claim to a continental shelf beyond 200 nautical miles in the Benham Rise Region before the Commission on the Limits of the Continental Shelf. He is also among the List of Experts on Marine Scientific Research for purposes of Special Arbitration under Annex VIII of the UNCLOS. He completed post-doctoral research on the US maritime security policy and the South China Sea disputes under the auspices of the US-ASEAN Fulbright Initiative Visiting Scholar Program. He most recently assisted the Philippines in securing the International Maritime Organization's designation of the Tubbataha Reef Natural Park in the Sulu Sea as a Particularly Sensitive Sea Area. He is regularly consulted for his independent views on maritime policy issues by government officials, diplomatic personnel, the press, and members of the academia. Currently, he serves as an associate professor at the University of the Philippines College of Law and is concurrently the Director of the Institute for Maritime Affairs and Law of the Sea of the U.P. Law Center.

Chen Qianping was born on February 10, 1955 in Nanjing. He earned his graduate degree from the Department of History, Nanjing University, in 1982, and his Ph.D. degree from Nanjing University in 2001. He is a special term professor at Nanjing University. He is the chairman of academic board of the Research Center for the History of Republic of China of Nanjing University.

His research field covers the political and diplomatic history of Republican area. He is a specialist in Sino-Western relations during the Republican period. He has published numerous books and articles in China and abroad. He is the author of *The Sino-British Negotiations on Tibet around Anti-Japanese War* (*Kangzhan Qianhou Zhi Zhongying*

Xizang Jiaoshe, 2003), *History Essay on the Foreign Relations During the Republican Period* (*Minguo Duiwai Guanxi Shilun*, 2013), *The Frontal Battlefield of China* (*Zhongguo Zhengmian Zhangchang*, 2015), and *History of a Century of Tibet* (*Xizang Bainianshi Yanjiu*, 2015). He is also the chief author of *The History of Anti-Japanese War of China, 1931–1945* (*Zhongguo Kangri Zhangzheng Shi*, 2016).

Vivian Louis Forbes is an adjunct research professor at the National Institute for South China Sea Studies, Haikou, and a distinguished research fellow and a guest professor at CIBOS and CICTSMR, Wuhan University, Wuhan, PRC. He has affiliations with many other institutions. He is a marine political geographer, a professional cartographer, and a former Merchant Naval Officer. He is an author of atlases, a number of books, chapters in books, and journals, and he has been consulted on matters pertaining to maritime and terrestrial boundaries delimitation. He has presented seminars and workshops on maritime boundary determination and archival research issues at numerous institutions. During 2017, he was involved in the publication of three books, numerous journal articles, and conference and research papers and presented workshops in his own right in many countries.

Tsu-Sung Hsieh is a professor at the School of Law, Ming Chuan University, Taiwan, ROC. He obtained his Juris Doctor and Master of Intellectual Property from the University of New Hampshire, Master of Science from the United States Naval Postgraduate School, and Bachelor of Science from the ROC Naval Academy. Prior to joining the Ming Chuan University, he was the dean of Humanity and Social College, and the director of Department of Law, Kainan University, Taiwan, ROC. His publications have appeared in various law journals covering topics mostly related to patent law, and he is a registered patent attorney of ROC. As a retired navy captain, naval history and maritime issues are also his areas of research interest.

Mulan-Lan Kao is an attorney-at-law since 1997, and an adjunct assistant professor in the College of Law at Ming Chuan University of the Republic of China (Taiwan). She obtained her Ph.D. degree in Laws from the Institute of the Law of the Sea at the National Taiwan Ocean University. She is also a participant of the International Foundation for the Law of the Sea (IFLOS) Summer Academy 2015 in Hamburg, Germany. Her research interests include international laws, maritime security, and maritime disputes in the East and South China Seas.

Dr. Nathan Kuanghua Liu earned his Ph.D. degree from the Department of Political Science, Northwestern University in December 1999. He is also a retired navy captain and served as the director of the Publishing & Research Office, National Defense University, from 2002 to 2004.

In August 2004, he retired from the military and took on a full-time teaching position in the Applied English Department, Ming Chuan University (MCU). In August 2006, he was appointed as MCU's first director of the Teaching Chinese as a Second Language Department (TCSL). He was the Deputy Director of International Education and Exchange Division (IEE/MCU) from 2007 to 2014 and was promoted to the Executive Director of Mainland China Education and Exchange Division (MCEE/MCU) in 2014. He has been appointed as the Executive Director of IEE since April 2017 when he completed his term in MCEE. He is currently a full-time associate professor and is concurrently the Director of International Affairs Master's/Diplomacy Bachelor's Program at MCU.

His major interests include global governance, Asia-Pacific studies, Cross-Strait issues, and strategic and defense policy issues. In addition, he is also an interpreter with a practical experience of 12 years.

Contents

Chapter 1

A Neglected Treaty for the South China Sea

Man-houng Lin

Institute of Modern History, Academia Sinica, Taipei, Taiwan

Abstract

Based upon the Republic of China's (ROC) Ministry of Foreign Affairs (MOFA) archives, United Nations' Treaty Series, Japanese wartime archives collected in Japan's Asia Historical Material Center, publications collected by pre-1945 Taiwan Governor-General Office's Library, and related studies, this chapter points out how the Taipei Treaty (TPT) could be a more effective legal basis to achieve the goal of Hague Arbitration (HA) of July 12, 2016.

Keywords: Asia-Pacific history, Hu Qingyu, South China Sea, sovereignty, strategic importance, Taipei treaty.

Introduction

Stein Tønnesson deems that there is no target for Japan's renunciation of Spratly Islands and Paracel Islands (S&P) in Article 2 of the San Francisco Peace Treaty (SFPT), which is the root cause of the current South China Sea (SCS) controversy.[1] This chapter points out that there is the Taipei Treaty (TPT), a sequel to the SFPT, to settle the sovereignty issue of S&P while these islands constitute the main part of the SCS. This chapter discusses (1) How the handling of S&P as stipulated in Article 2 of the TPT was framed; (2) Why was the Japanese renunciation of S&P exactly targeted at the ROC in Taiwan; and (3) How this treaty could be a more effective legal basis to achieve the goal of HA.

Process to Have TPT after SFPT

The ROC joined the preparatory meetings for postwar peace treaty with Japan since 1947. With more and more intensified conflict between the USSR and the US, about the handling of Taiwan, the exercise of veto right, and the participation of the People's Republic of China (PRC) in the peace treaty, the peace treaty was not realized before 1950. The making of the PRC–USSR Friendship, Alliance and Mutual Assistance Treaty on February 14, 1950 would be hostile to Japan when Japan cooperates with the capitalist countries. On the other hand, the US has planned to have a mutual security treaty with Japan. The outbreak of the Korean War on June 25, 1950, lessened the hostility of Asian and Australasian countries such as Australia, India, and the Philippines toward Japan and speeded up the peace treaty talk to be held at San Francisco.[2]

From October 20, 1950 to June 2, 1951, John Foster Dulles, US President Truman's adviser for SFPT, was in contact with Wellington Koo, the ROC ambassador at US, for SFPT. From June 2, 1951 to July 12, 1951, Dulles visited the UK. The UK opposed the ROC's

[1] Stein Tønnesson, The South China Sea in the age of European decline, *Modern Asian Studies,* vol. 40, no. I (February 2006), pp. 41, 48.

[2] Institute of Modern History, *Zhu Ri daibiaotuan dian waijiaobu Mei fujiang jiji tuijin duiRi heyue* 駐日代表團電外交部美復將積極推進對日和約 [Telegram of Chinese mission in Japan to the Ministry of Foreign Affairs for the enthusiastic move by the US for the peace treaty with Japan], in DuiRi heyue 對日和約 [*China–Japan Peace Treaty*], Archives of the Ministry of Foreign Affairs of the ROC, the Institute of Modern History, Academia Sinica, File no. 11-01-02-10-03-035.

attendance at the SFPT conference but agreed to have Articles 4 and 26 in the SFPT to prepare for the ROC's separate bilateral treaty with Japan.[3]

From July 12, 1951 to February 28, 1952, Karl L. Rankin, the US Chargé d'Affaires at the ROC contacted George Yeh, the ROC Minister of Foreign Affairs, to make preparations for the TPT at Taipei. The counterpart on the Japanese side was Yoshida Shigeru, who kept contact with Dulles. The TPT was negotiated between March 1, 1952 and April 28, 1952, but it was signed on a later date. The SFPT was signed on September 8, 1951 and did not come into force until the conclusion of the TPT on April 28, 1952, an intentional arrangement of the parties concerned. From April 28, 1952 to August 5, 1952 was the period from signature to ratifications done by Japan and the ROC, and to the coming into force of the TPT. Japan's domestic legislative approval took place on June 7, July 5, July 8, and July 9, respectively, by the Lower House, Upper House, cabinet, and the emperor. The ROC's domestic legislative approval took place on April 30, July 31, and August 2, respectively, by the Executive Yuan, the Legislative Yuan, and the president. The ROC Consulate in Japanese colonial Taiwan, 1931–1938, became Japan's embassy at the ROC on August 5, 1952 when the TPT came into force. Article 102 in Chapter 16 of the UN Charter recognizes only treaties registered at the UN. The TPT was registered at the UN on September 25, 1952 (Figure 1).[4]

[3] Institute of Modern History, *Waijiaobu duiRi heyuean banli jingguo jieyao* 外交部對日和約案辦理經過節要 [Summary prepared by the Ministry of Foreign Affairs of the handling process of China–Japan Peace Treaty], in DuiRi heyue 對日和約 [*China-Japan Peace Treaty*], Archives of the Ministry of Foreign Affairs of the ROC, the Institute of Modern History, Academia Sinica, File no. 11-01-02-10-03-063; *Guweijun huiyilu* 顧維鈞回憶錄 [*Ku Weijun Memoirs*], tr. by Chinese Academy of Social Sciences (Beijing: Chung Hwa Book Company, 1989), pp. 180–181.

[4] Man-houng Lin, Taiwan's sovereignty status: The neglected Taipei treaty, in Kimie Hara, ed., *The San Francisco System and Its Legacies: Continuation, Transformation, and Historical Reconciliation in the Asia-Pacific* (London and New York: Routledge, 2015), pp. 115–143.

No. 1858

CHINA
and
JAPAN

Treaty of Peace (with protocol, exchange of notes and agreed minutes). Signed at Taipei, on 28 April 1952

Official texts: Chinese, English and Japanese.
Registered by China on 25 September 1952.

CHINE
et
JAPON

Traité de paix (avec protocole, échange de notes et procès-verbaux approuvés). Signé à Taïpeï, le 28 avril 1952

Textes officiels chinois, anglais et japonais.
Enregistré par la Chine le 25 septembre 1952.

Figure 1. The TPT registered at the UN.
Source: https://treaties.un.org/doc/Publication/UNTS/Volume%20138/v138.pdf (accessed on January 9, 2012).

Process to Put S&P in the SFPT and the TPT

The Cairo Declaration required Japan to give up all Pacific islands that she had taken since 1914. The Cairo Declaration was succeeded by the Potsdam Declaration and the Japanese Surrender Instrument. When the SFPT was being negotiated, France initiated the move to ask Japan to renounce S&P. The UK and the US endorsed it and had

S&P written in Article 2 of the SFPT.[5] For S&P in the SCS, Japan renounced them in Chapter II of the SFPT entitled "TERRITORY."[6] It means that the SFPT acknowledges that S&P were Japanese territories obtained from war.

To legitimize the land won in war, before the formation of the UN, a legal war declaration process had to be followed. War declaration is the starting point of war status among countries. Peace treaty is the end of this status. Article 1 of the SFPT and Article 1 of the TPT both point out the end of war status with the entering into force of the said peace treaties. In the Anti-Japanese War period, it can be justified that the more Japanese you kill, the more you could be awarded. With the peace treaty, however, the more Japanese you kill, the more you would sit in the jail.[7] The war and treaty process also applies to the situation for the US territory. From independence to obtaining California or Hawaii, many US territories went through war and treaties.[8] For the sovereignty over islands and rocks, without treaties to determine the sovereignty, first discovery and effective rule would both count. With treaties, these two factors are still significant but not sufficient enough to claim sovereignty. This is the reason why the US could not explicitly say Senkaku Islands belong to Japan's territory, even though Japan has administrative rights over the Islands as described in the US–Japan Mutual Security Treaty.[9]

---

[5] Kimie Hara, *Cold War Frontiers in the Asia-Pacific: Divided Territories in the San Francisco System* (London and New York: Routledge, 2006), pp. 5, 61–68, 148–154.

[6] For the UN version of the San Francisco Peace Treaty, see https://treaties.un.org/doc/Publication/UNTS/Volume%20136/v136.pdf (accessed on October 17, 2016).

[7] Man-houng Lin, 林滿紅, Zhanzheng, heyue yu Taiwan 戰爭、和約與臺灣 [The resistance war, peace treaty and Taiwan], in Lü Fang-shang 呂芳上, ed., *Zhongguo Kanri zhanzhengshi xinbian* 中國抗日戰爭史新編 [*New History of China's War of Resistance against Japan*], Part 6: *Postwar China*, Chapter 4: The end of the hostility (Taipei: Academia Historica, 2015), pp. 465–522.

[8] For the territorial change of the US, see https://en.wikipedia.org/wiki/Territorial_evolution_of_the_United_States (accessed on February 14, 2017).

[9] Man-houng Lin, The May 26, 1971 note from the US on the Diaoyutai issue: Taiwan's sovereignty claim and the US response, in Tim F. Liao, Krista Wiegand, and

Regarding CHAPTER II of SFPT entitled "TERRITORY," its Article 2 states: Japan renounces all right, title, and claim to (a) Korea; (b) Formosa and the Pescadores; (c) the Kurile Islands and the South Sakhalin; (d) Pacific Islands under the mandate of Japan in the League of Nations; (e) the Antarctic area; and (f) the Spratly Islands and the Paracel Islands.

The ROC had influence on (a) Korea and (c) the Kurile Islands, even though the ROC did not attend the SFPT conference. On July 6, 1951, Wellington Koo sent a telegram to President Chiang Kai-shek about the draft that Foster Dulles had prepared for the SFPT. Koo forwarded Dulles' remarks that the independence of Korea and the same treatment of Kurile Islands and the South Sakhalin as Formosa and the Pescadores in the draft have been proposed by the ROC.[10] On September 1, 1947, Zheng Kangqi, the ROC ambassador in the UK pointed out in his telegram to the ROC Ministry of Foreign Affairs that all the inhabitants on the Kurile Islands were Japanese and therefore there was no reason for handing over those islands to Soviet Russia. If this was done, it would affect Chinese national security. As such, China should oppose this proposal.[11] However, talks regarding (f) the Spratly Islands and the Paracel Islands had not been initiated by the ROC. Wellington Koo sent a telegram to the Ministry of Foreign Affairs about whether to ask for the Spratly Islands in the SFPT, and Foreign Minister George Yeh

Kimie Hara, eds., *China and Japan Border Disputes: Islands of Contention in Multidisciplinary Perspective* (London: Ashgate, 2015), pp. 57–81.

[10] *Guweijundian Jiang Zhongzheng Mei Dulesi jiang dui Zi heyue gao songjiao* 顧維鈞電蔣中正美杜勒斯將對日多邊和約稿送交 [Telegram of Ku Weijun to Chiang Kaishek], in *Geming wenxian: duiRi yihe* (2) 革命文獻-對日議和（二）[*Literature of Revolution-Peace Treaty Negotiations* (2)], *Jiang Zhongzheng zongtong wenwu* 蔣中正總統文物 [*President Chiang Kai-shek Collection*], Academia Historica, Collection no. 002-020400-00054-001.

[11] *Zheng Kangqi dianjiao bu duiRi hehui Ying diguo zhubei huiyi taolun neirong* (2) 鄭康祺電交部對日和會英帝國準備會議討論內容（二）」 [Telegram of Cheng Kangqi to the Ministry of Foreign Affairs], in *DuiRi heyue* 對日和約 [*China–Japan Peace Treaty*], Archives of the Ministry of Foreign Affairs of the ROC, the Institute of Modern History, Academia Sinica, File no. 11-01-02-10-03-063.

replied about his and the Executive Yuan's negative stance so as not to be incongruent with the interest of the Philippines and France.[12]

When Article 2 of the TPT was negotiated in Taipei, the ROC prepared the treaty draft that fully copied Article 2 of the SFPT with the exception of the Kurile Islands and the South Sakhalin, with the sequence of (b) and (f) being changed to (a) and (b).

Japanese Vice Representative Kimura Shiroshichi said that if only Formosa and the Pescadores would be relevant for the TPT, then how would Korea and others be related with this TPT? However, the ROC Vice Representative Hu Qingyu pointed out that the Spratly had been subordinated to Taiwan when Taiwan was ruled by Japan and Japan had claimed "not to have occupied the Paracel." These two Islands were hence included in Article 2 of the TPT.[13] The ROC's record for "the Japanese not to have not occupied the Paracel" is inconsistent with the fact that Japan had actually occupied the Paracel from 1939 to 1945. Kimie Hara pointed out that Japan had not claimed internationally the Paracel islands as her territories as they had for the Spratly Islands. Even though Japan occupied the Paracel, Japan still asserted that these islands were the ROC's territory (p. 147).[14] Prof. Okazaki Koji went to the Japanese Diet record dated October 26, 1951 and validated the Japanese stance and inferred that the ROC record regarding "Japan had not occupied the Paracel" resulted from language misunderstanding.[15]

---

[12] *Yeh Gongchao dian Guweijun nansha qundao buying lieru gaoyue diasantiao* 葉公超電顧維鈞南沙群島不應列入約稿第三條 [Telegram of Ye Gongchao to Ku Weijun not to put the Spratly Islands in Article 3 of the SFPT], in *Dui Ri heyue* 對日和約 [*China–Japan Peace Treaty*], Archives of the Ministry of Foreign Affairs of the ROC, the Institute of Modern History, Academia Sinica, File no. 11-01-02-10-03-045.

[13] *Zhonghua minguo waijiao wenti yanjiuhui* 中華民國外交問題研究會 [Research Association for the ROC Diplomatic Issues], in *ZhongRi waijiao shiliao congbian* 中日外交史料叢編 [*Collected Series on the Historical Materials of the Diplomatic Relation between the Republic of China and Japan*], no. VIII: The relation between the SFTP and the TPT, *China–Japan Peace Treaty*, Archives of the Ministry of Foreign Affairs of the ROC, the Institute of Modern History, Academia Sinica, File no. 11-02-10-03-078, p. 53.

[14] Kimie Hara, *Cold War Frontiers*, p. 147.

[15] Prof. Okazaki Koji's letter to the present author dated June 3, 2017.

Background for Hu Qingyu's Claim that Spratly was Part of Taiwan

On September 3, 1937, Japan occupied the Pratas and the 37 coastal guard stations of the ROC on it, changed its name to Nishizawa, and put it under the Ministry of the Strategic Harbors at Magong of the Pescadores. In 1939, Japan also took over the Paracel and the Spratly Islands. Militarily, the SCS islands were directed by Makong Port Department. Pratas, Paracel, and Spratly were all administered by Takao (Gaoxiong) of Taiwan since 1939. It means that they were all under the jurisdiction of the Taiwan Governor-General Government.[16] The difference is that Spratly Island had registered inhabitants,[17] while the others did not.

On March 30, 1939, Japan integrated what it called "Shinnan Gunto" (comprising two-third of the Spratly Islands) into Takao Prefecture (today known as Kaohsiung City) through Announcement No. 122 of the Taiwan Governor-General Government.[18]

Taiwan's primary school textbooks from 1940 to 1945 taught the significance of Shinan Gunto (particularly the Taiping islands or Itu Aba) for Taiwan (Figure 2).[19] Taiwan Governor-General Government's public library held not only these textbooks but

[16] Zongjian 鍾堅, *Taiwan hangkong juezhan* 臺灣航空決戰 [*The Desperate Air Battle Over Taiwan*] (Taipei: Mitian Press, 1996), pp. 333–336.

[17] *Senkyuhyaku sanjukyunian machi, ohazabetsu koku 1939* 年町、大字別戶口 (*takaoshuu–takaoshi–heitoushi*) (高雄州--高雄市--屏東市), *Taiwan joujuu koku toukei* 台灣常住戶口統計 [*Taiwan Resident Statistics*], Taiwan sōtokufu kambou kigabu 台灣總督府官房企畫部 [The Government Planning Department, the Office of Taiwan Governor General], 1940, p. 134.

[18] Taiwan sōtokufu 臺灣總督府 [The Office of Taiwan Governor General], *Taiwan sōtokufu fuhō* 臺灣總督府府報 [*Gazette of the Office of Taiwan Governor General*], Shinnan Gunto ryouyuu koukoku 新南群島領有公告 [*Notice of the Occupation of Shinnan Gunto*], Notice no. 122, Showa 14th year (1939) March 30.

[19] W. Wenxin *et al.*, eds., *Rizhi shiqi Taiwan gong xuexiao yu guomin xuexiao Guoyu duben* 日治時期臺灣公學校與國民學校國語讀本 [*National Language Textbook for Taiwanese Public Schools and National Schools during the Japanese Colonial Period*], no. 4 (Taipei: Nantian Book Company, November 2013, reprinted according to the collection items held by Mr. Yang Yongbin), vol. 8, pp. 120–128.

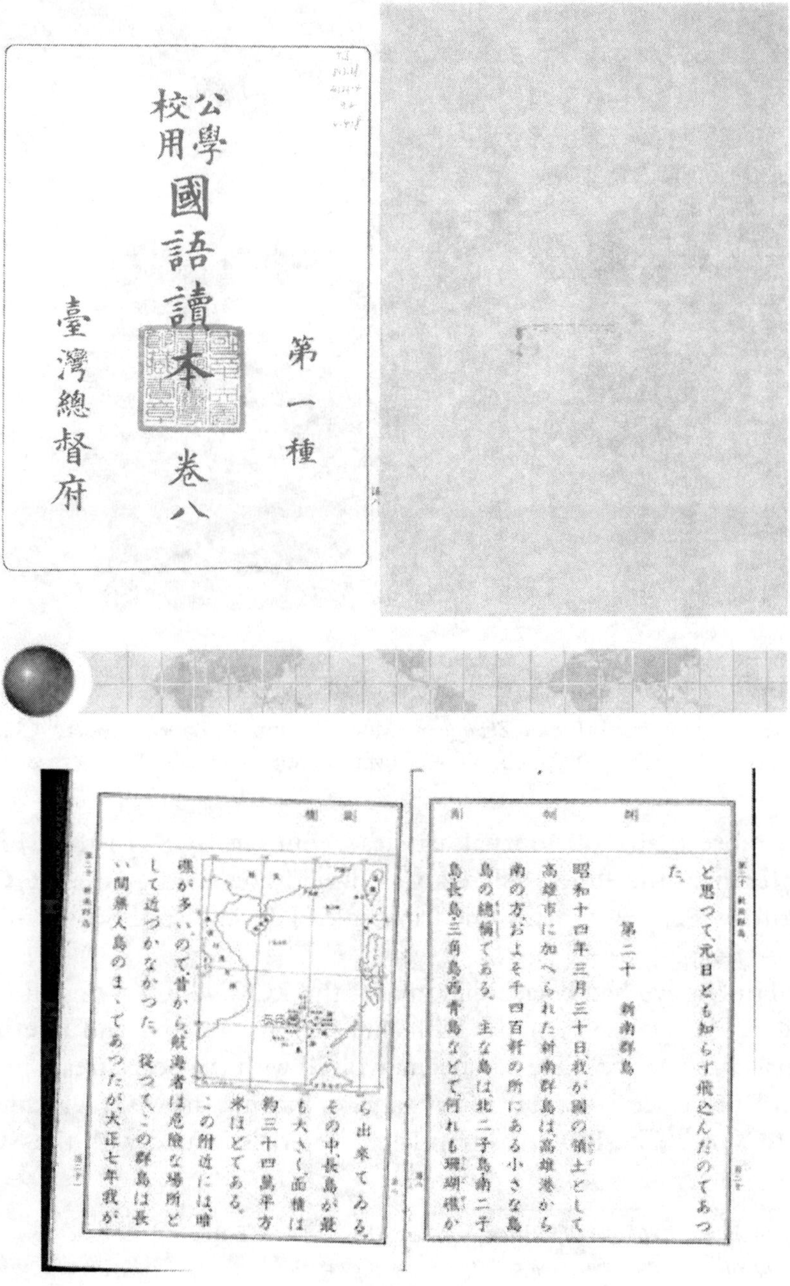

公學校用國語讀本
第一種　卷八
臺灣總督府

と思つて、元日とも知らず飛込んだのであつ
た。

第二十　新南群島

昭和十四年三月三十日、我が國の領土として
高雄市に加へられた新南群島は、高雄港から
南の方、およそ千四百粁の所にある小さな島
島の總稱である。　主な島は、北二子島・南二子
島・長島・三角島・西青島などで、何れも珊瑚礁か
ら出來てゐる。
その中、長島が最
も大きく、面積は
約三十四萬平方
米ほどである。
この附近には、暗
礁が多いので、昔から、航海者は危險な場所と
して近づかなかつた。　從つて、この群島は長
い間無人島のまゝであつたが、大正七年我が

Figure 2. Japanese Taiwan's textbook about the Spratly Islands.
Source: Wu Wenxin *et al.* (2013).

Figure 3. Hu Qingyu, who was crucial for S&P in TPT.

Source: Adapted from *Jindai Zhongguo* (Modern China) (Taipei: Modern China, Inc.), no. 148 (April, 2002), pp. 63–72, cover interior.

also more than 100 journal articles about the SCS. In the SFPT conference, the Pratas Islands was directly deemed as the ROC's territory. S&P was mentioned in the SFPT only (pp. 55, 61–68, 148–154).[20]

Hu Qingyu had been a diplomat at the ROC's MOFA since 1931 (Figure 3). He was familiar with international treaties and international organizations. He had been involved with the peace treaty issue with Japan since 1947. He took charge of moving the MOFA archives to Taiwan.[21] The ROC has translated materials related with the SCS

[20] Kimie Hara, *Cold War Frontiers*, pp. 55, 61–68, 148–154.

[21] *Zhonghua minguo waijiaobu dangan zixunchu* 中華民國外交部檔案資訊處 [The Ministry of Foreign Affairs, the Republic of China], ed., *Zhongguo zhuwai ge gongshiguan, dashiguan liren guanzhang xianming nianbiao* 中國駐外各公使館、大使館歷任

from Japanese into Chinese and put them in the MOFA archive of 1946–1947. In it, there was the Announcement No. 122 of the Taiwan Governor-General Government which subordinated the Spratly Islands into Takao.[22]

Strategic Importance of the SCS

After Taiwan was handed over to ROC on October 25, 1945, under General McArthur's Order No. 1, Chiang Kai-shek dispatched an order on October 3, 1946 to take over the SCS islands within 1 month.[23] Troops left Shanghai on October 29, 1946, and landed on Woody Island of the Paracel on November 28, 1946 and on Itu Aba (now Taiping Island) of the Spratly on December 12, 1946. From October 29, 1946 to December 12, 1946, it took one and a half months for the ROC navy to accomplish the mission (p. 60).[24]

Right after the end of the Sino-Japanese War, Chiang Kai-shek had a lot of things to do. He had to move the capital and people from Chongqing back to Nanjing and had to reconstruct the whole country. Particularly, the Chinese Communist Party became more and

館長銜名年表 [*Name Tables for the Ministers, Ambassadors in Various Embassies*], (Taipei: The Commercial Press, 1989); Academia Historica 國史館, ed., Guoshiguan xiancang minguo renwu zhuanji shiliao huibian 國史館現藏民國人物傳記史料彙編 [*Republican Biographies Collected by the Academia Historica*] (Taipei: Academia Historica, 1989), pp. 217–218; Wang Shijie niding duiRi heyue caoan weiyuan mingdan 王世杰擬定對日和約草案委員名單 [name lists proposed by Wang Shijie for the committee members for the draft of peace treaty with Japan], in DuiRi heyue 對日和約 [*China–Japan Peace Treaty*], Archives of the Ministry of Foreign Affairs of the ROC, the Institute of Modern History, Academia Sinica, File no. 11-01-02-10-03-034.

[22] Xinnan qundao diaocha baogao [Investigation report of the Xinnan qundao], in *Archives of the Ministry of Foreign Affairs of the ROC*, the Institute of Modern History, Academia Sinica, File no. 11-EAP-10-04152.

[23] The Ministry of Internal Affairs, ed., *Zhonghua minguo nanjiang shiliao xuanji* 中華民國南疆史料選輯 [*Selected Historical Materials about the Southern Territories of the Republic of China*] (Taipei: The Ministry of Internal Affairs, 2015), p. 62.

[24] *Ibid*, p. 60.

more a headache to him.[25] Why was he so eager to receive the SCS islands and include them in the TPT? We have to go back to the pre-1945 role of the SCS.

As part of Japan's Greater Asia military aggrandizement plans, until 1939, its land offenses included successful occupation of the coastal and major river regions of China. After a sea battle, Japan occupied the SCS in 1939, and the whole vast region was under its effective control continually for 4–5 years.[26]

In Japan's subsequent attack, the SCS was a springboard to some Southeast Asian countries. It can be used to refuel aircrafts and ships and supplement supplies; it can also be an anchorage for submarines.[27] Meteorological and hydrographical survey on these islands was crucial for the airplanes and warships.[28] Before taking the SCS, Taiwan was

---

[25] Man-houng Lin *et al.*, Zhanhou fuyuan yu wujia pengzhang (Reconstruction and inflation after the Sino-Japanese war) (co-authored with Sun Chen and Liang Chiyuan), in Chin Hsiao-yi 秦孝儀, ed., *Zhonghua minguo jingji fazhanshi* 中華民國經濟發展史 (*The Economic Development History of the Republican China*), Chapter 2, *Zhanhuo roulin xia de jingji* (The economy ravaged by the war) (Taipei: Modern China Press), pp. 737–1014.

[26] Crane Brinton, John B. Christopher, and Robert Lee Wolff, *A History of Civilization* (New Jersey: Prentice-Hall, Inc., 1960), vol. 2: *1715 to the Present*, pp. 553–564, 569, 625; Lu Shiqiang 呂實強, Jiang Yongjing 蔣永敬, eds., *Gaoji zhongxue biaozhun jiaokeshu* 高級中學標準教科書 (*Standard Textbook of the Senior High School*), vol. 3, (Taipei: Zhengzhong Press, 1999, 15th print), pp. 150–155; Zongjian, *Taiwan hangkong juezhan*, pp. 294–311.

[27] JACAR（*Ajia rekishi shiryou center*アジア歴史資料センター）Ref. B02031162900, *kakkoku ryoudo hakken oyobi kizokukankei zakken* 各国領土発見及帰属関係雑件 [*Miscellaneous Papers on Discovery and Subordination of Various Territory*] minamishinakai shoshoutou kizokukankei南支那海諸礁島帰属関係 [*Subordination of Various Rocks and Islands of the South China Sea*], *Shinanguntou kankei ni* 新南群島関係 [*Archives on Shinanguntou*], 第二巻 (A-4-1-0-2_1_1_002), *Gaimushou gaikou shiryou kan* 外務省外交史料館 [*Diplomatic Historical Center of Japan's Ministry of Foreign Affairs*].

[28] Zongjian, *Taiwan hangkong juezhan*, pp. 295–298. JACAR (*Ajia rekishi shiryou center* アジア歴史資料センター) Ref. C11110406000, *kanshi nisshi* 監視日誌 [Inspection diary], October 19, 1943–July, 27, 1944 (昭和18年10月19日-昭和19年7月27日), *Boueishou bouei kenkyuusho* 防衛省防衛研究所 [Institute of Defense Study, Japan's Ministry of Defense].

the southernmost territory of Japan, and so the SCS could defend Taiwan Strait and Bashi Channel and therefore Taiwan.[29] Japan's control of the SCS can prevent the British Borneo, American Philippines, and French Indo-China from offering assistance to Generalissimo Chiang Kai-shek.[30]

On February 4, 1947, the ROC Air Force General Headquarters sent soldiers to garrison the SCS islands and set up weather observation and radio stations to prevent others from invading the islands. The report from the military suggested establishing a string of "island bases in the SCS akin to American bases in the Pacific Ocean."[31]

This garrison was supported by the US government too.[32] Today, the PRC has built airports on the islands near Itu Aba, and often suggested joint use of the airport on these islands (pp. 49, 54).[33] It suggests the strategic military importance of the SCS, particularly Itu Aba.

---

[29] *kokka no ohzei ni junou seyo* 國家の大勢に順應せよ [Following the vivid trend of the development of the nation], in *Taiwan jichi hyouron* 臺灣自治評論 [*Review on Taiwan's Self-Governance*]. July 20, 1939, p. 10; Shinanguntou ryakushi 新南群島略史 [A brief history of Shinanguntou], in *Kagaku no Taiwan* 科學の臺灣[*Scientific Taiwan*], June 30, 1939, p. 23; *Taiwansotokufu bunkyoukyoku kakumuka* 臺灣總督府文教局學務課, in Kokumin seishin soudouin: kagayakuhinomaru 國民精神總動員輝く日の丸 [*Mass Mobilization of the National Subjects' Spirit: Glorifying Japan*], June 5, 1939, pp. 51, 55–57.

[30] *Taiwan keisatsu jihou henshuushitsu 臺灣警察時報編輯室, in Shinanguntou Taiwan no kenkatsu tonaru 西南群島臺灣の管轄となる* [*The Subordination of Shinanguntou to Taiwan*], May 10, 1939, *Taiwan keisatsu jihou* 臺灣警察時報 [*Taiwan Police Times*], p. 130; Denbuotoko 田醜男, *Daisan enShou ruto* 第三援蔣ルート [The third assisting Chiang Kai-shek route], in *Taiwan keisatsu kyoukai* 臺灣警察協會, *Taiwan keisatsu jihou* 臺灣警察時報 [*Taiwan Police Times*], September 10, 1939, pp. 70–72; *Hayashi Kyūjirō* 林久治郎 (南洋協會會長), in *Nanyou shisatsu kan* 南洋視察觀 [*A Perspective of the Southeast Asia after a Visit*], Taiwan: *Taiwan shinshoku kai* 臺灣神職會 [Association for Taiwan's Christian workers], 1940. pp. 13–16.

[31] Chris P.C. Chung, Since Time Immemorial: China's Historical Claim in the South China Sea, MA thesis, University of Calgary, 2013, pp. 49, 54.

[32] Xu Wentang, *Nansha yu Xisha de zhuquan Zhengyi*, p. 208.

[33] Chris P.C. Chung, Since Time Immemorial: China's Historical Claim in the South China Sea, Master's thesis, pp. 49, 54.

S&P and the Sovereignty of the ROC in Taiwan

While the UK dissuaded the ROC's participation in the SFPT conference and suggested a bilateral treaty between the ROC and Japan instead, it also insisted on noting the fact that this bilateral treaty's application scope should be limited to the territory that is now and will later be under the control of the ROC. This principle that reflected reality had been echoed by most of the allied countries, particularly the opposition party in Japan.[34]

Torao Ushiroku, the Director of the Second Division, Asian Affairs Bureau, Ministry of Foreign Affairs, Japan, was one member of the Japanese delegation for the TPT. He gave an address on June 25, 1952 about the process of negotiations and left a shorthand record. The record reveals that at the beginning, the Japanese Government ordered the delegation team never to approve the ROC's claims of sovereignty over Taiwan and the Pescadores, so as not to provoke the PRC (p. 4, the parentheses shows the page number in the record). Later on, the delegation team received a telegram from the Ministry of Foreign Affairs in Tokyo that began by telling them to judiciously adopt the ROC's claims and make repeated efforts to reach an amicable agreement, as long as it did not go against the intention of the Yoshida Notes (p. 7). The delegation team then prepared a second draft for the treaty. Besides Taiwan and the Pescadores, the delegation team added to Article 2 both the Spratly and Paracel Islands, which the ROC was concerned about. Eiji Wajima, the Director-General of the Asian Affairs Bureau, explained at the Committee on Foreign Affairs in the Upper House on May 27,

[34] *Waijiaobu cheng Jiang Zhongzheng ZhiongRi hehui lici huiyi shaungfang daibiao tanhua jilu zhaiyao* 外交部呈蔣中正中日和會歷次會議非正式會議雙方代表談話紀錄摘要 [Memorandum of the Ministry of Foreign Affairs to Chiang Kaishek], in Geming wenxian: duiRi yihe 革命文獻-對日議和（二）〉 [*Literature of Revolution-Peace Treaty Negotiations* (2)], *Jiang Zhongzheng zongtong wenwu* 蔣中正總統文物 [*President Chiang Kaishek Collection*], Academia Historica, Collection no. 002-020400-00054-029; *Chen Yanjeong cheng Jiang Zhongzheng Wodaoshi dui ZhongRi heyue wenti tanhua yishu* 陳延炯呈蔣中正倭島氏對中日和約問題談話憶述 [Memorandum of Chen Yanjiong to Chiang Kaishek], in ibid, Collection no. 002-020400-00054-034.

1952 that of the territories prescribed in Article 2 of the SFPT, those closely relating to the ROC are also mentioned in Article 2 of the Japan–ROC Peace Treaty (p. 8). In other words, the guiding principle of the delegation team was not to approve the ROC's claims on critical problems, e.g. sovereignty over Mainland China. Regarding other issues, they would take the ROC's sincerity into consideration and accept its claims, recognizing the fact that the ROC had also made a compromise (p. 11).[35]

In Article 2 of the TPT, the ROC received from Japan all right, title, and claim to the Paracel and the Spratly Islands in addition to Taiwan and Penghu. For an understanding of what the terms "all right, title and claim" mean, we have to go back to the Shimonoseki Treaty which ceded Qing China's full sovereignty in perpetuity of Taiwan, Penghu, and the islands appertaining or belonging to the said Islands of Formosa.

In 1895, S&P were not islands appertaining or belonging to the said Islands of Formosa. Nevertheless, after 1952 in a legal sense they were. On the other hand, nowadays the ROC just has real control over the island Itu Aba. For Itu Aba, the ROC in Taiwan has full sovereignty in perpetuity.

When Japan and the PRC established diplomatic relations in 1972, Japan's Foreign Minister, Ohira Masayoshi, announced the unilateral termination of the TPT in a press conference. But international law specialist L. Oppenheimer took the view that a treaty consists of an executory treaty and an executed treaty. Alliances, trade, administration, and extradition belong to the former, while boundaries, cession, and transfer of territory belong to the latter. Once executed, the terms of the treaty become permanent; if the parties to the treaty do not sign new treaties for amendment, the *status quo* must

[35] Hattori Ryuji, *Ushiroku Torao Ajia kyoku daini kachou kenshuujo kouen sokki* 「*nikka heiwajouyaku koushou keii*' (1952 *nen* 6 *gatsu* 25 *nichi*), in Chuuoudaigaku ronshuu, no. 34 (February 20, 2013), pp. 1–22. 後宮虎郎アジア局第二課長研修所講演速記「日華平和条約交渉経緯(1952年6月25日), "中央大学論集, 第34号, pp. 1–22, 2013-02-20, http://ir.c.chuo-u.ac.jp/repository/search/item/md/rsc/p/4759/. Prof. Okazaki Koji kindly informed the author of the important message of this note on June 13, 2017.

persist.[36] The unilateral termination of the TPT in 1972 by Japan canceled the transactional articles related to trade, fisheries, and diplomacy, but not the articles related to the state of peace, the shift of sovereignty over Taiwan, Penghu, the S&P, and the nullification of old treaties, including the Shimonoseki Treaty.

This is also the principle set by the 1969 version of the Vienna Convention on the Law of Treaties. Its Article 63 says "The severance of diplomatic or consular relations between parties to a treaty does not affect the legal relations established between them by the treaty except in so far as the existence of diplomatic or consular relations is indispensable for the application of the treaty."[37]

At Spratly, the PRC has real control over six islands or islets with military stations. The ROC has one, Philippine, three, Vietnam, four, and Malaysia, one.[38] In Paracel, Vietnam has control over 29 small islands or rocks, the PRC has the main Woody Islands and other five bigger small islands[39] (data varies for these numbers).

---

[36] See Cui Shuqin 崔書琴, *Guojifa* 國際法 [*International Law*], vol. 1 (Taipei: Commercial Press, 1961), p. 272; Charles G. Fenwick, *International Law* (New York: Appleton-Century-Crofts, 1965, 4th ed.), p. 519; Chen Zhishi 陳治世, "*TaiPeng de falu diwei*" 臺澎的法律地位 [The legal status of Taiwan-Penghu], in *Dongfang zazhi* 東方雜誌 [*The Eastern Miscellany*], vol. 4 of republished edition, no. 12 (June 1, 1971), p. 37.

[37] Zhongri duanjiao qian zhengqing ziliao 中日斷交前後政情資料 [*Political Situation Before and After the Severance of Diplomatic Relations Between the ROC and Japan*], Archives of the Ministry of Foreign Affairs of the ROC (Department of Asia-Japan), the Institute of Modern History, Academia Sinica, File no. 012.1, 0002. About Vienna Convention on the Law of Treaties, see the United Nations, Treaty series, Vienna Convention on the Law of Treaties, 1980, p. 347, https://treaties.un.org/doc/Publication/UNTS/Volume%201155/v1155.pdf, p. 341 (accessed on May 2, 2017).

[38] Annonymous 佚名, *Nanhai zhengba tujie* 南海爭霸圖解 [An illustration for the rivalry of hegemony over the South China Seas], in *Mingbao* 明報 (Hong Kong), June 12, 2016, p. A16.

[39] Xu Wentang 許文堂, *Nansha yu xisha de zhuquan zhengyi: tazhe de guandian* 南沙與西沙的主權爭議：他者的觀點 [Sovereignty controversy over the South China Seas: a perspective from others], in Xu Wentang 許文堂 ed., *Qiling niandai dongya fengyun: Taiwan yu liuqiu, Diaoyutai, nanhai de guishu wenti* 七零年代東亞風雲：臺灣與琉球、釣魚臺、南海諸島的歸屬問題 [*East Asian turmoil in the 1970s: the*

In the Second World War (WWII) period, those islands and rocks could have served to allow planes or ships to refuel or to supplement supplies, or to have on-the-spot understanding of the weather or hydrography, to make them strategically important. Other than fishing, Spratly Islands have not been used as submarine resources after the 1960s. Hence, for S&P in the TPT, basically, it would only be islands and rocks that would be involved.

For the SCS dispute, another treaty often mentioned is the Treaty of Paris signed on December 10, 1898, between Spain and the United States that provided the exact longitude and latitude coordinates to delimit the Philippines from the SCS.[40]

Even though the TPT has been so important for the SCS controversy, after the TPT was effectuated, the Cold War made the US exercise its influence to seat the ROC at the Security Council of the UN instead of the PRC. The ROC's mainland background and this Cold War factor made the TPT so important, which has been linking the ROC with Taiwan but was oft-neglected in and out of Taiwan.[41] It also provides the basis for the insufficiency of the HA.

Dialogue with HA

The main spirit of the HA is to (1) negate the PRC's exclusive right in the SCS; (2) downgrade many islands in the SCS as rocks so as not being able to set the Exclusive Economic Zone (EEZ) as UNCLOS 121.3 allows; and (3) allow the Philippines to have its continental shelf claim starting from its coastal baselines.[42]

---

sovereignty issue of Taiwan, Okinawa, Diaoyutai, and the South China Sea] (Taipei: Taiwan Professors' Association, 2015), p. 197.

[40] United States Department of State Bureau of Oceans and International Environmental and Scientific Affairs, Limits in the Seas, No. 142, the Philippines: Archipelagic and other Maritime Claims and Boundaries, September 15, 2014, pp. 7–8, http://www.state.gov/documents/organization/231914.pdf (accessed on August 29, 2016) Kimie Hara, *Cold War Frontiers*, p. 146.

[41] Man-houng Lin, *Taiwan's Sovereignty Status: The Neglected Taipei Treaty*, pp. 128–135.

[42] Permanent Court of Arbitration, The South China Sea Arbitration, July 12, 2016, 6, https://pcacases.com/web/sendAttach/1801 (accessed on October 20, 2016).

On p. 6 of the HA, it says

> The Tribunal accepted that there is a dispute between the Parties concerning sovereignty over islands in the South China Sea, but held that the **matters submitted to arbitration by the Philippines do not concern sovereignty**. The Tribunal considered that it would not need to implicitly decide sovereignty to address the Philippines' Submissions and that doing so would not advance the sovereignty claims of either Party to islands in the South China Sea.

It is generally held that only sovereignty could confer exclusive right. Without going into the sovereignty issue, the HA could not convince the PRC to accept its arbitration.

Page 6 of HA also points out "In its Position Paper, China advanced the following arguments: The essence of the subject-matter of the arbitration is the territorial sovereignty over several maritime features in the South China Sea." Such a position taken by the PRC is well-grounded.

On the other hand, China's nine-dash line is not sufficient to to claim sovereignty.

Legally speaking, the ROC has full sovereignty in perpetuity over the S&P, but the ROC just had effective jurisdiction over Itu Aba among the S&P. It is a historical irony! However, it provides a significant opportunity for legal solution to the SCS controversies.

For the SCS, the PRC's Vice-Chairman of the Chinese People's Political Consultative Conference National Committee, Dong Jianhua, has referred to the TPT and the UN 2758 resolution to serve as the PRC's basis for its claim for S&P.[43] As the TPT had been registered at the UN, unless the ROC signed another treaty with some other countries to alienate its sovereignty over the S&P, the S&P's sovereignty is still in the hands of the ROC. Articles 58 and 63 of the ROC's Constitution require the approval of the ROC's

---

[43] Dong Jianhua 董建華, '*Nanhai caijue*': *houguo yanzhong*: 「南海裁決」後果嚴重 (The outcome of the Hague resolution would be very serious), *Jianada shangbao*加拿大商報 (*Canadian Commercial News*), July 15, 2016, http://www.Today commercialnews.com /hk/14860 (accessed on October 17, 2016).

Executive Yuan, Legislative Yuan, and the President to sign a treaty with another country. The UN 2758 resolution is not such a treaty.

The PRC is right in that the Hague Tribunal is not the right place for settling this issue. As sovereignty is involved, it is the UN that has to solve the issue. One way is to revisit the UN 2758 resolution, which decided the UN representation issue regarding the seat held by China. That moment missed what Dulles had proposed: Let the PRC enter the Security Council and the ROC stay as a member.[44]

With the S&P's sovereignty clarified, the neighboring countries could claim or share continental shelf or EEZ as justified by the UNCLOS.

As Territorial Seas and EEZ can only be extended from the territory with sovereignty,[45] there is no need to downgrade the SCS islands to rocks, as most of them were under the effective control of various countries without sovereignty. Some people might deem this proposal as going against the One China Policy. Both the Democratic People's Republic of Korea and the Republic of Korea have their own unification policy and their seats have coexisted in the UN for years. The existence of the DPRK, ROK, PRC, ROC, UN, and the SFPT system were all post-WWII arrangements for the whole world to go ahead.

Without the attendance of the PRC at the SFPT, the PRC often negates the SFPT system. Yet, it is the SFPT which confers to Japan national sovereignty. The PRC's embassy in Tokyo or having Japan in the UN is the expression of the general acceptance of the SFPT. The denial of this treaty would subvert the international order.

Why was the peace treaty between China and Japan signed in Taiwan, which was then a Japanese colony? It was because the PRC

---

[44] Nancy B. Tucker, John Foster Dulles and the Taiwan root of the two China policy, in Richard H. Immerman. ed., *John Foster Dulles and the Diplomacy of the Cold War* (Princeton, NJ: Princeton University Press, 1990), pp. 235–262; Tu Chengji, *Zhonghua minguo zai Lian Heguo de zuihou rizi* [*The Final Days of the ROC at the UN*] (Taipei: Xiuwei, 2008), p. 32.

[45] The UN, *UNCLOS*, December 10, 1982, http://www.un.org/depts/los/convention_agreements/texts/unclos/UNCLOS-TOC.htm (accessed on October 20, 2016).

drove the ROC to Taiwan in December 1949. However, the ROC had helped for 8 years, if counting from the Marco Polo incident, or for 14 years, if counting from the Mukden incident, in protecting China from Japanese conquest, which the Qing dynasty of China failed during the 5 months of the First Sino-Japanese War. The Shimonoseki Treaty, in which the Qing government was requested by the US to prevent the Japanese conquest, actually had sacrificed Taiwan in order to maintain China as a whole.[46]

The sacrifice of the Chinese mainland people was compensated by the PRC's entering the UN Security Council in 1971, to which Japan is still not admitted.

The 1994 UNCLOS is an illustration of the PRC's power exercised in this position. Before the 1994 UNCLOS, the territorial sea was 3 NM off the coast, after that it became 12 NM. The 200 NM continental shelf or EEZ is also a new arrangement of the 1994 UNCLOS. With a comparatively long coastline, the PRC has gained to some extent.

With this UNCLOS, the rules set by it need to be observed by every country in the world. Even though the US did not ratify it and the ROC was not in the UN, the *erga omnes* principle (universal principle) in the international law could still apply.

For the effective control without sovereignty claim of various countries in the SCS, the UN could form committees to set acceptable conduct for all of them. The rule that is applied to the SCS should also be applied to other sea areas.

Conclusion

The ROC (Taiwan) has been farther away from the SCS dispute than any other SCS claimants. Without the understanding that Taiwan was ceded to Japan because of the Shimonoseki Treaty, Japan took S&P from 1939 to 1945 and put them under Taiwan's jurisdiction, and so it would be difficult to understand why S&P's sovereignty has been held by the ROC (Taiwan) through both the SFTP and the TPT.

---

[46] Man-houng Lin 林滿紅, *Zhanzheng, heyue yu Taiwan* pp. 502–506, 521–522.

The lack of such understanding of the SCS controversy among scholars has been caused to some extent by an epistemological blind spot in modern history. The understanding of modern Chinese history has long been bound by the limits of China, and the understanding of modern global history during the 16th to 19th century has long been focused on the Atlantic Ocean. Such a mindset neglects the increasing cooperation between the US and Meiji Japan after the US boundary had reached the Pacific Ocean in 1848 and the latter's rise to be an Asia-Pacific Power in the 20th century.

In signing the Shimonoseki Treaty, Li Hongzhang was the representative on the Chinese side. He had an American adviser on international treaties, John Watson Foster, for negotiating this treaty. Foster helped to cut indemnity or to reduce the ports to be opened for Japan. Foster also played an important role for China to have ceded Taiwan to Japan.

The US as well as the European countries would not welcome the Japanese full conquest of China, which was actually an imminent threat before the US came forth to help formulate the peace treaty. To cede an island far away from Beijing and to make that island also serve as an outpost for Japan, a rising Asia-Pacific Power, was a win–win arrangement for the international powers in 1895 (Figure 4).

This John Watson Foster happens to be the maternal grandfather of John Foster Dulles who helped to shape the SFTP and the TPT. It was his maternal grandfather's inspiration that prompted him started to learn international laws. Both of them had served as State Secretary of the US. This familial relation with the treaties that were connected with Taiwan and S&P was actually a microcosm that led to the rise of Asia-Pacific Powers in the modern world.[47]

The SCS controversy has been threatening world peace considerably. Without reference to sovereignty, the HA has been unfair to both the ROC and the PRC across the Taiwan Strait. The main spirit of the HA is to (1) negate the PRC's exclusive right in the SCS and

[47] Man-houng Lin, *Taiwan's Sovereignty Status: The Neglected Taipei Treaty*, pp. 116–118, 132–135.

Figure 4. Conference for the Shimonoseki Treaty, 1895.

Source: Woodblock Print of Treaty of Shimonoseki negotiations (courtesy of Freer Gallery of Art, Smithsonian Institution, Washington, D.C.), https://www.pinterest.jp/pin/512988213788480921/ (accessed on July 14, 2017).

(2) downgrade many islands in the SCS as rocks so as not being able to set the EEZ. The goal is to open the SCS as much as possible.[48]

In the Greater East Asian War period, S&P only involved the island and rocks, which could serve to refuel the planes or ships, or to have on-the-spot understanding of whether the weather or hydrography would be suitable for domestic planes or ships to move, or to hit the enemy ships or planes. With these legal premises, the SCS is no more the inner sea of any country. All the countries surrounding the SCS could have their EEZs from their coastal baseline with the

[48] Permanent Court of Arbitration, "The South China Sea Arbitration." https://pcacases.com/web/sendAttach/1801 (accessed on October 20, 2016).

condition to respect the midline with the neighboring countries.[49] This would be favorable for the PRC as well as Southeast Asian countries.

As the ROC has not referred to the Asia-Pacific history, the Shimonoseki Treaty, and the TPT to elaborate fully its sovereignty claim for S&P, various SCS claimants referred only to the historical involvement before the SFPT and the TPT, thereby confusing the world. The neglected TPT should not be overlooked any more.

In the SCS as well as other sea areas, there are so many islands and rocks under some countries' effective control but without their sovereignty. There is a real need for the UN Security Council to set rules for their conduct for the purpose of peacekeeping.

Today, with the outstanding trade surplus of the PRC in international finance, and the preeminence of military power of the US, an era of Sino-American condominium or Chinamerica or G-2, a bipolar system, has come into being.[50] Based upon the Shimonoseki Treaty and the TPT, which had been signed by both China and the US, their further cooperation at present time would bring about peace for the SCS.

---

[49] Treaty Collections of United Nations, United Nations Convention on the Law of the Sea, December 10, 1982, https://treaties.un.org/Pages/showDetails.aspx?objid=0800000280043ad5 (accessed on October 20, 2016).

[50] John F. Cooper, Trump's Decision to Honor the One-China Policy: How Best to Explain It? http://www.ChinaUSFriendship.com, May 2017 Publication (accessed on May 1, 2017).

Chapter

2

The Nationalist Government's Efforts to Recover Chinese Sovereignty Over the Islands in the South China Sea after the End of World War II

Chen Qianping

Department of History, Nanjing University, Nanjing, China

Abstract

Utilizing substantial archival materials, this chapter examines the process through which the Nationalist government reasserted Chinese sovereignty over the islands in the South China Sea, including China's stationing of troops on the Dongsha Islands, Yongxing Island, and Taiping Island. Well-prepared militarily, economically, and diplomatically, the Nationalist government achieved this strategic goal after overcoming various difficulties including insufficient ships and funds, unfavorable weather and maritime conditions, and the obstruction of the French colonial government in Vietnam. The Nationalist government also sent technicians to survey the islands and map out the sphere of Chinese maritime territory in the South China Sea, and it built two weather stations. These actions were publicized on December 1, 1947. During this process, the government of the United States adopted a policy of acquiescence due to its close collaboration with China. When the French government occupied one of the Xisha Islands and attempted to take firmer actions, the US and Britain pressured France to make concessions to China, which led the French government to seek a diplomatic solution.

Keywords: Nationalist government, war of resistance against Japanese aggression, sovereignty over the South China Sea, affirmation of South China Sea territorial sphere.

Introduction

Chinese frontiers faced serious crises in the 20th century, including the French and Japanese imperialist encroachment on the islands in the South China Sea. In 1907, Huang Zhongying, captain of the battleship *Feiying* of the Southern Ocean Fleet, led two warships of Qing China to survey the Dongsha (East Sand) Islands [known in English as the Pratas Islands]. On August 11 of that same year, Nishisawa Yoshitsugu, a Japanese citizen, landed on the Dongsha Islands without authorization, and he "raised a Japanese flag, built residential quarters, and dug guano"; moreover, he named the island after himself: "Nishisawa Island."[1] After several rounds of negotiations, the Qing government took back the Dongsha Islands on October 11, 1909. To safeguard Chinese sovereignty over the islands in the South China Sea, Zhang Renjun, the Governor-General of Guangdong and Guangxi, dispatched the assistant general Wu Jingrong to survey the Xisha (West Sand) Islands [known in English as the Paracel Islands], who was followed by an official "bureau established to manage [island affairs]." On May 19, 1909, Commander Li Zhun led 170 sailors in the battleships *Fubo*, *Chenhang*, and *Guangjin* to survey the Xisha Islands; he renamed three of the islands after his three ships.[2] Li also

[1] Zhang Dajun, *Zhongyue guojie yanjiu* 中越国界研究 [*A Study of the Sino-Vietnamese Border*] (Taipei: Guangfu dalu sheji weiyuanhui), 1977, p. 159.

[2] In the name of the Qing government, Li Zhun changed the name of Drummond Island to Fubo Island, Duncan Island to Chenhang Island, and Palm Island to Guangjin Island.

planted the Qing national flag, the yellow dragon, and erected a stone stele to mark the occupation.[3]

The Republic of China, founded in 1912, effectively governed the islands in the South China Sea. Between 1917 and 1923, multiple business enterprises applied to develop these islands, which were then a part of Qiongzhou Prefecture of Guangdong Province, that is, today's Hainan Island. After its founding in 1928, the Guangdong provincial government, under the government of the Republic of China in Nanjing, dispatched the battleship *Hairui* to survey Woody Island (then known as Lin Island, now known as Yongxing Island).[4]

After the Mukden Incident of 1931, Japan occupied Manchuria, and the French colonial government in Indochina seized the opportunity to take over nine small islands in the South China Sea in early April 1933.[5] The Chinese government lodged numerous protests with the French government, emphasizing that these islands had been inhabited by the Chinese people and affiliated with the Chinese government for generations. To officially publicize Chinese sovereignty over the South China Sea islands, the Censoring Commission of Land and Water Maps of the Ministry of the Interior of the Republic of China drew a "Map of the Islands in the South China Sea," which for the first time affirmed that the southernmost Chinese maritime territory reached the James Shoal on the fourth parallel north, and for the first time, the Chinese government divided the islands into four groups: Dongsha, Xisha,

[3] See Zhonghuaminguo Nanhai sida qundao jielüe 中华民国南海四大群岛节略 [A Brief Summary of the Republic of China's Four Island Groups in the South China Sea] (mimeographed copy), printed by Neizhengbu dizheng si 内政部地政司 [Ministry of the Interior, Department of Local Governance], February 23, 1974. *ngfu dalu sheji weiyuanhui*, 1977, quoted in Zhang Dajun, *Zhongyue guojie yanjiu* 中越国界研究 [*A Study of the Sino-Vietnamese Border*] (Taipei: Guangfu dalu sheji weiyuanhui), 1977, p. 168.

[4] See Zhang Dajun, *Zhongyue guojie yanjiu* 中越国界研究 [*A Study of the Sino-Vietnamese Border*] (Taipei: Guangfu dalu sheji weiyuanhui), 1977, p. 170.

[5] Xu Gongsu, "*Faguo zhanling jiuxiaodao shijian* 法国占领九小岛事件" [Incident of the French Occupation of the Nine Small Islands]. *Waijiao pinglun* 外交评论 [Diplomatic Commentaries] 2, no. 9 (September 1933), pp. 13–14. These nine small islands are part of what is now known as the Nansha Islands.

Nansha (South Sand, now known as Zhongsha [Middle Sand]), and Tuansha (Round Sand, now known as Nansha).

In July 1938, the French took advantage of the Sino-Japanese War and seized the Xisha Islands. After Japanese troops took over Hainan Island in February 1939, they encroached upon the Xisha and Tuansha Islands right away. On March 30 of that same year, the Japanese government renamed the Tuansha Islands the New Southern Islands [Shinangunto in Japanese] and placed them under the jurisdiction of Kaohsiung City, Taiwan.

After World War Two (WWII), the government of the Republic of China, as one of the Big Four, took back the sovereignty of the islands in the South China Sea in accordance with international law and the new international order in the Asia-Pacific region laid down by the Cairo Declaration and the Potsdam Proclamation. The Nationalist government not only stationed naval ships at the important islands in the South China Sea, reestablished territorial steles, conducted surveys, and exercised governance but also confirmed on December 1, 1947, the official names of the islands and reefs belonging to the Dongsha, Xisha, Zhongsha, and Nansha Islands. By doing all of this, the Chinese government declared its sovereignty to the world.

There is some influential scholarship on the Nationalist Government's efforts to recover its sovereignty over the islands in the South China Sea after WWII. For example, based on abundant primary sources, Li Guoqiang examined the Nationalist government's takeover of the Nansha Islands after WWII.[6] Wu Shicun used archival materials preserved in the Number Two Historical Archives of China to study the topic from the three perspectives of negotiation of sovereignty, administrative governance, and development.[7] Tan Weiyuan focused on the Chinese government's administrative governance of

---

[6] Li Guoqiang, "*Minguo zhengfu yu Nansha qundao* 民国政府与南沙群岛" [The Nationalist Government and the Nansha Islands], *Jindaishi yanjiu* 近代史研究 [*Modern Chinese History Studies*], no. 2 (1994), pp. 163–174.

[7] Wu Shicun, "*Minguo shiqi de Nanhai zhudao wenti* 民国时期的南海诸岛问题" [Problems of the Islands in the South China Sea in the Republican Period], *Minguo dang'an* 民国档案 [*Republican Archives*], no. 3 (1996), pp. 127–132.

the islands in the South China Sea. His article, which discusses the postwar period as well, is outstanding among the most recent scholarships, because it provides new ideas based on various historical sources and a broad research horizon.[8] As a complement to existing scholarship, this research is grounded in archival documents in Taipei in the Academia Historica and the Institute of Modern History of the Academia Sinica, in addition to the materials on the islands in the South China Sea donated to the Nanjing University by Zheng Ziyue, a famous geographer who surveyed the islands in the South China Sea with the Nationalist fleet that took over those islands. In this chapter, I will elaborate on the whole process of the Nationalist Government's takeover of the islands in the China South Sea and its demarcation of Chinese maritime territory there.

The Nationalist Government's Plan to Reestablish Rule Over the Islands in the South China Sea

Due to the crucial strategic position of the South China Sea islands, Jiang Jieshi had long considered taking them back after the end of WWII. In November 1945, the Chinese Nationalist government received a request from the British government asking if the British could send a small battleship to "survey the Dongsha Islands and build a weather station there"; however, the British request was "rejected for political reasons" by Jiang Jieshi.[9] Jiang then directed the army commander-in-chief He Yingqin to order Zhang Fakui, the chief of the Military Commission's Guangzhou office, to "station troops on the Dongsha and Xisha Islands." Zhang Fakui replied in

---

[8] Tan Weiyuan, "*Minguo shiqi Zhongguo zhengfu dui Nanhai zhudao shezhi guanxia de lishi kaocha* 民国时期中国政府对南海诸岛设治管辖的历史考察" [Historical Examination of the Chinese Government's Establishment of Governance and Jurisdiction over the Islands in the South China Sea during the Republican Era], *Zhongguo bianjiang shidi yanjiu* 中国边疆史地研究 [*China's Borderland History and Geography Studies*], no. 2 (2016), pp. 135–145.

[9] Chen Cheng cheng Jiang zhuxi shiyue wuri qiancheng [Chen Cheng's Memorial Submitted to Chairman Jiang], October 5, 1946, Jiang Zhongzheng zongtong dang'an, File no. 002-020400-00050-045-001x_05_04 _2016.

early 1946 by telegraph, "The voyage will be feasible only in March because of strong ocean winds." Jiang followed up with an inquiry dated March 24, asking Zhang "whether the island garrison troops have been dispatched."[10]

On April 4, 1946, Chen Yi, governor of Taiwan Province, requested permission to take over the three archipelagoes, the Xisha, Dongsha, and New Southern Islands. In the telegram, Chen Yi stated that

> (1) The Xisha Islands to the west of Hainan Island are Chinese territories that were occupied by France in 1934. After the outbreak of the Pacific War, they were occupied by the Japanese. The former [Japanese colonial] governor's office of Taiwan once established a survey office on the islands. Now our provincial Bureau of Meteorology has sent staff to conduct surveys and photograph the islands, and wooden marks evidencing Chinese sovereignty have been erected. [...] Should these islands be ruled by Taiwan Province?
>
> (2) The Dongsha Islands to the southwest of Taiwan are close to Kaohsiung County and they contribute a lot to the fishery industry of the province. These islands were occupied by the Japanese, and we propose to take them under our province's jurisdiction and make them part of Kaohsiung County.
>
> (3) The New Southern Islands near the Philippines include 13 Islands and are 770 nautical miles away from Kaohsiung Harbor. These islands were put under the governance of Kaohsiung City in 1938, when the Japanese ruled Taiwan. We are now actively engaged in the handover of government for them.

To accomplish the handover of the New Southern Islands, Chen Yi requested the Nationalist government to "ask the US Army headquarters in the Philippines for assistance."[11]

---

[10] Jiang Zhuxi zhi Zhang Fakui jing dian [Jiang Jieshi's Telegram to Zhang Fakui], March 24, 1946, Jiang Zhongzheng zongtong dang'an, File no. 002-090106-00017-242-001a_05_05_2016.

[11] Chen Yi zhi xingzhengyuanzhang Song Ziwen dai dian [Chen Yi's Telegram to Prime Minister Song Ziwen (T. V. Soong)], April 4, 1946, Waijiaobu dang'an, Xisha qundao 5 [Foreign Ministry Archives: Xisha Islands (5)]. (Taipei: *Guoshiguan* 国史馆 [Academia Historica]), 1947, File no. 020-049904-0005-0013a.

Upon receiving Chen Yi's telegram, the Executive Yuan immediately ordered "the Ministry of the Interior and the Foreign Ministry to check the situation and report back as soon as possible." The Ministry of the Interior found only that "the Dongsha and Xisha Islands were under the jurisdiction of Guangdong Province prior to WWII," yet it "did not know much" about "the population, size, economy, communications, culture, and distance among the counties on the islands (calculated in nautical miles)."[12]

The Foreign Ministry's reply to the Ministry of the Interior demonstrated a thorough understanding of the situation of the Dongsha and Xisha Islands and a lack of information about the New Southern Islands. The Foreign Ministry pointed out that the Xisha Islands "have long been listed as our country's territory, but we have not exercised actual occupation." It went on to say:

> According to Article 3 of "Zhongfa jiewu zhuantiao wutiao [the Sino-French Five-article Treaty of Border Affairs]" signed on June 26, 1887, "the islands in the sea shall be demarcated southward along the red line drawn by the border negotiation ministers from both countries. This line cuts across the eastern hilltop at Chagushe (in Chinese it is called Wanzhu, located south of Mangjie and southwest of Zhushan), and this line should be taken as the borderline. All the islands to the east of the line belong to China, and the Jiutou Hill in the sea to the west of the line, along with other small islands, belongs to Vietnam."

The report also emphasized that although the Sino-French treaty did not mention the name of the islands, yet "their position indicates that they belong to the Chinese sphere to the east of the demarcation line. These islands (Xisha) were occupied by the French and then taken over by the Japanese, and naturally we should recover them. "The Dongsha Islands, according to the Foreign Ministry, "were originally part of Chinese territory, and there was never international

[12] Neizhengbu zhi waijiaobu dai dian [Telegram from the Ministry of the Interior to the Foreign Ministry], April 24, 1946, Waijiaobu dang'an, Xisha qundao 5 [Foreign Ministry Archives: Xisha Islands (5)]. (Taipei: *Guoshiguan* 国史馆 [Academia Historica]), 1947, File no. 020-049904-0005-0013a.

dispute. These islands were occupied by the Japanese, and due to the geographic proximity, it is appropriate to put them under the jurisdiction of Taiwan Province after we recover them."[13]

Meanwhile, the Department of European Affairs of the Foreign Ministry telegraphed the Chinese Consulate General in Manila and the Chinese delegate to Japan Zhu Shiming on April 30 and June 17, respectively, urging them to contact the US Army in the Philippines and General Douglas MacArthur to ask for assistance to Taiwan Province in taking over the New Southern Islands.[14] However, the reply from the Consulate General in Manila was delayed for unknown reasons. Foreign Minister Wang Shijie followed up with another telegram to Zhu Shiming in June saying, "Our government is prepared to take over the New Southern Islands near the Philippines," and "please negotiate for [US] assistance in the takeover from the place nearby."[15]

Due to a temporary failure to locate the exact position of the New Southern Islands, the Foreign Ministry actively engaged the Ministry of Military Command and the Ministry of Military Administration to deliberate on the takeover of the Dongsha and Xisha Islands. On May 21, the Minister of Military Command Xu Yongchang telegraphed Foreign Minister Wang Shijie, saying that Jiang Jieshi had ordered Zhang Fakui, the chief of the Military Commission's Guangzhou office, to send troops to occupy the Dongsha and Xisha Islands.

[13] Waijiaobu wei jieshou Dongsha Xisha ji Xinnan qundao zhi xingzhengyuan mishuchu han [Letter from the Foreign Ministry to the Secretariat of the Executive Yuan Regarding Receiving the Dongsha, Xisha and New Southern Islands], April 30, 1946, Waijiaobu dang'an, Xisha qundao 5 [Foreign Ministry Archives: Xisha Islands (5)]. (Taipei: *Guoshiguan* 国史馆 [Academia Historica]), 1947, File no. 020-049904-0005-0029x.

[14] Waijiaobu zhi manila zonglinshiguan dian [Telegram from the Foreign Ministry to the Chinese Consulate General in Manila], April 30, 1946, Waijiaobu dang'an, Xisha qundao 5 [Foreign Ministry Archives: Xisha Islands (5)]. (Taipei: *Guoshiguan* 国史馆 [Academia Historica]), 1947, File no. 020-049904-0005-0030x.

[15] Wang Shijie zhi zhuri zhu daibiao [Telegram from Wang Shijie to the Chinese Delegate to Japan, Zhu Shiming], June 17, 1946, Waijiaobu dang'an, Xisha qundao 5 [Foreign Ministry Archives: Xisha Islands (5)]. (Taipei: *Guoshiguan* 国史馆 [Academia Historica]), 1947, File no. 020-049904-0005-0041x.

Yet Xu also said that he "had not yet received reports about the movement and stationing of the troops."[16]

Zhou Shikai, a secretary at the Foreign Ministry, later reported to Wang Shijie what he had learned about the reasons for the troops' delay. First, the First Department of the Ministry of Military Command, which was supposed to supervise the takeover, had been merged into the newly founded Ministry of Defense in June 1946, and no one had temporary responsibility for overseeing the islands. Second, ships were in great demand for transportation and supply, but none were available in southern China. Third, "Chairman (Jiang) telegraphed Chief Zhang Fakui to dispatch troops to the islands, and the deadline was set for the end of November last year. The action has been postponed to April of this year."[17] Wang Shijie then followed up with a telegram to Zhang Fakui inquiring about "when the troops will arrive" at the Dongsha and Xisha Islands.[18] Zhang Fakui replied, "The stationing was delayed in the past due to the shortage of suitable transport ships." He confirmed that the troops assigned to take over the Xisha Islands would reach their destination by the end of June if no other obstacles arose and that the troops assigned to the Dongsha Islands "could only be transported in early July."[19]

---

[16] Xu Yongchang zhi Wang Shjie dai dian [Xu Yongchang's Telegram to Wang Shijie], May 21, 1946, Waijiaobu dang'an, Xisha qundao 5 [Foreign Ministry Archives: Xisha Islands (5)]. (Taipei: *Guoshiguan* 国史馆 [Academia Historica]), 1947, File no. 020-049904-0005-0032a.

[17] Zhou Shukai zhi Wang Shijie qiancheng [Report Submitted to Wang Shijie by Zhou Shukai], June 1, 1946, Waijiaobu dang'an, Xisha qundao 5 [Foreign Ministry Archives: Xisha Islands (5)]. (Taipei: *Guoshiguan* 国史馆 [Academia Historica]), 1947, File no. 020-049904-0005-0033x.

[18] Wang Shijie zhi Zhang Fakui dian [Wang Shijie's Telegram to Zhang Fakui], June 4, 1946, Waijiaobu dang'an, Xisha qundao 5 [Foreign Ministry Archives: Xisha Islands (5)]. (Taipei: *Guoshiguan* 国史馆 [Academia Historica]), 1947, File no. 020-049904-0005-0034x.

[19] Zhang Fakui zhi Wang Shijie dian [Zhang Fakui's Telegram to Wang Shijie], June 12, 1946, Waijiaobu dang'an, Xisha qundao 5 [Foreign Ministry Archives: Xisha Islands (5)]. (Taipei: *Guoshiguan* 国史馆 [Academia Historica]), 1947, File no. 020-049904-0005-0035a.

The actual obstacle at the time was China's lack of large ships, which was exacerbated by treacherous weather conditions and waves in the South China Sea. The landings had to be postponed to ensure the safety of the troops. Fortunately, Lin Zun, commander of the Chinese fleet in the US was just then on his way back to China from Guantanamo Naval Base, leading a fleet given by the US government as aid to China during the later period of WWII.[20] Lin's fleet would subsequently play an important role in taking over the islands in the South China Sea.

Another obstacle was the Chinese government's lack of information about the New Southern Islands. On July 5, Jiang Menglin, the secretary general of the Executive Yuan, wrote to the Foreign Ministry urging it to provide a quick answer about "whether 'New Southern Islands' was just another name for the Nansha Islands."[21] On July 24, Jiang Menglin telegraphed the Office of the Chief Executive of Taiwan Province demanding an investigation of the exact name and position of the New Southern Islands.[22] This inquiry to the Foreign Ministry eventually garnered detailed data regarding the New Southern Islands from two sources. The first was a report from Duan Maolan, the Chinese Consul-General in Manila, who met with the

[20] The fleet included the destroyers *Taikang* and *Taiping*, the minesweepers *Yongsheng*, *Yongshun*, *Yongding*, and *Yongning*, and the coastal patrol boats *Yongtai* and *Yongxing*, The US Navy also sent another 10,000-ton supply ship as Commander Lin Zun's flagship. Upon arrival in Shanghai in July 1946, this supply ship was also transferred to China and renamed the *Emei*.

[21] Xingzhengyuan mishuchu gonghan [Memorandum of the Secretariat of the Executive Yuan], Waijiaobu dang'an, Xisha qundao 5 [Foreign Ministry Archives: Xisha Islands (5)]. (Taipei: *Guoshiguan* 国史馆 [Academia Historica]), 1947, File no. 020-049904-0005-0042x.

[22] Taiwansheng xingzheng zhangguan gongshu zhi waijiaobu dai dian [Telegram from the Office of the Chief Executive of Taiwan Province to the Foreign Ministry], August 17, 1946, Waijiaobu dang'an, Nansha qundao (jieshou Tuansha qundao) (July 1946–April 1947) [Foreign Ministry Archives: Nansha Islands (Recovering the Tuansha Islands) (July 1946–April 1947)], 1947. (Taipei: Taiwan *zhongyang yanjiuyuan jindaishi yanjiusuo dang'anguan* 台湾中央研究院近代史研究所档案馆 [Archives of the Institute of Modern History, Academia Sinica]), File no. 11-EPA-04152, pp. 202857–202859.

Philippine Foreign Minister on August 5. Duan was told that the New Southern Islands:

> were nothing but coral islands without economic value.... They are two hundred miles away from Palawan Island in the Philippines and two thousand miles away from the Asian continent. The islands were first discovered by the British and then occupied by the French, who sent ships to gather guano. The islands were later occupied by the Japanese as a bastion from which to attack the Philippines.[23]

The Chinese Foreign Ministry then checked the *Updated World Atlas* compiled by Tan Lian and published in March 1938 and discovered that "what the Philippine Foreign Minister referred to as the New Southern Islands was called the Tuansha Islands in Tan's book; it seems it was just one place that has two names, and New Southern Islands was the Japanese name." The Foreign Ministry then reported to the Executive Yuan, "According to Tan's atlas, the Tuansha Islands belong to China."[24] The Office of the Chief Executive of Taiwan Province also confirmed with the Foreign Ministry on August 17 that the New Southern Islands under the jurisdiction of Kaohsiung City were the same as the Tuansha Islands, which had been seized illegally by the French Vietnamese government and the Japanese.[25] So far, the information coming from both the Consulate-General in Manila and the Office of the Chief Executive of Taiwan affirmed that the

---

[23] Waijaobu zhi xingzhengyuan mishuchu gonghan [Foreign Ministry's Memo to the Secretariat of the Executive Yuan], August 5, 1946, Waijiaobu dang'an, Xisha qundao 5 [Foreign Ministry Archives: Xisha Islands (5)]. (Taipei: *Guoshiguan* 国史馆 [Academia Historica]), 1947, File no. 020-049904-0005-0059-0060x.

[24] *Ibid.*

[25] Taiwansheng xingzheng zhangguan gongshu zhi waijiaobu dai dian [Telegram from the Office of the Chief Executive of Taiwan Province to the Foreign Ministry], August 17, 1946, Waijiaobu dang'an, Nansha qundao (jieshou Tuansha qundao) (July 1946–April 1947) [Foreign Ministry Archives: Nansha Islands (Recovering the Tuansha Islands) (July 1946–April 1947)], 1947. (Taipei: Taiwan *zhongyang yanjiuyuan jindaishi yanjiusuo dang'anguan* 台湾中央研究院近代史研究所档案馆 [Archives of the Institute of Modern History, Academia Sinica]), File no. 11-EPA-04152, pp. 202857–202859.

so-called New Southern Islands were actually the Tuansha Islands, determined to be Chinese territory by the Chinese government as early as April 1935.

Military Preparation by the Nationalist Government to Take Over the South China Sea Islands

After confirming the status of the New Southern Islands, which was Tuansha Islands in prewar Chinese maps, as Chinese territory, the Executive Yuan "ordered the Guangdong provincial government to temporarily take over the Dongsha, Xisha, Nansha, and Tuansha Islands" on August 8, 1946.[26] On September 13, the Foreign Ministry, the Ministry of the Interior, the Ministry of Defense, and the Naval Command each sent delegates to the Foreign Ministry for a meeting to discuss the takeover of the New Southern or Tuansha Islands. The delegates brought with them relevant books and resource materials.[27]

On October 3, 1946, Jiang Jieshi issued the following handwritten order to General Chief of Staff Chen Cheng: "Ground troops transported by the navy should be stationed on the Dongsha Islands and the Xiasha Islands (and this should be completed within the month). Not too many troops are needed; it is sufficient to assign one company to one place. Each year, however, there should be a rotation."[28] Chen Cheng agreed that the South China Sea islands should be garrisoned as important fortresses of national defense, but

---

[26] Waijiaobu zhi Manila Duan zonglingshi dian [The Foreign Ministry's Telegram to Consul-General Duan in Manila], August 9, 1946, Waijiaobu dang'an, Xisha qundao 5 [Foreign Ministry Archives: Xisha Islands (5)]. (Taipei: *Guoshiguan* 国史馆 [Academia Historica]), 1947, File no. 020-049904-0005-0059-0062x.

[27] Xingzhengyuan guanyu huishang jieshou xinnan qundao banfa de tongzhi [The Executive Yuan's Notice Concerning the Collaborative Takeover of the New Southern Islands], September 8, 1946, Waijiaobu dang'an, Xisha qundao 5 [Foreign Ministry Archives: Xisha Islands (5)]. (Taipei: *Guoshiguan* 国史馆 [Academia Historica]), 1947, File no. 020-049904-0005-0067a.

[28] Jiang Zhongzheng shouling [Handwritten Order of Jiang Jieshi], October 3, 1946, Jiang Zhongzheng zongtong dang'an, File no. 002-080200-00553-181-001a_05_04_2016.

he also thought that the dispatch could only be implemented "with the backup of all kinds of equipment and marine forces" due to the difficulties of maritime supply. Jiang Jieshi criticized Chen Cheng's procrastination, ordering him to send troops rapidly. Jiang pointed out, "No matter what, one platoon with tents should be stationed on each of the Xisha and Nansha Island[29] archipelagoes. This must be done within one month, and no delay will be tolerated. The survey of local conditions can be done at the same time."[30]

After the intervention of Jiang Jieshi, the Defense Ministry invited personnel from the Foreign Ministry, the Ministry of the Interior, and the Naval Command to hold a "highly confidential" meeting to discuss the following issues related to sending troops to the islands.

The first issue discussed was timing. The meeting decided to follow Jiang Jieshi's guideline stipulating that stationing and inspection could be carried out simultaneously, because "if the troops arrive after the scouting is done, it will take too long and may draw the attention of other countries, or we may even lag behind them."[31]

The second issue was the initial occupation plan. This was to include a field trip by staff from the Ministry of the Interior, the Foreign Ministry, the Ministry of Defense, and the Naval Command, with the collaboration of Guangdong Province. The team was to adopt the method of "landing simultaneously or taking turns to land" when approaching the islands.[32] National territorial boundaries were to be demarcated and maps were to be drawn. The plan also included collaboration among different troops, coordination of transport and

---

[29] What Jiang Jieshi meant here is actually islands now known as Nansha Islands, namely islands called Tuansha Islands in prewar Chinese maps. From this point onward, I will use "Nansha lslands" to refer to those islands called Tuansha Islands before.

[30] Chen Cheng cheng Jiang zhuxi shiyue wuri qiancheng [Chen Cheng's Memorial Submitted to Chairman Jiang], October 5, 1946, Jiang Zhongzheng zongtong dang'an, File no. 002-020400-00050-045-001x_05_04_2016.

[31] Guofangbu zhi waijiaobu dai dian [Telegram from the Ministry of Defense to the Foreign Ministry], October 8, 1946, Xisha qundao 5 [Foreign Ministry Archives: Xisha Islands (5)]. (Taipei: *Guoshiguan* 国史馆 [Academia Historica]), 1947, Waijiaobu dang'an, File no. 020-049904-0005-0068a-0072x.

[32] *Ibid.*

escort ships, building of weather stations, and selection of communication and medical personnel, as well as funding, equipment, housing, immigration and development, and constructions and supplies.

The third issue was permanent construction plans for the islands. These included proposed permanent governance institutions, surveying, naming of islands, composition and rotation of the marine troops, port equipment, immigration and development, and expenditures for all construction plans.

The fourth issue was diplomatic preparedness. The meeting concluded that "with regard to the sovereignty issue, it is better to create established fact," and thus, the government of the Republic of China "would not raise the issue of sovereignty for the time being." "All source materials concerning sovereignty" would be "compiled by the Ministry of the Interior, the Ministry of Defense, and Naval Command and transmitted to the Foreign Ministry for future use."[33] The Ministry of Education would be responsible for the revision of geography textbooks.

The meeting also discussed the relations among the islands, for example, the temporary administrative affiliation, future military relations, and so on.

The National Government's Takeover of the South China Sea Islands

In fact, military action aimed at taking over the islands in the South China Sea had started in April 1946.

The Recovery of the Dongsha Islands

Nationalist government personnel landed on the Dongsha Islands in three groups. The first group consisted of the 35 officers and soldiers of the naval weather station. They landed on May 23, 1946, and weather broadcasting began on June 15. The second group was made up of 24 soldiers from the 64th Division of the army. They embarked for the Dongsha Islands on the battleship *Wanning*. Unfortunately,

[33] *Ibid.*

the ship encountered storms at sea to the southwest of Dongsha Islands, and it sank. Ten surviving soldiers, who were rescued by British and American naval ships, landed on the Dongsha Islands on August 15.[34] After that, the Military Commission's Guangzhou office sent "a platoon of ground troops assisted by a radio squad" to land on the Dongsha Islands on September 12.[35]

The sinking of the *Wanning*, which had been transporting supplies from Guangzhou to the Dongsha Islands, caused logistical difficulties for the stationed troops. On September 18, Zhang Fakui telegraphed Chen Cheng reporting "50 extra troops stationed on Dongsha Island have suffered a shortage of food for two days due to the sinking of the *Wanning*." Chen Cheng immediately ordered, "Air-drop by the air force and a naval ship to carry on transportation."[36] Thus, the stationing of troops on the Dongsha Islands had been completed.

Due to the Chinese navy's lack of large ships, the military occupations of the Xisha and Nansha Islands were not completed until after Lin Zun's fleet arrived in Nanjing in July 1946. According to Lin's report later on, "In the fall of 1946, Naval Command dispatched four battleships, the *Taiping*, *Yongxing*, *Zhongjian*, and *Zhongye*, to form a fleet with Lin Zun as the commander of the fleet stationed in the Xisha and Nansha Islands and Yao Ruyu as deputy commander. The fleet departed from Wusongkou port near Shanghai on October 29, 1946 and arrived at Humen, Guangzhou, on November 2. It reached Yulin port on Hainan Island on the ninth."[37]

---

[34] Gao Sulan, *Jiang Zhongzheng zongtong dang'an: Shilüe gaoben* [Presidential Archives of Jiang Jieshi: Brief Accounts of Matters] (68), December 1946–February 1947 (Taipei: *Guoshiguan*), 2012, p. 138.

[35] Guofangbu zhi waijiaobu dai dian [Telegram from the Ministry of Defense to the Foreign Ministry], October 8, 1946, Waijiaobu dang'an, Xisha qundao 5 [Foreign Ministry Archives: Xisha Islands (5)]. (Taipei: *Guoshiguan* 国史馆 [Academia Historica]), 1947, File no. 020-049904-0005-0068a-0072x.

[36] Yu Jishi cheng Jiang zhuxi shiyue liuri qiancheng [Memorial Submitted to Jiang Jieshi by Yu Jishi], October 6, 1946, Jiang Zhongzheng zongtong dang'an, File no. 002-020400-00050-045-001x_05_04_2016.

[37] Gao Sulan, *Jiang Zhongzheng zongtong dang'an: Shilüe gaoben* [Presidential Archives of Jiang Jieshi: Brief Accounts of Matters] (69), March to May 1947 (Taipei: *Guoshiguan*), 2012, p. 504.

The Recovery of the Xisha Islands

The Naval Command dispatched the First Independent Platoon and a weather station, led by Recovery Deputy Xiao Ciyin and Vice-Commander Yao Ruyu, to land on Woody Island, one of the Xisha Islands, on November 28, 1946. According to a record, "The platoon has 33 officers and soldiers equipped with two light machine guns and 16 rifles. The weather station with 11 officers and 32 soldiers is equipped with a radio of 250 watts RMS, which has established direct communication with Naval Command."[38] The personnel involved in the takeover of the Xisha Islands totaled 76. Lin Zun's report states, "The ships *Yongxing* and *Zhongjian* departed for Yongxing Island in the Xisha Islands, and they arrived on the twenty-eighth and unloaded materials and personnel. The two ships returned on December 3, passing Robert Island and Pattle Island and reached Yulin port." Lin Zun also reported on the conditions on Yongxing Island, "No residents living on the island, [yet] there are houses, bridges, trees, ponds, and wells, as well as oxen, pigs, and dogs left by the Japanese."[39]

The Takeover of the Nansha Islands

The Second Independent Platoon and a weather station, totaling 76 members, were sent by Naval Command to recover the Nansha Islands, on the battleships *Taiping* and *Zhongye* led by Recovery Deputy Mai Yunyu, Commander Lin Zun, and a staff member from the Ministry of the Interior. According to Lin Zun, "The two ships *Taiping* and *Zhongye* made two attempts to reach the Nansha Islands on November 12 and 18 and both times failed due to storms, and the ships returned. On December 9, the two ships succeeded on their third try and reached Taiping Island [known as Itu Aba Island in English and Nagashima when occupied by the Japanese, later renamed

---

[38] Haijun zongsilingbu, "Xi, Nansha qundao jianshe shishi," January 1947, Waijiaobu dang'an, Xisha qundao 6 [Foreign Ministry Archives: Xisha Islands (6)]. (Taipei: *Guoshiguan* 国史馆 [Academia Historica]), 1947, File no. 020-049904-0006-0024x-0025x.

[39] Gao Sulan, *Jiang Zhongzheng zongtong dang'an: Shilüe gaoben* (69), p. 505.

Taiping in Chinese after the battleship that landed there], one of the Nansha Islands. Troops landed on the island and cargo was unloaded. The two ships returned on the fifteenth, passing the islands of Loaita [Nanyue in Chinese] and Thitu [Zhongye in Chinese] and North Danger Reef [*Shuangzi Dao* in Chinese]. They arrived at Yulin port on December 17."[40] Lin Zun also described the conditions on Taiping Island: "Taiping Island in the Nansha Islands has lush trees, houses, remnants of docks, wells, and ponds. It seems that the island was bombarded by Allied aircraft."[41]

Naval Command also summarized the conditions on Taiping Island, pointing out that after occupying the island, the Japanese army built a 620-m-long dike on its south shore, inside of which they constructed a 2.5-m-deep dock with an area of 1,300 m^2. A 172-m-long dock and warehouses were built at the port. Although the facilities had been damaged, Naval Command reported, "We can repair and expand them after takeover."[42]

The National Government's Naming of and Construction on the Xisha and Nansha Islands

After the occupation of Woody (Yongxing) Island and Itu Aba (Taiping) Island, Naval Command drafted a "Proposal to Implement Construction on the Xisha and Nansha Islands," revealing the Chinese government's determination to carry out military deployment and construction on the Xisha and Nansha Islands. The document pointed out that these islands "are close to Guangdong and Hainan to the north, face Vietnam to the West, and check the Philippines to the east," and "they hold the throat of the transportation line between Hong Kong and Singapore and have an extremely important position in military as well as commercial transportation."

[40] *Ibid*, p. 504.

[41] *Ibid*, p. 505.

[42] Haijun zongsilingbu, "Xi, Nansha qundao jianshe shishi," January 1947, Waijiaobu dang'an, Xisha qundao 6 [Foreign Ministry Archives: Xisha Islands (6)]. (Taipei: *Guoshiguan* 国史馆 [Academia Historica]), 1947, File no. 020-049904-0006-0024x-0025x.

Furthermore, the document asserted, "All countries in this region covet these two groups of islands." For the Chinese navy, Woody Island in the Xisha islands and Itu Aba Island in the Nansha Islands had the greatest military value. In addition, islands such as Robert Island and Pattle Island[43] in the Xisha Islands; and Thitu Island, North Danger Reef, Loaita Island, and Storm Island in the Nansha Islands were small, but their "positions are also crucial," and they "should all be transformed into outposts of our country's national defense."[44]

The occupation of the Xisha Islands centered on the military deployment on Woody Island. To minimize supply difficulties caused by inconvenient sea transportation, the navy decided to reduce the number of troops stationed on the island. Yet the allocation of fire-power was not to be discounted: "The weapons system is to be upgraded and mainly composed of 25-millimeter cannons, backed up by machine guns." In addition, "Troops with machine guns should be redeployed to Robert Island and Pattle Island," because "these two islands are so close to Vietnam, and they may be seized by the Vietnamese before we get there." In addition to military facilities, the Chinese navy also planned to "build dikes, harbors, docks, warehouses, and dormitories for shelter and storage and to make the lives of the staff and troops more comfortable." All the occupied islands were also to "build lighthouses, tidal monitoring stations, signals, and navigation markers," in order to "indicate waterways and record tidal conditions," facilitating safe navigation of vessels. The Naval Command also decided to order its Administration of Nautical Surveying to "dispatch a survey squad to provide detailed data about the small islands and seaways and to draw accurate nautical maps as a reference for future navigation." The Naval Command also recommended, "Woody Island should be equipped with a five-to-six-ton transport

---

[43] In Chinese, Robert Island is known as Ganquan [Sweet Springs] Island, and Pattle Island is known as Shanhu [Coral] Island.

[44] Haijun zongsilingbu, "Xi, Nansha qundao jianshe shishi," January 1947, Waijiaobu dang'an, Xisha qundao 6 [Foreign Ministry Archives: Xisha Islands (6)]. (Taipei: *Guoshiguan* 国史馆 [Academia Historica]), 1947, File no. 020-049904-0006-0024x-0025x.

ship or a scouting vessel that can patrol all the islands, and all small islands should also have their own small ships and boats for purposes of self-defense."[45]

In the Nansha Islands, the navy not only decided that Itu Aba Island should "enhance firepower and increase cannons" but also planned to "select two or three small islands to occupy so that they could flank Itu Aba Island." Naval Command pointed out that the Nansha Islands could "appropriately mimic the Xisha Islands" when carrying out construction of dikes, harbors, docks, channels, and lighthouses. Yet because "Itu Aba Island is a good sea anchorage," it "should be able to accommodate ships with deep draughts." For the navy, the measurement of the South China Sea's water routes became a priority due to the long distance between Itu Aba Island and Hainan Island. According to the navy report, for many civilian vessels "see navigation in this area as a challenge," so the navy should "conduct surveys as soon as possible ... and hopefully the outcome will benefit ships earlier." The Naval Command also recommended that "the control ship at Yulin port should undertake the transportation between Itu Aba Island and Hainan Island." Quicker rotations of the troops on Itu Aba Island were also recommended in order to maintain fighting ability. Above all, the Naval Command planned to build Itu Aba Island into a "fortress in the sea" just like Midway Island.[46]

On January 16, 1947, the Ministry of Defense convened the "Conference Concerning the Implementation of Construction on the Xisha and Nansha Islands," attended by Defense Minister Bai Chongxi and Deputy Ministers Lin Wei, Qin Dechun, and Liu Shiyi. The conference invited Fu Jiaojin, the chief of the Department of Territory of the Ministry of the Interior; Ye Gongchao, the chief of the Department of European Affairs of the Foreign Ministry; and Zhu Qi, the chief of Customs Affairs of the Ministry of Finance. Bai Chongxi reported to the attendees that the Xisha and Nansha Islands had "recently been occupied by our navy." He pointed out that

---

[45] *Ibid.*

[46] *Ibid.*

"we should complete the necessary facilities on the islands rapidly in order to demonstrate to those nations friendly to us our constructive attitude." Bai also emphasized that because "France used to say that these islands were not our territory," diplomatic negotiations "should back up military deployment after the occupation."[47] Zhou Xianzhang, the chief of staff of the navy, briefed the conference on current conditions in the Xisha and Nansha Islands, and Ye Gongchao discussed the process of Sino-French negotiations.

The conference made the following final decisions. (1) With regard to the issue of sovereignty, the Foreign Ministry was charged with collecting historical source materials and diplomatic documents and replying to the French government after careful deliberation. (2) The Naval Command was in charge of increasing weapons and building batteries on the islands. (3) Lighthouses on the islands were to be built by the Customs on orders from the Ministry of Finance. Naval Command was to take the initiative to set up weather stations on Woody Island and Robert Island in the Xisha Islands. (4) Land surveys were to be completed by the Ministry of the Interior, and a water survey was to be conducted by the Naval Command; these could be done separately. (5) The Xisha and Nansha Islands were to be explicitly listed as Chinese territories, and the Ministry of the Interior was to be responsible for endorsing the demarcation line based on exact latitude and longitude. The outcome was to be implemented by publishing institutions and circulated among institutions of education by the Ministry of Education. (6) With regard to administrative affiliation, the Xisha and Nansha Islands would belong to Hainan Island after the founding of the Hainan Special Administrative Region, but for the time being, they were to be under the supervision of the navy. (7) The Ministry of Agriculture and Forestry was charged with having soil specialists investigate the suitability of the island soil for planting, in preparation for immigration and development. (8)

[47] Guanyu xinansha qundao jianshe shishi huiyi jilu [Minutes of the Conference Concerning the Implementation of Construction on the Xisha and Nansha Islands], January 16, 1947, Jiang Zhongzheng zongtong dang'an, File no. 002-020400-00050-054-003x_05_04_2016.

Previously, the Guangdong provincial government had issued passports to those who went to the Xisha and Nansha Islands to fish and cultivate land. The Guangdong provincial government was to be consulted for details that could be used for reference. (9) Upon the completion of lighthouses and weather stations on the islands, the Foreign Ministry was to notify friendly nations about the formal takeover of the Xisha and Nansha Islands. (10) From then on, no foreign ships passing the Xisha and Nansha Islands were to be permitted to land, except when seeking shelter. Any foreign sailors who landed were to be notified that the islands were not open to foreigners. Naval Command and the Foreign Ministry were to meet to deliberate on a temporary method of exclusion. (11) All the costs for constructing camps, forts, docks, and warehouses were to be covered by a special fund earmarked by the Ministry of Finance.[48]

Beginning in 1947, the Department of Territory of the Ministry of the Interior called a series of meetings on the sphere of Chinese sovereignty in the South China Sea and how to affirm and publicize it. These meetings laid down a basic framework for the demarcation of Chinese sovereignty in the South China Sea. Based on survey data, specialists such as Zheng Ziyue worked on drawing maps of the Dongsha, Xisha, Zhongsha, and Nansha Islands and compiling an index of island names. On March 15, 1947, the Nationalist government approved a proposal to entrust the islands to the "temporary management of the navy."[49] On April 3, 1947, Minister of the Interior Zhang Lisheng notified all ministries and commissions that the Nationalist government had approved changing the name of Woody Island to Yongxing Island and Itu Aba Island to Taiping Island and that the renaming of other islands would follow.

---

[48] *Ibid.*

[49] Zhonghuaminguo lingyou Nansha ji Xisha qundao genju zhi shuotie [Republic of China's Statement on the Foundation for Occupying and Governing the Nansha and Xisha Islands], January 1974, Waijiaobu dang'an, Nansha qundao (Zhong Yue bufen) (January 1974-?) [Foreign Ministry Archives: Nansha Islands (China–Vietnam) (January 1974–?)]. (Taipei: Taiwan *zhongyang yanjiuyuan jindaishi yanjiusuo dang'anguan* 台湾中央研究院近代史研究所档案馆 [Archives of the Institute of Modern History, Academia Sinica]) 1947, File no. 11-EPA-04590, p. 105537.

In May 1947, 36 members of the National Assembly, represented by Hu Mulan, proposed a motion entitled "Urging the Government to Protect Sovereignty, Define Demarcation Lines, Enhance National Defense Construction, and Reward Outstanding Personnel in Recovering Territory for the Purpose of Consolidating National Defense and Building the Xisha and Nansha Islands," which was warmly supported by the attending assemblymen. The meeting passed a resolution aimed at "developing the Xisha and Nansha Islands, enhancing national defense, and urging the government to protect our sovereignty, clearly demarcate national nautical boundaries, and enhance national defense." They also requested that the motion "be submitted to the Ministry of Defense and the Foreign Ministry," that the Chinese government "negotiate with foreign governments using reason and facts [and that the government] urge the French army to withdraw, or expel them if necessary."[50] In response, the Ministry of Defense directed Naval Command to devise a more detailed construction plan for the Xisha and Nansha Islands.

In September 1947, Naval Command submitted to the Executive Yuan a "Draft Plan of Construction for the Xisha and Nansha Islands," which focused mainly on military construction. The main items were as follows.

The first item was the construction plan. (1) Construction funds. Since the navy occupied Yongxing and Taiping Islands, lack of funds "limited construction in this region" and thus "work cannot be done." The navy requested the allocation of funds, to be coordinated by a designated office. (2) Increase the number of garrison troops on the islands. The troops should be "mainly composed of soldiers who are familiar with the conditions and life on Hainan Island." (3) The islands should all be put under the supervision of the navy, "according to the practice in other countries." The plan also suggested that "revenue generated by exploiting the natural resources of the islands,

---

[50] Guofangbuzhang Bai Chongxi zhi waijiaobuzhang Wang Shijie dai dian [Minister of Defense Bai Chongxi's Telegram to Foreign Minister Wang Shijie], August 15, 1947, Waijiaobu dang'an, Xisha qundao 9 [Foreign Ministry Archives: Xisha Islands (9)]. (Taipei: *Guoshiguan* 国史馆 [Academia Historica]), 1947, File no. 020-049904-0009-0076a.

such as phosphate fertilizer production and fisheries, should all be used for construction projects in the region."

The second item in the Naval Command's draft plan was the concrete method of implementation. Because the terrain and climate on the Xisha and Nansha Islands were "inappropriate for long-term stationing of large ships and long-term training of military corps," the draft plan recommended a two-stage process of military and economic construction.

Stage One

(1) Enhancement of defense works. Since troops were stationed on Yongxing and Taiping Islands, the construction of defense works had been partially completed. In the future, antiaircraft guns and flat trajectory guns should be added.

(2) Increase in living facilities for personnel. The addition of people involved in construction would exacerbate the shortage of fresh water, food, and fuel on the islands. With regard to fresh water, priority should be given to "building reservoirs with the capacity to support daily use." The draft plan also recommended, "Tall, dry, and solid warehouses should be built to store a three-month supply of grains and fuel," because these materials "had to be purchased and shipped from the mainland." "In case of adverse weather or accident, the people on the islands would experience difficulties without timely aid." Moreover, lodging for officers and soldiers needed to be improved, and the plan suggested "building more houses to accommodate future personnel who will work in the islands."

(3) Transportation of materials and construction of navigation and harbor equipment. The plan pointed out that the garrison troops' morale suffered for a while because of the inadequate supplies in the winter of 1946, when "transport ships such as the *Yongxing*, *Taiping*, *Zhongjian*, and *Zhongye* delivered only half of their quota of blankets, food, equipment, and miscellaneous objects before returning, due to the terrible weather, violent tides, and lack of shelters and docks." The plan suggested that "simple docking facilities should be built first to enable ships to berth and unload

materials" so that the quantities of transported materials "can increase dozens of times over that of last winter." The plan also recommended that "havens ought to be built on the southwestern tip of Yongxing Island and inside the coral reefs on the western side of Taiping Island," and "markers should be erected in these places so that shipped materials could be transferred to small boats, which in turn could enter the harbor for unloading." Moreover, "two or three fast boats can berth inside the shelter and venture out to scout all the islands when weather permits."

(4) Establishment of a weather station and radar stations. The plan recommended that "one radar station should be built on Yongxing Island and one on Taiping Island for military purposes" to monitor foreign vessels passing in the South China Sea.

Stage Two

(1) Building a weather station on Taiping Island. Because "The Xisha Islands and the Nansha Islands are far from each other and the weather conditions in the two places are not identical," the plan argued, "a weather monitoring station should be established on Taiping Island in the Nansha Islands," and the daily data recorded should be "reported to the weather station on Yongxing Island."

(2) Setting up a radio station. The Xisha and Nansha Islands "witnessed many ship wrecks due to their complicated coral reefs and violent tidal waves," and "navigation is extremely challenging." The plan recommended that "a radio station should be built on each island for safety purposes."

(3) Speedy construction of typhoon shelters should continue until completed.

(4) Improving the living standards of the stationed personnel. "The Xisha and Nansha Islands are far from the mainland, and their land area is too limited for growing plants. The climate is brutal due to the low latitude, and hurricanes often strike the islands," the plan states. "Timely improvement is needed in the facilities for the daily life of the stationed personnel." The most important thing, according to the plan, was "to install two large generators,

> one on Yongxing Island and one on Taiping Island, to make water and ice, and for communications and other purposes that require power." In addition, "camps and workshops should be solid and comfortable and fully equipped with recreation facilities, in order to mitigate the personnel's homesickness and loneliness."[51]

On October 9, 1947, Prime Minister Zhang Qun transmitted the Naval Command's draft plan to "the Ministry of the Interior; the Ministries of Defense, Finance, the Economy, Agriculture and Forestry, and Transportation; and the Foreign Ministry" for deliberation. On October 15, Fu Jiaojin, the chief of the Department of Territory of the Ministry of the Interior, convened a meeting of delegates from the Ministries of Defense, the Economy, Agriculture and Forestry, Communications, and Finance, as well as the Foreign Ministry and Naval Command. This meeting concluded with a consensus that "the Xisha and Nansha Islands are more significant militarily than economically." Thus, the focal point of the discussion was military-related construction and the funds needed for it. The meeting made three final decisions. (1) The Ministry of Defense was to coordinate with army, navy, and air force commands to put together an investigation team with technicians from the Ministries of the Economy, Communications, Agriculture and Forestry, and the Customs. (2) Upon the completion of their investigation, all involved sectors should submit the data collected concerning local conditions and construction to the Ministry of Defense for overall review. (3) After the investigation team returned to Nanjing, the Ministry of the Interior should call another meeting of all concerned sectors to discuss the data collected and to come up with concrete methods.[52]

---

[51] Xi, nansha qundao jianshe jihua (junshi bufen) cao'an [Draft Plan of Construction for the Xisha and Nansha Islands: Military Part], proposed by Naval Command in September 1947, Waijiaobu dang'an, Xisha qundao 10 [Foreign Ministry Archives: Xisha Islands (10)]. (Taipei: *Guoshiguan* 国史馆 [Academia Historica]), 1947, File no. 020-049904-0010-0011x-0018x.

[52] Liu Jiaju guanyu huishang xinansha qundao jianshe jihua de baogao [Liu Jiaju's Report on a Joint Meeting to Deliberate on the Plan of Construction for the Xisha and Nansha Islands], October 16, 1947, Waijiaobu dang'an, Xisha qundao 10

The Affirmation and Declaration of the Sphere of Chinese Sovereignty Covering the South China Sea Islands

The French Indochinese colonial government had occupied nine small islands in the South China Sea in 1933, and it had encroached on the Xisha Islands in 1938. Consequently, Nationalist government used caution when sending troops to the Xisha (West Sand) Islands and the Nansha (South Sand) Islands, trying to preclude news of their activity from leaking before the final announcement. When the Naval Command telegraphed the Foreign Ministry in early December of 1946 that the ships *Yongxing* and *Zhongjian* "had arrived at Woody Island in the Xisha Islands on November 28, and troops with light equipment had landed," it made a special request: "Please do not announce [the occupation] before the takeover of the Nansha Islands, [which was delayed] for climatic reasons."[53] The Naval Command was worried that an early announcement might lead to the French Indochinese government's seizure of Itu Aba (Taiping) Island.

Only after the ships *Taiping* and *Zhongye* unloaded troops on Itu Aba Island in the Nansha Islands on December 12 did the Chinese Foreign Ministry's spokesperson announce to the world at a press conference on January 7, 1947, that "the Chinese government has taken back the Xisha Islands from Japanese occupation" and that "sovereignty over this island group belonged to China originally, so there is no need to ask any party to authorize this recovery."[54]

[Foreign Ministry Archives: Xisha Islands (10)]. (Taipei: *Guoshiguan* 国史馆 [Academia Historica]), 1947, File no. 020-049904-0010-0007x-0008x.

[53] Haijun zongsilingbu zhi waijiaobun dai dian [The Naval Command's Telegram to the Foreign Ministry], December 7, 1946, Waijiaobu dang'an, Xisha qundao 5 [Foreign Ministry Archives: Xisha Islands (5)]. (Taipei: *Guoshiguan* 国史馆 [Academia Historica]), 1947, File no. 020-049904-0005-0068a-0075x.

[54] "ZhongFa guanyu Xisha qundao jiaoshe dalüe" [A Brief Account of the Sino-French Negotiations over the Xisha Islands], February 1, 1947, Waijiaobu dang'an, Xisha qundao 7 [Foreign Ministry Archives: Xisha Islands (7)]. (Taipei: Guoshiguan 国史馆 [Academia Historica]), 1947, File no. 020-049904-0007-0010x; Zhaoyi Fa dashiguan yijiusiqi nian yi yue shisan ri guanyu Xisha qundao shi zhi benbu [Chinese Translation of the French Ambassador's Memo to Our Ministry dated January 13, 1947], Waijiaobu dang'an, Xisha qundao 5 [Foreign Ministry Archives: Xisha

The Chinese takeover of the Xisha Islands attracted immediate attention from the international media.

On January 9, the British Broadcasting Company announced the news about the Chinese takeover of the Xisha Islands and said the French government was surprised and puzzled by the sudden Chinese takeover, because the French army was stationed there before and after the Japanese occupation. One day later, Agence France-Presse reported that the French navy's reconnaissance aircraft had confirmed that there were no Chinese troops on the Xisha Islands, which had just recently been occupied by the Chinese army. The French news agency also said that the French Foreign Ministry spokesperson had also confirmed the hoisting of the Chinese flag over the Xisha Islands.[55]

On January 13, 1947, the French embassy in Nanjing presented a memorandum to the Foreign Ministry of the Chinese Nationalist government stating that "although the French government maintains its demand as proposed in the memorandum of July 1937, which advocated peaceful settlement of the issue between our two governments, we have to express our explicit reservation regarding your ministry's statement concerning the Chinese army's exercise of rights of occupation of the islands and any possible consequences."[56]

On the morning of January 17, 1947, a French ship filled with marine troops dropped anchor at Woody Island on the pretext that "the Xisha Islands are French territories." The captain declared that "he was landing under the orders of his government, and he was to

---

Islands (5)]. (Taipei: *Guoshiguan* 国史馆 [Academia Historica]), 1947, File no. 020-049904-0005-0015x-0016x.

[55] Haijun zongsilingbu, "Xi, Nansha qundao jianshe shishi," January 1947, Waijiaobu dang'an, Xisha qundao 6 [Foreign Ministry Archives: Xisha Islands (6)]. (Taipei: *Guoshiguan* 国史馆 [Academia Historica]), 1947, File no. 020-049904-0006-0024x-0025x.

[56] Zhaoyi Fa dashiguan yijiusiqi nian yi yue shisan ri guanyu Xisha qundao shi zhi benbu [Chinese Translation of the French Ambassador's Memo to Our Ministry dated January 13, 1947], Waijiaobu dang'an, Xisha qundao 5 [Foreign Ministry Archives: Xisha Islands (5)]. (Taipei: *Guoshiguan* 国史馆 [Academia Historica]), 1947, File no. 020-049904-0005-0015x-0016x.

ship the Chinese personnel off the island." He went as far as to set 8 a.m. on January 18 as a deadline for Chinese departure or he would "land by force." The French demand was firmly rejected by the Chinese garrison, which was "determined to resist." The French ship finally left Woody Island early on the morning on January 19 and went to occupy Pattle Island 50 nautical miles away.[57]

In response to the forced French landing on Woody Island and France's occupation of Pattle Island, the Chinese Foreign Ministry and Chinese Ambassador to France Qian Tai presented multiple protests to the French government, and negotiations ensued. On January 19, 1947, in a meeting with the secretary general of the French Foreign Ministry, Qian Tai requested him to "order the withdrawal of the French ship." The secretary general, however, denied the responsibility of the French government, claiming, "It was an action based on the free choice of the captain." He also said that he had ordered the French Indochinese governor Georges Thierry d'Argenlieu to "stop it as soon as possible," and he urged the Chinese government to "calm down." The director of the Department of Asian Affairs of the French Foreign Ministry followed up by explaining to Qian Tai that "the French government hopes for a peaceful settlement, and it does not want the Sino-French friendship to be undermined," and that the French also "hope the Chinese government will not escalate matters." When Qian Tai pursued the issue, inquiring whether the ship was dispatched under orders from the French government, the director reiterated, "It was not the intention of the French Foreign Ministry, which had telegraphed d'Argenlieu to withdraw."[58]

On January 23, Ye Gongchao announced to the press, "The Xisha Islands have been occupied by the Chinese army after the surrender

[57] S. Gao, *Jiang Zhongzheng zongtong dang'an: Shilüe gaoben* (68), pp. 443–444.

[58] Qian dashi Tai you Bali zhi waijiaobu cheng Jiang zhuxi dian [Ambassador Qian Tai's Telegram to Chairman Jiang Jieshi via the Foreign Ministry, Sent from Paris], January 19, 1947, Guomin zhengfu dang'an [Archives of the Nationalist Government], File no. 200 000000A-0662.20-8350.01-01 (Taipei: *Guoshiguan* 国史馆 [Academia Historica]); Qian Tai yu Zheng Tianxi cheng zhu Fa, Ying qingbao [Information on France and Britain Submitted by Qian Tai and Zheng Tianxi], dated from April 13, 1946 to December 10, 1948, Guomin zhengfu dang'an, File no. 200 000000A-0662.20-8350.01-01.

of the Japanese, and now the Chinese flag has been hoisted. The island group will continue to be Chinese territory."[59] However, the Chinese government concealed the fact that Chinese troops had been stationed on Taiping Island, mainly because it was still investigating how to define the range of the Nansha Islands (then known as the Tuansha Islands).

To address this issue, the National government directed the Ministry of the Interior to convene a discussion meeting of all concerned parties. On April 14, 1947, Fu Jiaojin invited Ma Dingbo, a staff member of the Defense Ministry; Shen Mo, a staff member from the Department of the Americas of the Foreign Ministry; and Lin Zun, commander of the fleet stationed in the South China Sea to meet and discuss related issues. Fu pointed out,

> The territorial boundaries of our South China Sea are in urgent need of definitive demarcation. As early as 1931, the official map of China included James Shoal as the southernmost border. Now the Dongsha, Xisha, and Nasha islands have been taken over from the Japanese, and we need to discuss two points: First, how do we define the range of the Nansha Islands? Second, what is the best way to publicize the range of the island groups?[60]

The meeting reached three conclusions. (1) "The southernmost territorial boundary should reach James Shoal," and "this sphere has been confirmed by pre-WWII Chinese government institutions and

---

[59] Zhu Fa dashiguan cheng waijiaobu [Memo Submitted by the Chinese Embassy in Paris to the Foreign Ministry], January 24, 1947, no. 240. Waijiaobu dang'an, Nansha qundao (Zhong Yue bufen), June 9, 1956 to November 12, 1959 [Foreign Ministry Archives: Nansha Islands (China–Vietnam) (June 9, 1956–November 12, 1959)] (Taipei: Taiwan *zhongyang yanjiuyuan jindaishi yanjiusuo dang'anguan* 台湾中央研究院近代史研究所档案馆 [Archives of the Institute of Modern History, Academia Sinica]), 1947, File no. 11-EPA-04141, p. 200065.

[60] Waijiaobu Chen Zegui guanyu Nansha qundao fanwei ji zhuquan zhi queding yu gongbuan huiyi baogao [Report on Affirming and Publicizing the Scope of the Xisha and Nansha Islands and Chinese Sovereignty over Them, Submitted by Chen Zegui], April 15, 1947, Waijiaobu dang'an, Xisha qundao 8 [Foreign Ministry Archives: Xisha Islands (8)]. (Taipei: *Guoshiguan* 国史馆 [Academia Historica]), 1947, File no. 020-049904-0008-0095x-0096x.

schools and has been endorsed by the Ministry of the Interior. There should be no change to it." (2) The announcement of Chinese sovereignty over the Xisha and Nansha Islands should be made after the naming and mapping have been completed by the Ministry of the Interior and submitted to the Nationalist government. The Ministry of the Interior will be responsible for making it known throughout the country. Before publicizing this information, the Naval Command should try to station troops on the islands. (3) The fishing season in the Xisha and Nansha Islands is coming soon, and the fishermen who are to depart for these islands from the mainland should be protected by the Naval Command and Guangdong provincial government and supported with convenient transportation and telecommunication.[61]

In May 1947, Lin Zun wrote to the Nationalist government, urging a timely announcement of "the Chinese recovery of the Xisha and Nansha Islands." He recommended, "The Xisha Islands should be treated as a whole when publicizing." He had two suggestions concerning the Nansha Islands. "(1) Declare that all the islands are to be recovered by China. (2) If the easternmost islands are inside the territorial sea of the Philippines, we may give them up, and declare the recovery of the islands within the area between latitudes 7 degrees and 12 degrees north and longitudes 111 degrees and 115.30 degrees east."[62] In response, the National government directed the Executive Yuan to call another meeting to deliberate.

On June 10, 1947, the secretariat of the Executive Yuan convened a meeting of officials from the Ministry of the Interior, the Foreign Ministry, and the Defense Ministry to discuss Lin Zun's proposals. Guan Ou from the Executive Yuan presided. At the meeting,

---

[61] Xi, Nansha qundao fanwei ji zhuquan zhi queding yu gongbuan huiyi jilu [Minutes of the Meeting on Affirming and Publicizing the Scope of the Xisha and Nansha Islands and Chinese Sovereignty over Them], April 14, 1947, Waijiaobu dang'an, Xisha qundao 8 [Foreign Ministry Archives: Xisha Islands (8)]. (Taipei: *Guoshiguan* 国史馆 [Academia Historica]), 1947, File no. 020-049904-0008-0086x-0091x.

[62] Xingzhengyuan minshuchu gonghan [Letter from the Secretariat of the Executive Yuan], June 2, 1947, Waijiaobu dang'an, Xisha qundao 9 [Foreign Ministry Archives: Xisha Islands (9)]. (Taipei: *Guoshiguan* 国史馆 [Academia Historica]), 1947, File no. 020-049904-0009-0035x.

Fu Jiaojin advocated "following the resolution on this issue, as passed at the last meeting of the Ministry of the Interior," namely, "using the pre-WWII government and school publications concerning the South China Sea territorial scope as the standard." With regard to the timing of the official announcement, Fu suggested that "it should occur after the Ministry of Defense occupies all accessible islands." Gan Lijing from the Ministry of Defense pointed out that "the Japanese occupation of the Nansha Islands had its own scope, which included all islands but did not cover the open sea to the west of the Nansha Islands. Since we are taking over from the Japanese, we can simply use the old Japanese scope." Shen Mo from the Foreign Ministry said that following the direction of Jiang Jieshi, "It seems appropriate for the Ministry of Defense to continue military occupation of the important islands, and the means and scope of the announcement should be determined after the stationing of troops is finished."[63]

The meeting concluded with a resolution that included the following items. (1) The territorial scope publicized "should follow the territorial scope in the South China Sea that has been endorsed by the Ministry of the Interior." (2) The information should be publicized via "domestic news release, followed by historical/geographic basics and condition of local facilities [of these islands], accompanied by illustrations, compiled by the Ministry of the Interior," and "the data should be submitted to the Nationalist government for archiving and should be transmitted to all government institutions and schools." (3) The announcement should be made "after the important islands such as Nanwei [Spratly] Island and the Shuangzi Islands [Northeast Cay and Southwest Cay] are occupied and after territorial markers have been erected on the less important

[63] Waijiaobu Liu Jiaju cheng guanyu shencha gongbu Xi, Nansha qundao wei wo shoufu an huiyi taolun yu jueyi qingxing [Summary of Deliberations and Decisions Concerning the Review and Publicizing of Our Recovery of the Xisha and Nansha Islands, Submitted by Liu Jiaju of the Foreign Ministry], June 11, 1947, Waijiaobu dang'an, Xisha qundao 9 [Foreign Ministry Archives: Xisha Islands (9)]. (Taipei: *Guoshiguan* 国史馆 [Academia Historica]), 1947, File no. 020-049904-0009-0029a-0033a.

neighboring islands."[64] Jiang Jieshi approved the recommendations of this meeting and directed the Executive Yuan to "carefully research and report the evidence of the Nansha Islands' belonging to China."[65]

On June 16, 1947, Zhang Qun sent duplicates of the resolution to the Defense Ministry, the Ministry of the Interior, and the Foreign Ministry. The revised "Review Report" had the following content. (1) Confirmation of the scope of the Xisha and Nansha Islands. The report stated that the scope of the Xisha Islands should "follow the original recommendation and cover all the islands, as this will accord with the scope of the islands as demarcated earlier by the Ministry of the Interior." The report then turned to the Nansha Islands, whose scope "has been defined by the Ministry of the Interior as all of its islands," and whose "easternmost island is still one hundred nautical miles away from the Philippines, which has not yet presented a territorial claim to it." Thus, it continued, we "should also claim all the Nansha Islands." (2) Announcement of the Chinese recovery of all of the islands. The "Review Report" asserted first, "Our government has made numerous statements regarding Chinese sovereignty over all of the Xisha islands, and there seems to be no need to announce recovery (Pattle Island is still under the military occupation of France, and the Foreign Ministry is now negotiating with the French)." It then stated a second point, "At present, it is not deemed necessary to declare that the Nansha Islands fully or partially belong to China (our actual control is only exercised over one of the islands, namely Taiping Island)." (3) Stationing troops on other important islands in the Xisha and Nansha archipelagoes. Here, the "Review Report" urged "the Defense Ministry to send troops to occupy important islands" such as Nanwei Island and the Shuangzi Islands. (4) The time and means of announcing the Chinese takeover of the Xisha and Nansha Islands. "The time and means of indicating that the islands belong to China and that China had recovered them should be left to the Ministry of the Interior, in collaboration with other concerned

[64] *Ibid.*

[65] Xingzheng yuan xunling [Directive from the Executive Yuan], July 16, 1947, Waijiaobu dang'an, Xisha qundao 9 [Foreign Ministry Archives: Xisha Islands (9)]. (Taipei: *Guoshiguan* 国史馆 [Academia Historica]), 1947, File no. 020-049904-0009-0042x-0043x.

sectors, based on the situation of the actual control of the Xisha and Nansha Islands."[66]

To concretize the scope of Chinese territory in the Xisha and Nansha Islands, the Department of Territory of the Ministry of the Interior printed a "Map of the South China Sea Islands," which has become an indispensable blueprint for modern Chinese maps of the South China Sea. The map has several features. (1) It used 11 broken dashes, which form a "U"-shaped circle, to demarcate Chinese sovereign waters in the South China Sea. This demarcation line has become the source of the current nine-dash line, which is now used by China to make territorial claims, and it has become crucial legal grounds on which to claim Chinese territorial sovereignty over the islands in the South China Sea. (2) The map adjusted the names of the island groups. For instance, the Tuansha Islands were renamed "the Nansha Islands," and the former Nansha Islands were renamed "the Zhongsha [Middle Sand] Islands." (3) It reconfirmed the southernmost tip of Chinese maritime territory was "Zengmu tan" [James Shoal], which was renamed "Zengmu ansha" [literally "James Hidden Reef"].[67]

In August 1947, the Minister of the Interior created the following maps: "Simplified Map of the Island Positions in the South China Sea," "Map of the Xisha Islands," "Map of the Zhongsha Islands," "Map of the Nansha Islands," "Map of Taiping Island," and "Map of Yongxing Island and Shi Island," along with a "Chart of New and Old Names of the Islands in the South China Sea." All these were submitted to the Executive Yuan for approval. The same month, Jiang Jieshi, chairman of the Nationalist government, decided after reviewing the "Simplified Map of the Island Positions in the South China Sea" that "the scope [of Chinese sovereignty] should cover all these island groups."[68]

In November 1947, the first book in a series "Chinese territory authorized by the Ministry of the Interior [Neizhengbu fangyu congshu]," titled *A Brief Account of the Geography of the Islands in the*

---

[66] *Ibid.*

[67] Neizhengbu gonghan [Letter from the Ministry of the Interior], September 4, 1947, Waijiaobu dang'an, Xisha qundao 10 [Foreign Ministry Archives: Xisha Islands (10)]. (Taipei: *Guoshiguan* 国史馆 [Academia Historica]), 1947, File no. 020-049904-0010-0039x.

[68] *Ibid.*

South China Sea [*Nanhai zhudao dili zhilüe*], edited by Zheng Ziyue, was published by the Commercial Press. The "Simplified Map of the Island Positions in the South China Sea" and other maps, as well as the "Chart of New and Old Names of the Islands in the South China Sea" were included in the book, which was distributed by the Department of Territory of the Ministry of the Interior to all other ministries and commissions on November 19 for reference.[69] On December 1, 1947, the Ministry of the Interior officially endorsed the names of all the islands and reefs in the Dongsha, Xisha, Zhongsha, and Nansha Islands, which were then published in the print media at home and abroad and became known to the world. There was full compliance with all measures stipulated by international law. The islands in the South China Sea formally returned to China, and China asserted its sovereignty over these territories in accordance with international law. On April 1, 1949, the Hainan Special Administrative Region was founded, and the Dongsha, Xisha, Zhongsha, and Nansha Islands came under its jurisdiction.[70]

Conclusion

First, there are solid grounds in history and international law for Chinese sovereignty over the islands in the South China Sea.

[69] Z. Zheng 郑资约, ed. *Nanhai zhudao dili zhilüe* 南海诸岛地理志略 [*A Brief Account of the Geography of the Islands in the South China Sea*] (Beijing: Commercial Press), 1947. Neizhengbu fangyusi han [Letter from the Department of Territory of the Ministry of the Interior], November 19, 1947, Waijiaobu dang'an, Xisha qundao 10 [Foreign Ministry Archives: Xisha Islands (10)]. (Taipei: *Guoshiguan* 国史馆 [Academia Historica]), 1947, File no. 020-049904-0010-0042x.

[70] Zhonghuaminguo lingyou Nansha ji Xisha qundao genju zhi shuotie [Republic of China's Statement on the Foundations for Occupying and Governing the Nansha Islands and the Xisha Islands], January 1974, Waijiaobu dang'an, Nansha qundao (Zhong Yue bufen) (January 1974-?) [Foreign Ministry Archives: Nansha Islands (China–Vietnam) (January 1974–?)] (Taipei: Taiwan *zhongyang yanjiuyuan jindaishi yanjiusuo dang'anguan* 台湾中央研究院近代史研究所档案馆 [Archives of the Institute of Modern History, Academia Sinica]), 1947, File no. 11-EPA-04590, p. 105537.

On June 26, 1887, the Treaty between China and France Concerning Delimitation of the Border between China and Tonkin [Convention relative à la Délimitation de la Frontière entre la Chine et le Tonkin] was signed. This treaty demarcated the border between China and French Indochina. According to Article 3 of the treaty,

> The islands in the sea shall be demarcated southward along the red line drawn by the border negotiation ministers from both countries. This line cuts across the eastern hilltop at Chagushe (in Chinese it is called Wanzhu, located south of Mangjie and southwest of Zhushan), and this line should be taken as the borderline. All the islands to the east of the line belong to China, and the Jiutou Hill in the sea to the west of the line, along with other small islands, belongs to Vietnam.[71]

The borderline between Vietnam and Guangdong is located at Zhushan (21°30′ north, 108°2′ east), so the maritime borderline between the two countries is the longitude line of 108°2′ east. Although the ministers from China and France who negotiated the border disagreed with each other at the beginning, after they had reached a consensus, they agreed "to abide with all the resolutions forever," and "they reviewed and signed the agreement and the map of the borderline without disagreement."[72] Thus, the maritime borderline between China and Vietnam was defined according to this international treaty. The Vietnamese coast is to the west of the longitude line of 108°2′ east, and all of the South China Sea islands are located to the east of this line. Therefore, these islands are Chinese territory without any question. In other words, as early as 1887, the French government had admitted that the islands in the South China Sea belong to China

---

[71] F. Zhong *"Xu yi jiewu zhuantiao" di san kuan* 中法《续议界务专条》第三款 [Special Sino-French Treaty of Continued Discussion of the Borderline]. *Waijiaobu dang'an* 外交部档案 [Foreign Ministry Archives]. File no. 11-EPA-04590, p. 105561 (Taipei: Taiwan *zhongyang yanjiuyuan jindaishi yanjiusuo dang'anguan* 台湾中央研究院近代史研究所档案馆 [Archives of the Institute of Modern History, Academia Sinica]), June 26, 1887.

[72] *Ibid*, p. 105560.

and that China has sovereignty over them. Based on this treaty, the Nationalist government used the longitude line of 108°2′ east as the starting point to demarcate Chinese maritime territory.

From time immemorial, Chinese fishermen from Hainan Island frequently went to the islands in the South China Sea to fish, and they took up irregular residence on the islands. After WWII, both the Chinese government's stationing of troops on the islands and its establishment of the Nansha Administrative Bureau to exercise governance indicated indisputable Chinese sovereignty.

Second, the victory of China's War of Resistance against Japanese Aggression and the international antifascist war, as well as the postwar international order, all granted China the right to recover its sovereignty over the South China Sea. Right after WWII, the US and British governments, and the US government in particular, took a pro-China stance with regard to the issue of Chinese sovereignty over the South China Sea. On January 28, 1947, the American and British ambassadors to France met with French Foreign Minister Georges-Augustin Bidault, and both requested "France to carefully consider the historical materials presented by the Chinese government concerning Chinese sovereignty over the Xisha Islands, according to the instructions of their own governments [namely the US and British governments]." Before the meeting, both ambassadors "reached an agreement in principle that, regarding the issue of the Xisha Islands, France should seek a solution through diplomatic channels and without undermining Sino-French friendship."[73]

As a victor in WWII and a permanent member of the United Nations Security Council, China recovered the four provinces in the northeast, Taiwan, the Penghu (Pescadores) Islands, and the islands in the South China Sea, and reaffirmed the map of the Republic of China. This was China's right granted by the United Nations and the Allies after WWII. More importantly, it was China's legal right based on the post-WWII international order.

---

[73] Baomiju cheng Jiang zhuxi er yue qi ri qingbao [Information Submitted to Jiang Jieshi by the Bureau of Military Intelligence], February 11, 1947, Jiang Zhongzheng zongtong dang'an, File no. 002-020400-00050-056-001x_05_04_2016.

Chapter

3

Archival Research to Enhance Territorial and Sovereignty Claims

Vivian Louis Forbes

Adjunct Research Professor, NISCSS, Haikou, China
Distinguished Research Professor, CIBOS, Wuhan University, China

Abstract

In an endeavor to establish certainty over territorial and sovereignty claims, research at National Archives could prove invaluable. A period of research, whether in your nation's capital city or elsewhere, at home or in other countries, that may or may not have trading relations or administrative linkages, could uncover a wealth of information contained in the original documents such as agreements, Memoranda of Understanding, treaties, and particularly, in files maintained by the relevant departments and ministries such as foreign and home affairs and trade. Examples of where such research has produced documents that were presented at international courts and arbitration tribunals to prove sovereignty claims include the cases in which Malaysia was party to disputes with Indonesia and Singapore at the International Court of Justice, in 2002 and 2008, respectively. In January 2017, reports emerged that Malaysia had "discovered" three important documents at the UK National Archives that had become available to the public. Such a discovery may go some way forward to turn a decision set by the ICJ in 2008 in Malaysia's favor. This chapter demonstrates, illustrates, and discusses the manner in which research at national archives, public and private libraries, and other institutions that are depositaries of primary documents, and by inference also secondary, may support claims to territory may be conducted.

Keywords: National archives, sovereignty, territory, official correspondence, secret files.

> *...historical materials are the cells and tissues of history; when incomplete or inaccurate, history cannot be reconstructed*
>
> Philosopher, Liang Qichao (1873–1929).

Introduction

Anyone who has cleaned out a family house or attic will know the importance of retaining family documents — birth and marriage certificates and photographs — of important events that the family or even close friends were involved in and even newspaper clippings. In the words of Akita,[1] "Historical gap is created due to missing written records"; gaps in historical records may cause problems in securing title to territory and proving sovereignty over a parcel of land. History cannot be reconstructed if documents are missing.

Perseverance in research could pay dividends as shown by the Government of Malaysia when its team found three vital documents at the National Archives, UK between August 2016 and January 2017.[2] In its Application, Malaysia contends that there exists a new fact of such a nature as to be a decisive factor within the meaning of Article 61 according to the ICJ on February 4, 2017 in referring to the three documents discovered.

---

[1] Lailah Gifty Akita, *Think Great, Be Great* (New York: Createspace Independent Publishing Platform, 2014).

[2] News of the find was announced by the Ministry of Foreign Affairs, Malaysia, and given due publicity in the local media and by the International Court of Justice in February 2017.

On undertaking academic research in national archives, it will come as no surprise to "discover" a wealth of information that may prove to be important in obtaining proof of sovereignty over a territory that was lost due to some administrative oversight, or indeed a misunderstanding or misinterpretation of a phrase in the narrative of an agreement.

In an attempt to establish a database by searching thousands of government-generated documents, there are nearly as many generally related individual items mentioned in them, as illustrated in Figure 1 — a typical archival document that could support territorial and sovereignty claims in that activity was undertaken at some earlier time.

There is excitement and joy of opening the files and folders, rolls of map, sepia prints, and black and white photographs, not really knowing what one may find to read. Between the aging covers of files on these

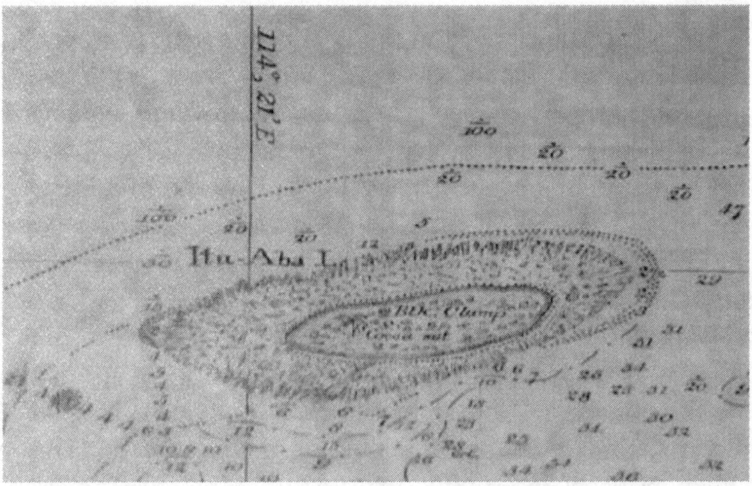

Figure 1. Survey of Itu Aba Island by HMS Rifleman, 1866.[3]

[3] The map extract is from a hydrographic survey plan held at the United Kingdom Hydrographic Office Archives (UKHO), Taunton. Such plans were compiled from original surveys undertaken by the Royal Navy's Admiralty Hydrographic Office during the 1700 and 1800s.

shelves in the archives, contained in tiny, abstract black, blue, or red marks and scribbles on sheets of paper, are voices from the past. Voices that may now wish to reach into the present and convey what once may be perceived as "secret," and these may be of importance for the future.

The stale, musty, and dusty odor of the files that have been stored for 50 years or more, from sheets of paper and pages of books gently wafts up and smells like the very old books in public and university libraries that no one ever really opens let alone reads but yet are readily admired for their ability to survive the contemporary "cull on physical materials," or in the words of political correctness — "surplus to present requirements" or "it is now available online"; however, please do not mention words like "discard" or "dump" as these infer destruction of culture, educational value, and social heritage.

Archival Material

At times, while reading through the documents that have been handwritten straining to decipher the words, it may occur to the researcher whether the authors' peers had as much difficulty reading their inked scribbles. Consider the cover of the archive file FE 13/116/1 (Figure 2) that discusses two topics: (1) Violation of the Freedom of Navigations in the Area of the China Sea by Kunmingtang (yes, this may be a guess based on the handwriting; the correct spelling is "Kuomintang"); and (2) Soviet Tanker in Acts of Aggression against China.[4] The file was created on November 9, 1953. Amazing that even in 1953 there was discussion of the concept of "freedom of navigation" and "hijacking" in the China Sea. Nothing has changed in the last 60 years! The geographical definition of insular features has been challenged by legal interpretations, for example, Itu Aba Island in 1866 (see Figure 1); in 2016, the island was considered a "rock" according to the provisions of Article 121 of the 1982 UN Law of the Sea Convention.[5]

---

[4]This file is part of the collection held by the UK National Archives located at Richmond. Details of holdings may be shown UK National Archives, http://www.nationalarchives.gov.uk/.

[5]The Ruling of the Permanent Court of Arbitration on July 12, 2016 in the case brought by the Philippines against China relating to insular features of the Spratly

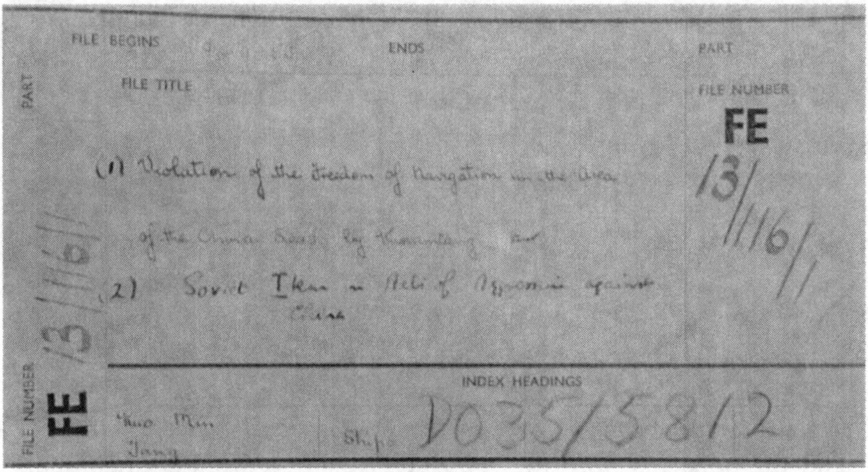

Figure 2. Front page cover of a file in UK National Archives.

Archival material is vital not only to the writer of historical fiction but also to academics, government officials, and lawyers who are required to delve into the written word to seek facts to prove a point of view. See the range of selected images in Annex 1.

A level of miscommunication is unrealistic and belies the agency of diplomats as more than messengers, but the exercise points to a very real problem in diplomacy. Miscommunication is a nightmare to diplomats whose nuanced words are so carefully pulled apart by their contemporaries, as is the case in the US, especially during March and April 2017. There is an enjoyment in reading these documents, because the foreign office staffers write so clearly and crisply, mostly. At times, it is as if the words jump out of the page, and some of these documents show little chinks in the formalities of government and glimpses in the margins that may suggest cynicisms and joys.

The present author had the opportunity to visit many national archives, libraries, and museums to examine documents, charts, and maps for the purposes of boundary studies and geopolitical issues. The

---

Group held that none of the features were capable of generating an Exclusive Economic Zone, only a Territorial Sea Zone where applicable. Refer to the PCA's webpages.

following descriptions of a few national archives namely, Japan, Taiwan, US, and UK are offered with examples of records and reports that are held at these facilities. How does one search the records in an Archive?

UK National Archives

In the instance of the UK National Archives, a search may be conducted using "Discovery," the catalogue, or the "Search Box" online.[6] This is a keyword search so the results will show all instances of the term(s) that was searched from within the Archives' catalogue descriptions for these records. To find out which types of records are held and whether one needs to physically visit the facility to access them, the details are on the webpage. To access original documents, a reader's ticket is required; however, if one wishes to access documents online only, they will not need a reader's ticket.

The records of the UK National Archives, consist of correspondence, reports, memoranda, and other papers documenting the work of, for example, of a Foreign Secretary, or Home Secretary, and are particularly a rich source for the study of diplomacy during, for example, the Second World War. Such records will include material additional to, or expanding on, the papers contained in the main functions of the Foreign Office (Foreign Affairs) political records for this period, where the paperwork passing through the private office was not passed on into the departmental registry system.

- Use AND find more than one term in a description
- Use "double quotation marks" to find exact phrases

For example, a search for the papers relating to Sir Anthony Eden's private office papers 1935–1946 the particular file is FO 800/750–851, perhaps one of many files containing the papers of the then former Prime Minister of UK, at the time of World War II. The records contained in the files may look like the illustration in Figure 3, which

[6] See UK National Archives webpage mentioned in Footnote 3.

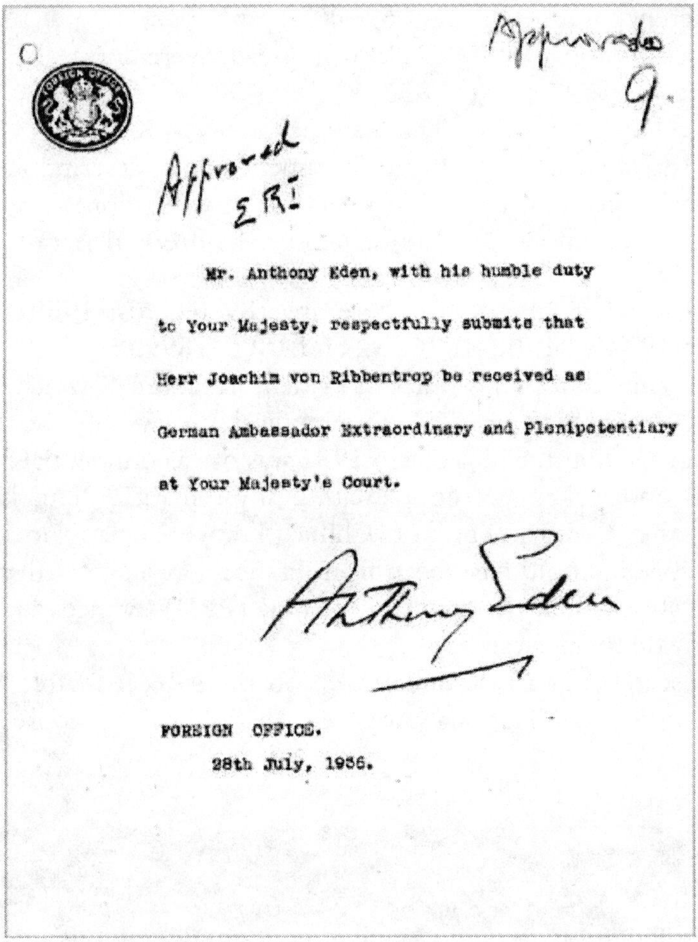

Approved

9.

Approved
ERI

Mr. Anthony Eden, with his humble duty to Your Majesty, respectfully submits that Herr Joachim von Ribbentrop be received as German Ambassador Extraordinary and Plenipotentiary at Your Majesty's Court.

Anthony Eden

FOREIGN OFFICE.
28th July, 1936.

Figure 3. Document held in the National Archive.

is a submission for the appointment of Joachim von Ribbentrop as German Ambassador (FO 954/10a).[7]

A Search made on the UK National Archive on April 13, 2017 with subject matter "Falkland Island Sovereignty" presented the following tabulation:

[7] UK National Archive File: FO 954/10a (FO = Foreign Office of UK).

Reference	FO 6/500[8]
Description	Falkland Islands (sovereignty)
Date	1833
Held by:	The National archives, Kew
Closure status:	Open document, Open description
Restrictions on use:	3 working days' notice to produce
Access conditions:	Normal closure before FOI Act

The search revealed that there are 189 records: 1950+ (135), 1925–1949 (45), 1900–1924 (6), and 1800–1899 (5).

The range of topics is varied as evident in Figure 4, which implies that the HMS "Iroquois'" hydrographical surveys off the Paracel Islands in the South China Sea in 1931 was of "a confidential nature" and was undertaken "without exciting any remark." Remarks from whom: the Governments of China, France, Japan or others? Presumably, it would have been from France and Japan at that point of time. Research at the archives in China (PRC), France, and Japan may provide the answer.

If a search was to be undertaken on the subject matter "Hong Kong" at the UK National Archives, an "online" response would

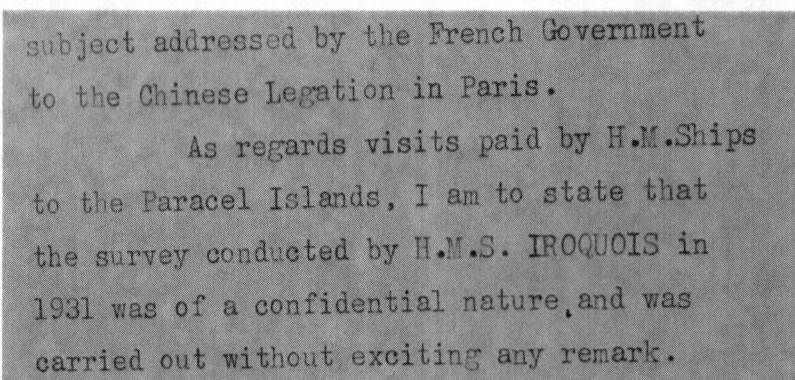
subject addressed by the French Government to the Chinese Legation in Paris.

As regards visits paid by H.M.Ships to the Paracel Islands, I am to state that the survey conducted by H.M.S. IROQUOIS in 1931 was of a confidential nature, and was carried out without exciting any remark.

Figure 4. An extract of a primary document held at the UK National Archives.

[8] UK National Archive File: FO 6/500.

reveal that the facility holds 54,884 documents of which 3,201 are available for download. Other Archives in the UK hold 2,640 items. The time frames for the documents are:

Date unknown	570
1950+	30,831
1925–1949	24,496
1900–1924	8,365
1800–1899	2,513
1700–1799	24
1600–1699	7
1500–1599	2

In another search on the subject matter "Straits Settlement" with reference to the territories that were administered by the British, in what is present-day Malaysia and Singapore,[9] the following summary was offered:

The National Archives	226
Available for download	1
Other archives	23
Dates unknown	5
1950+	7
1925–1949	152
1900–1924	61
1800–1899	49
1700–1799	8
1600–1699	7
1500–1599	3

The range of themes and topics covered in the files vary. For example, three files are mentioned hereunder to illustrate the spatial, temporal, and thematic nature of the files held in national archives.

[9]The number of items held by the UK National Archives with the search words "Straits Settlement" as listed in the webpages of that institution.

Straits Settlement, Act Regulating Pilots

Board of Trade Harbour Department: Correspondence and papers. Board of Trade Department: Correspondence and papers. Straits Settlement Act Regulating Pilots.[10]

Held by:	The National Archives — Ministries of Transport and related bodies
Date:	1869
Reference:	MT 10/81/3
Subjects:	Asia | Trade and Commerce

Colonial Office: Straits Settlement Acts

Reference:	CO 274[11]
Title:	Colonial Office: Straits Settlement Acts
Description:	This series contains acts passed by the government of the Straits Settlements.
Date:	1867–1949
Related material:	For later Singapore Acts see CO 925
Held by:	The National Archives, Kew
Legal status:	Public Record(s)
Language:	English
Physical:	23 volume(s)

Johore Boundary Agreement Correspondence; Draft Bill; Copy of Agreement; Anglo-Italian Treaty (East African Territories)

Colonial Office: Straits Settlements Original Correspondence. Johore boundary agreement correspondence; draft bill; copy of the agreement; Anglo-Italian Treaty (East African Territories) Act, 1925.[12]

---

[10] UK National Archives File: MT 10/81/3 (MT = Ministry of Transport of UK).

[11] UK National Archives File: CO 274 (CO = Commonwealth Office, UK).

[12] UK National Archives: in this file correspondence within relate to three geographical areas. Caution is advised to ensure each file is thoroughly examined for the subject matter.

Held by:	The National Archives — Colonial Office Commonwealth and Foreign and Commonwealth Offices
Date:	1927–1928
Reference:	CO 273/536/9
Subjects:	Asia | International | Treaties and Alliances

Files relevant to national security are released once an embargo is lifted, or as stated in the jargon of the archivist — the file is de-classified — the SECRET label no longer applies to the status of the record. For example, on April 11, 2017, while compiling the present narrative, the latest files of MI5 were released. On this day, 24 previously "top secret" files from the UK Security Service, or MI5 were made available to the public.[13] These records cover a range of subjects and span the inter-war years — Second World War and post-war era up to the mid-1960s. Personal files include individuals classed as Second World War German intelligence agents, Soviet intelligence agents, communists, and suspected communist and Russian sympathizers. They are searchable from KV 2/4315 to KV 2/4345. Among the files released was the following title and record number:

Westland Helicopters: part 1A

Catalogue reference: PREM 19/1415
Date range: April 30, 1985 to December 10, 1985

This file PREM 19/1416[14] provides useful material on the background to the Westland Crisis of December 1985 to January 1986. Apparently, there were mounting tensions between ministers of the then Government about the future of the company. Michael Heseltine, then Secretary of State for Defence, wrote to the then Prime Minister, Margaret Thatcher, on April 30, 1985 about the ailing Westland helicopter company. By May and June 1986, the possibility of Westland going into receivership was mooted and questions were raised as to whether the Government should provide assistance.

[13] UK National Archives webpages.

[14] UK National Archives File: PREM 19/1415 and 1416.

The aforementioned examples, gleaned from the UK National Archives, offer a representative sample of records held. Although all the examples shown do not necessarily relate to territory and sovereignty, they do illustrate the diverse range of themes and spatial and temporal extent of documents held. Likewise, a peek at archives in other countries, for example the US, Taiwan, and Japan, to name just a few, reveals a similar diversification of valuable documents for the researcher to delve into.

National Archives and Records Administration (NARA), US

The National Archives and Records Administration (NARA) of the US is the nation's record keeper. Records belong to the people is the rationale, and for more than seven decades, the NARA has preserved and provided access to the records of the US. Records help the citizens claim their rights and entitlements, hold their elected officials accountable for their actions, and document the history as a nation. In short, the NARA ensures continuing access to the essential documentation of the rights of American citizens and the actions of their Government. The research rooms are open to the public. Each of the locations holds different groups of records. To make the most efficient use of time, the researcher is encouraged to write, telephone, or send an email in advance to make sure that the documents or the microfilm they wish to consult are at the location they intend to visit.

In the first two decades of the 20th century, the relationship between the US and Japan was marked by increasing tension and corresponding attempts to use diplomacy to reduce the threat of conflict. Each side had territory and interests in Asia that they were concerned the other might threaten. US treatment of Japanese immigrants as well as competition for economic and commercial opportunities in China also heightened tensions. At the same time, each country's territorial claims in the Pacific formed the basis for several agreements between the two nations, as each government sought to protect its own strategic and economic interests. Files or records document all these political and social issues.

The NARA was established in 1934; however, its major holdings date back to 1775.[15] The NARA only keeps those Federal Records that are judged to have continuing value — about 2–5% of those generated in any given year. There are approximately 10 billion pages of textual records; 12 million charts, maps, and architectural and engineering drawings; 24 million aerial photographs; 300,000 reels of motion picture film; 400,000 video and sound recordings; and 133 terabytes of electronic data. All of these materials are preserved because they are perceived to be important to the workings of government, have long-term research significance, or provide information of value to citizens.

For example, in the words of the then President of US, made on December 15, 1945, the record states:

> The Government of the United States holds that peace and prosperity of the world in this new and unexplored era ahead depend upon the ability of sovereign nations to combine for collective security in the United Nations organization.
>
> It is the firm belief of this Government that a strong and united democratic China is of the utmost importance to the success of the UNO and for world peace. China disorganized and divided either by the foreign aggression, such as that undertaken by the Japanese, or by violent internal strife, is an undermining influence to world stability and peace, now and in the future. The United States Government has long subscribed to the principle that the management of internal affairs is the responsibility of the peoples of the sovereign nations. Events of this century, however, would indicate that a breach of peace anywhere in the world threatens the peace of the entire world. It is thus in the most vital interest of the United States and all the United Nations that the people of China overlook no opportunity to adjust their internal differences promptly by methods of peaceful negotiations.

Closer to the Northeast Asia region, if the focus of research relates to the islands in the Sea of Japan and the East and South China Seas,

---

[15] The USA National Archives, NARA https://www.archives.gov/.

a search on the webpages of the National Archives of the US may offer a plethora of files with the key words search of "Cairo Declaration" or "Treaty Of San Fransisco." In the Gerald R. Ford Presidential Library and Museum, a file relating to Philippines and Vietnam Incident in Spratly Islands contained Box 39 labeled — IF/NS File for the President, 7,603,086 — contains instructions to Ambassador Williams to take appropriate actions as deemed necessary (www.fordlibrarymuseum.gov/library/guides/findingaid/nsalogged.asp).

National Archive of Taiwan

Former President Ma Ying-jeou allegedly observed that the 1952 "Treaty of Taipei" (refer to Annex 1) affirmed the transfer of Taiwan's sovereignty from Japan to the Republic of China (ROC). President Ma's statement deviated from his previous claim that it was the 1943 Cairo Declaration that gave the ROC its claim to Taiwan.

> While the 1952 treaty does not specify the legal successor government [of Taiwan], it was clear between the lines, Japan would not have signed the accord with the ROC if it did not intend to concede the territories to the ROC.

However, the 1943 Cairo Accord and the Potsdam Declaration of 1945 gave China the right to resume sovereignty over Taiwan and Penghu. It is alleged that the Cairo Declaration was a legal document that established the Republic of China's claim. Independence activists, however, doubt the validity of the 1943 Declaration, saying that it was little more than a press release and cite the 1952 treaty to argue that Taiwan's international status remains undefined. To check the accuracy of these statements, a potential source for research would be the National Archives of Taiwan with its vast holdings of government-generated files.

Members of the public who intend to read, copy, or duplicate an archive document can search the catalogues via the Archives Access Service (A+, https://aa.archives.gov.tw)[16] or visit the Archives Access

[16] The National Archives of Taiwan, https://www.archives.gov.tw/english/Publish.aspx?cnid=1232.

Centre (AAC) located on the first floor of the National Archives Administration (NAA) of the National Development Council to fill in an application form for access to the archives. Researchers may also submit an application to NAA via mail, fax, email, or using a citizen digital certificate to apply via the NAA website. The application form for access to archives may be downloaded from the NAA website or obtained from the AAC.

On December 15, 1999, the Government of the ROC passed the "Archives Act" to improve the management and transparency of important documents relating to the history and development of the Republic. On March 1, 2000, the Research, Development, and Evaluation Commission (RDEC) set up the NAA Preparatory Office, laying the foundation and developing plans for a centralized management of documentation organization. On October 24, 2001, the "Organic Act of the National Archives Administration" was passed, and a month later, the NAA was formally established as a part of the RDEC. The legislation entered into effect on January 1, 2002, and provided a legal foundation for an archives administration system.

On August 21, 2013, the President promulgated the "Organic Act Establishing the National Archives Administration," National Development Council. This legislative instrument established the administration as a part of the newly named National Development Council effective on January 22, 2014.

The National Archive accepts donations, trusteeship, and acquisition of valuable documents from private sectors to ensure the archives is worthy of long-term preservation value to be properly stored, preserved, and utilized after cataloguing description, arrangement, and conservation. By late-2016, 19 categories of approximately 18 km of national archives were collected by NAA, including those related with government policies, interior affairs, cross-strait relations, legislative, and control of national affairs.

To facilitate public access to the archives, the latest information about the national archives has been provided since 2010 by the quarterly Newsletter of the national archives. The data in the national archives (divided into four major categories) of 160 m length were collected between July and September 2016. They are interior affairs

(4.5%), fiscal and financial (89%), transportation (6.25%), and local affairs (0.25%).

As of September 30, 2016, the National Archives of Taiwan collection totaled 17,918.575 m linear of shelf space in length. Paper files accounted for 17,450.75 m; non-paper files totaled 467.825 m, including 202.73 m of photographic files; 244.64 m of video and audio tape files; 12.815 m of electronic media files; and 7.64 m of restructured agency used seals.[17] The numbers and proportions of the various types of files include about 4.5% relating to Foreign and Overseas Chinese Affairs and a mere 0.15% on the Government's Policies. However, fiscal and financial issues represent over 20% of the collection, and National Defense and Veteran Affairs slightly over 17%.

National Imperial Palace Museum, Taiwan

The National Imperial Palace Museum in Taipei is highly commended for its collection of primary documents and in particular its collection of maps, scrolls, treaty narratives, and scripts relating to China's northern and south-eastern boundaries of the Qing era and earlier.

Published by the National Imperial Palace Museum of Taiwan in early-2017, *The Green Borderlands* "Treaties and maps that defined the Qing's Southwest Boundaries" is a catalogue of the primary documents (treaties) and maps that were, in March 2017, on display at the Museum.[18] The present author was fortunate to view the display. If there was a regret, it was that he was not permitted to capture on camera images of the displayed maps and the documents. Scholars of boundary studies and sociological issues relating to borderland interactions will find this volume of immense interest. There are at least 76 colored maps and documents of surveys and treaties in this volume consisting of 252 pages.

[17] The statistics were accessed from the Archive's web pages on May 25, 2017.

[18] This volume offers many maps depicting the terrestrial boundary between China and its south-eastern neighbors.

The reprographics and the quality of production are of a high standard, and the volume, at the time, was available only at the National Palace Museum at a cost of NT$ 850. This volume is of tremendous value for administrators who wish to understand the implication of historical primary documents in dealing with contemporary issues and problems over territorial disputes and in the background of the geopolitical complexities in the South East Asian region as we are witnessing in early 2017 and the preceding years.

The reproduction of the narrative of the agreements, in essence, every map and series of primary documents is essential for reading and examination, if the reader wishes to comprehend why and how the borders along the southern part of China were determined and demarcated.

National Archives, Japan (NAJ)

Public access to the Specified Historical Public Records and Archives is principally ensured unless there is a risk of harm to the rights and interests of an individual or there are any other reasonable grounds to restrict it.[19] The principal public records holdings of the archives include the following:

"Goshomei Genpon" that includes the Constitution of the Empire of Japan (1889), the Constitution of Japan (promulgated 1946), various Imperial Rescripts, laws, and treaties. These documents are securely preserved in the special repository, because these signed and sealed documents, for example, the Imperial Rescript Ending the War in 1945, are especially important.

"Dajo Ruiten" consists of typically collected material compiled by the records section of the "Dajokan," or Cabinet of the early Meiji (1869–1912) Government. It comprises fair copies of various regulations selected from cabinet diaries, daily journals, public records ("Kobunroku"), and other material. The collection is classified into

[19] National Archives of Japan, http://www.archives.go.jp/english/.

19 categories and is arranged chronologically starting in October of the third year of the Keio period (1867) and ending in the 14th year of the Meiji period (1881).

The "Kobunroku" are the official documents and records created or received by the Cabinet of the first 18 years of the Meiji period (1868–1885). They are arranged chronologically and by ministries and agencies, and constitute the basic governmental records of early Meiji. They are designated as National Important Cultural Property of Japan in 1998.

The "Kobun Ruishu" were first edited under the name "Dajo Ruiten," but took their present name in 1882. Aside from some special categories, they are chronologically arranged and classified into 23 categories ranging from the system of government to foreign affairs. After 1886, they came to consist principally of the original documents of laws and regulations.

The "Kobun Zassan" records are those miscellaneous documents created or received by the Cabinet that are not part of the "Kobun Ruishu." Dating from 1886, its contents are arranged chronologically and by ministries and agencies (Annex 1).

The "Naikaku Kobun" are official documents composed of the Constitution, Imperial rescripts, acts, cabinet Orders, treaties, and other preserved documents related to the Cabinet (excluding personal affairs) since 1955. Documents are classified following the Preserved Documents Classification Chart and are compiled according to their retention periods.

In addition to the above-listed collections, there are special collections referred to as Principal Antique Documents Holdings and Important Cultural Properties of Japan. One particular section in the Antique documents is NAJ that holds foreign books on the history, politics, and law of western countries, which the early Meiji Government researched and translated, and other legal books purchased from the UK, US, and France during the Meiji and Taisho periods. Many French and German books were destroyed during the air raids in 1945.

UK National Archive Files Reveal

With specific reference to the sovereignty over Itu-Aba and other islands in China Sea, a number of files were examined (see Figure 5).[20] Two in particular offer these insights, which are summarized as listed below:

FILE: British Embassy, Paris March 27, 1935
Office dispatch No. 1678 (w11786/1391/17) of October 3, 1933, Naval attaché.
Subject: Annexation by France of certain islands, namely:

- Seratly (Spratly) Date of possession: April 13, 1930
- Caye D'Amboine and islets — April 7, 1933
- Itu-Aba and islets — April 10, 1933
- Two-Island Group — April 10, 1933
- Loaito islet — April 11, 1933
- Thi-Tu and islets — April 12, 1933

These islands are henceforward under French sovereignty.

FILE: F.O. Letter F62634499/6T September 12, 1937

- April 1930 — "Malicieuse" visited Spratley Is (*sic.*); took formal possession
- April 1933 — "Astrolabe" took formal possession of Amboine, Itu-Aba and Loaita
- Cruiser La Motte-Picquet carried out reconnaissance in 1937; however, it did not take formal possession
- Ownership discussion with Chinese Government to be held
- French Govt. informed Japanese Govt. that they claimed "full sovereignty" over the islands
- The Japanese Government was never given any rights or privileges whatsoever in these islands

[20] For historical documents on the South China Sea, the UK National Archives and the UKHO Archives hold substantial volumes. Additional information available in the UK may also be found in the National Libraries and some Library holdings in Universities.

- British advise the French Government to make French occupation of islands more effective
- The British Government's desire to claim the Spratly Group was weak although it surveyed and charted the sea and the insular features but never took possession
- Apparently, the French never made the claim official (according to the correspondence)
- HMS "Herald" observed Japanese naval hydrographers busily surveying and fishing activities by Japanese fishers in the vicinity of Itu-Aba
- The UK Air Ministry viewed these islands as potential advanced air bases
- They would be cheap and efficient way to watch over the main sea-way from Japan to Singapore
- The British considered reviving its claim or obtain a lease of the islands from the French
- Concern that Japanese was forming an advanced base for raids on Singapore and sea-borne commerce in the region

The then UK Government's intentions and thoughts were to:

- Review the whole position/situation
- Encourage French Government to exercise sovereignty more actively
- Prevent the Japanese encroachment and possible creation of Japanese title to sovereignty (by continuous occupation)
- The British considered using Spratly Island as a landing-ground
- Mischief Reef was targeted as a potential seaplane anchorage (Yes, in the 1930s)
- Now (2017), it is transformed into an island

Did a Japanese group plan to purchase the islands? The response to the question was "The news is very improbable. From the time taken to produce the reply I infer that the enquiry did not go beyond the 'Chef de 2me Bureau' and his staff."

It must be recalled that Mischief Reef was targeted as a potential seaplane anchorage by the British Government. Yes, even in the

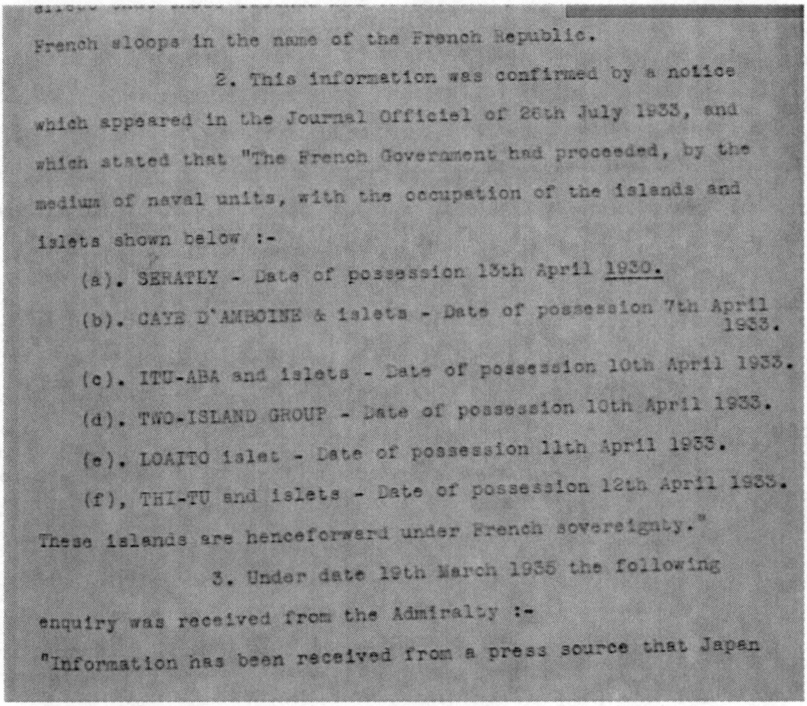

French sloops in the name of the French Republic.

2. This information was confirmed by a notice which appeared in the Journal Officiel of 26th July 1933, and which stated that "The French Government had proceeded, by the medium of naval units, with the occupation of the islands and islets shown below :-

(a). SPRATLY - Date of possession 13th April <u>1930.</u>

(b). CAYE D'AMBOINE & islets - Date of possession 7th April 1933.

(c). ITU-ABA and islets - Date of possession 10th April 1933.

(d). TWO-ISLAND GROUP - Date of possession 10th April 1933.

(e). LOAITO islet - Date of possession 11th April 1933.

(f), THI-TU and islets - Date of possession 12th April 1933.

These islands are henceforward under French sovereignty."

3. Under date 19th March 1935 the following enquiry was received from the Admiralty :-

"Information has been received from a press source that Japan

Figure 5. Taking possession of certain islands by the French Government.

1930s. It is ironic that between 1994 and 2017, this feature has been transformed from a humble reef into an artificial island with alleged military facilities and major port development and is the subject of sovereignty dispute between two or three littoral States of the South China Sea.

Consider This Research Topic

In examining the great power rivalry among Britain, Japan, France, and US during 1930–1945, the discussion of the sovereignty of various islands, including the Paracel and Spratly archipelagoes and other insular features, the catalyst could be the expansion of civil and military aviation. The British, Japanese, and US militaries recognized the importance of having naval and air bases in order to attain force projection in areas not previously reachable. Both Governments embarked on a series of investigations into the suitability of various islands as bases, sparking off a decade or more of disputes. Compounding this rivalry was the intense competition between commercial aviation companies for international routes. For example, the Pacific Islands were essential as re-fuel stops for trans-Pacific flights connecting New Zealand and Australia to Hawaii and the mainland US. With US-owned Pan-Am securing landing rights in New Zealand in 1935, the British Government attempted unsuccessfully to secure landing rights for British or dominion airlines to land in Hawaii.

Since 1990, scores of previously unseen British government documents have been released and deposited in the UK National Archives that provide greater insight into these events. The same could possibly apply to the National Archives in Australia, China, France, Japan, Germany, and the US, and indeed, in Taiwan.

The focus of such a research theme has broad intellectual and political significance because it looks at a case study of an area of conflict between two or more allied partners within a time of larger global

Figure 6. Wood carving of Japanese surrender, WWII.

Source: Zhejiang Provincial Museum, PRC.

conflict with implications that rear its ugly head in 2017 and beyond. It demonstrates how local and global conflicts affect the dynamics of a particular alliance between major powers at a particular instance of time. It could examine in greater detail these disputes between the various government and commercial actors and situates this rivalry within the contemporary global arena. Even an item such as a wooden sculpture to commemorate a significant historical geopolitical event can prove an important piece in the overall narrative of archival research (Figure 6).

Summary

This study offered a brief analysis of four major national archives which are considered valuable resource centers in which to conduct research to delve into the files and records that may hold clues and solutions to resolve the maritime disputes and to settle the sovereignty issues that are placing burden on citizens of the littoral states, external users, and, of course, a strain on limited budgets and funds. It also highlighted a summarized version of the events that led to the processes of claiming sovereignty over a few islands of the South China Sea, in particular the Spratly Group. The study was complimented with a PowerPoint Presentation at a conference in Taipei, on June 1, 2017 that demonstrated the effectiveness of undertaking research at National Archives to enhance territorial and sovereignty claims in disputed maritime zones.

Annex 1

Examples of select documents held in various National Archives: Japan, Taiwan, and UK.

British Ships (Attacks)

30. **Sir L. Plummer** asked the Secretary of State for Foreign Affairs how many British ships have suffered damage as a result of attacks made upon them by assailants known or suspected to have come from Formosa, the Pescadores, the islands of Quemoy, Matsu or the Tachens since 1st January, 1952.

32. **Mr. Hale** asked the Secretary of State for Foreign Affairs the number of attacks on British ships in the last 12 months to the most recent convenient date which have been made by the forces engaged in the Chinese civil war ; and the number which, on investigation, have been found to be due to the forces of General Chiang Kai-shek, and those due to the forces of the Chinese Government.

34. **Mr. Foot** asked the Secretary of State for Foreign Affairs on how many occasions in the past four years protests

Sir L. Plummer : May I ask the right hon. Gentleman whether, in view of that reply and the number of incidents which have taken place, and in view of the tension in this part of the world, he would consider calling another Nyon Conference to protect our ships from these acts of piracy?

Sir A. Eden : This is not on all-fours with the situation then. If the hon. Gentleman would like me to discuss the Nyon Agreement I will do so, but not at this moment. We have put in certain claims and some have been met and some not, and we shall continue to pursue our claims.

Mr. Foot : Can the right hon. Gentleman say in how many of these cases representations have also been made to the United States Government about the matter, particularly in view of his own legal interpretation of the situation in Formosa, which apparently means that

Formal Questions and Answers on Record relating to Formosa.

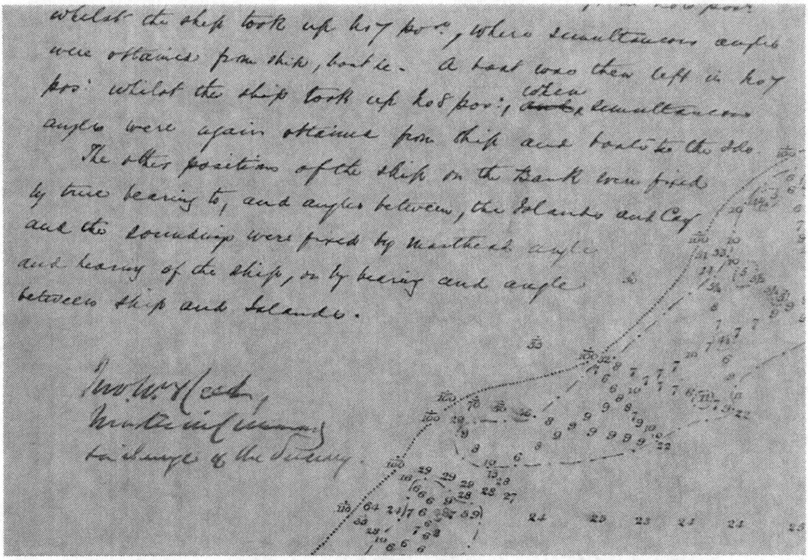
whilst the ship took up No 7 posn, where simultaneous angles were obtained from ship, boat &c. A boat was then left in No 7 posn whilst the ship took up No 8 posn, when simultaneous angles were again obtained from ship and boats to the Islds.

The other positions of the ship on the Bank were fixed by true bearing to, and angles between, the Islands and Cay and the soundings were fixed by masthead angle and bearing of the ship, or by bearing and angle between ship and Islands.

Master in Command,
In charge of the Survey.

Survey notes relating to Tizard Bank and Itu Aba Island, 1866.

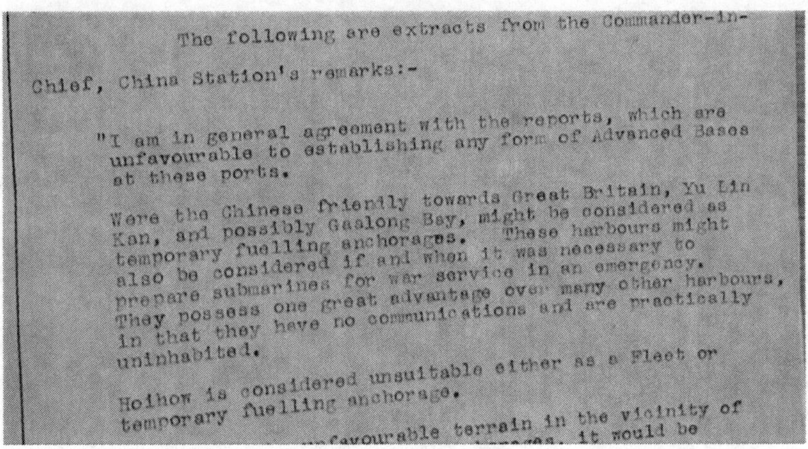
The following are extracts from the Commander-in-Chief, China Station's remarks:-

"I am in general agreement with the reports, which are unfavourable to establishing any form of Advanced Bases at these ports.

Were the Chinese friendly towards Great Britain, Yu Lin Kan, and possibly Gaalong Bay, might be considered as temporary fuelling anchorages. These harbours might also be considered if and when it was necessary to prepare submarines for war service in an emergency. They possess one great advantage over many other harbours, in that they have no communications and are practically uninhabited.

Hoihow is considered unsuitable either as a Fleet or temporary fuelling anchorage.

... unfavourable terrain in the vicinity of ... it would be

Proposal to use Yu Lin Kan and Gaalong Bay as fueling anchorages.

Files in National Archives of Taiwan

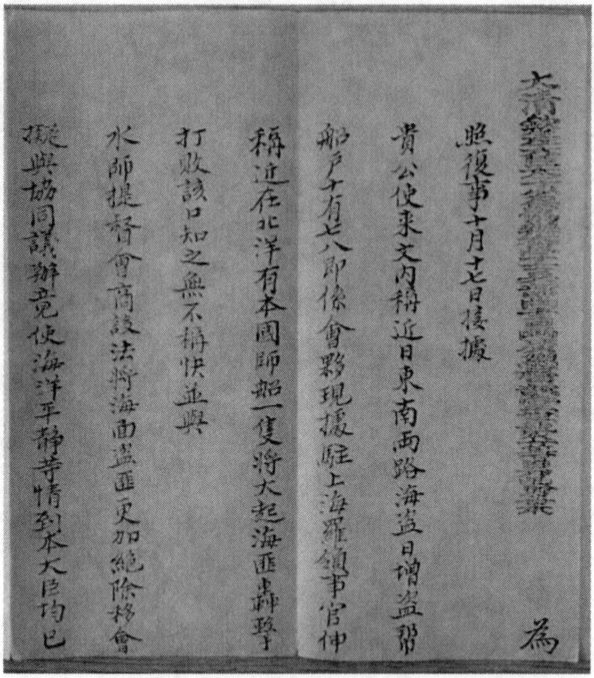

照復事十月十七日接據
貴公使來文內稱近日東南西路海盜日增盜幫
船戶十有七八即係會匪現據駐上海羅領事官伸
稱近在北洋有本國師船一隻將大起海匪擒拏
打敗該口知之無不稱快並與
水師提督會商設法將海南盜匪更加絕除移會
擬與協同議辦竟使海洋平靜等情到本大臣均已

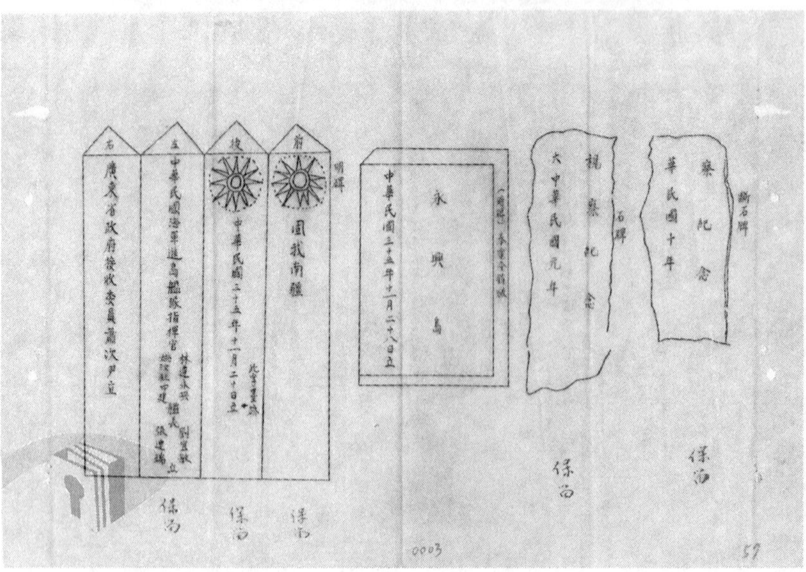

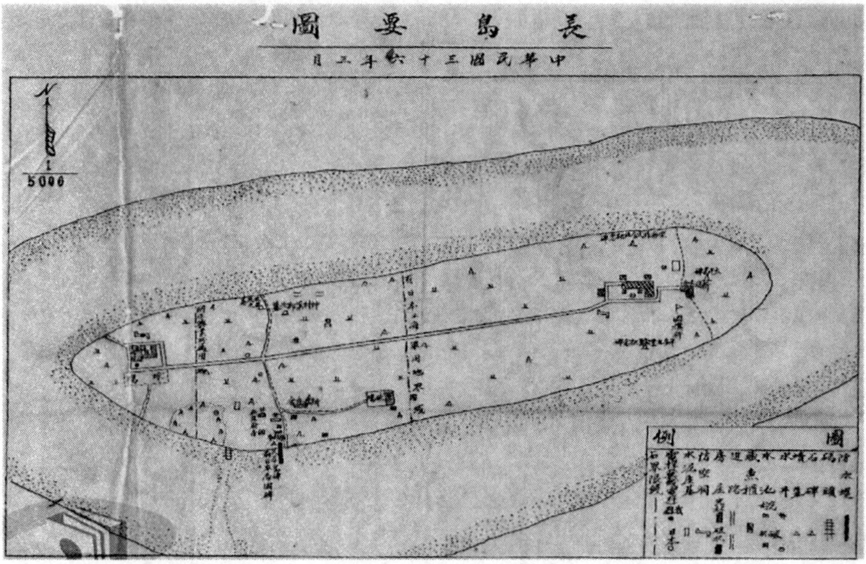

Plan of Itu Aba Island held in National Archives of Taiwan.

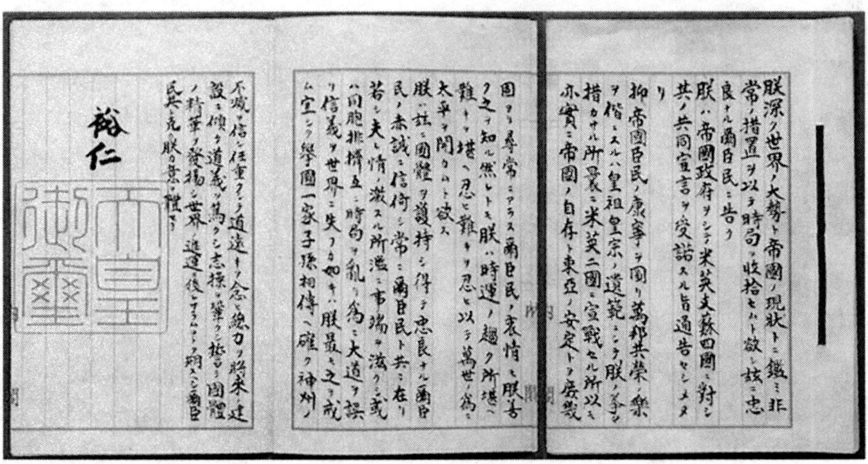

朕深ク世界ノ大勢ト帝國ノ現狀トニ鑑ミ非
常ノ措置ヲ以テ時局ヲ收拾セムト欲シ茲ニ忠
良ナル爾臣民ニ告ク
朕ハ帝國政府ヲシテ米英支蘇四國ニ對シ
其ノ共同宣言ヲ受諾スル旨通告セシメタ
リ
抑々帝國臣民ノ康寧ヲ圖リ萬邦共榮ノ樂
ヲ偕ニスルハ皇祖皇宗ノ遺範ニシテ朕ノ拳々
措カサル所曩ニ米英二國ニ宣戰セル所以モ
亦實ニ帝國ノ自存ト東亞ノ安定トヲ庶幾

固ヨリ尋常ニアラス爾臣民ノ衷情モ朕善
ク之ヲ知ル然レトモ朕ハ時運ノ趨ク所堪ヘ
難キヲ堪ヘ忍ヒ難キヲ忍ヒ以テ萬世ノ爲ニ
太平ヲ開カムト欲ス
朕ハ茲ニ國體ヲ護持シ得テ忠良ナル爾臣
民ノ赤誠ニ信倚シ常ニ爾臣民ト共ニ在リ
若シ夫レ情ノ激スル所濫ニ事端ヲ滋クシ或
ハ同胞排擠互ニ時局ヲ亂リ爲ニ大道ヲ誤
リ信義ヲ世界ニ失フカ如キハ朕最モ之ヲ戒
ム宜シク擧國一家子孫相傳ヘ確ク神州ノ

不滅ヲ信シ任重クシテ道遠キヲ念ヒ總力ヲ將來ノ建
設ニ傾ケ道義ヲ篤クシ志操ヲ鞏クシ誓テ國體
ノ精華ヲ發揚シ世界ノ進運ニ後レサラムコトヲ期スヘシ爾臣
民其レ克ク朕カ意ヲ體セヨ

裕仁

天皇御璽

The Imperial Rescript ending the war (1945).

Treaty of Peace

The Republic of China and Japan,

Considering their mutual desire for good neighborliness in view of their historical and cultural ties and geographical proximity; Realizing the importance of their close cooperation to the promotion of their common welfare and to the maintenance of international peace and security; Recognizing the need for a settlement of problems that have arisen as a result of the existence of a state of war between them; Have resolved to conclude a Treaty of Peace and have accordingly appointed as their Plenipotentiaries,

His Excellency the President of the Republic of China: Mr. YEH KUNG-CHAO;

The Government of Japan: Mr. ISAO KAWADA

Who, having communicated to each other their full powers found to be in good and due form, have agreed upon the following Articles:—

Article 1

The state of war between the Republic of China and Japan is terminated as from the date on which the present Treaty enters into force.

Article 2

It is recognized that under Article 2 of the Treaty of Peace which Japan signed at the city of San Francisco on 8 September 1951 (hereinafter referred to as the San Francisco Treaty), Japan has renounced all right, title, and claim to Taiwan (Formosa) and Penghu (the Pescadores) as well as the Spratley Islands and the Paracel Islands.

Article 3

The disposition of property of Japan and its nationals in Taiwan (Formosa) and Penghu (the Pescadores), and their claims, including debts, against the authorities of the Republic of China in Taiwan (Formosa) and Penghu (the Pescadores) and the residents thereof, and the disposition in Japan of property of such authorities and residents and their claims, including debts, against Japan and its nationals, shall be the subject of special arrangements between the Government of the Republic of China and the Government of Japan. The terms nationals and residents include juridical persons.

Article 4

It is recognized that all treaties, conventions, and agreements concluded before 9 December 1941 between Japan and China have become null and void as a consequence of the war.

Article 5

It is recognized that under the provisions of Article 10 of the San Francisco Treaty, Japan has renounced all special rights and its interests in China, including all benefits and privileges resulting from the provisions of the final Protocol signed at Peking on 7 September 1901, and all annexes, notes, and documents supplementary thereto, and has agreed to the abrogation in respect to Japan of the said protocol, annexes, notes, and documents.

Article 6

(a) The Republic of China and Japan will be guided by the principles of Article 2 of the Charter of the United Nations in their mutual relations.

(b) The Republic of China and Japan will cooperate in accordance with the principles of the Charter of the United Nations and, in particular, will promote their common welfare through friendly cooperation in the economic field.

Article 7

The Republic of China and Japan will endeavor to conclude, as soon as possible, a treaty or agreement to place their trading, maritime, and other commercial relations, on a stable and friendly basis.

Article 8

The Republic of China and Japan will endeavor to conclude, as soon as possible, an agreement relating to civil air transport.

Article 9

The Republic of China and Japan will endeavor to conclude, as soon as possible, an agreement providing for the regulation or limitation of fishing and the conservation and development of fisheries on the high seas.

Article 10

For the purposes of the present Treaty, nationals of the Republic of China shall be deemed to include all the inhabitants and former inhabitants of Taiwan (Formosa) and Penghu (the Pescadores) and their descendants who are of the Chinese nationality in accordance with the laws and regulations which have been or may hereafter be enforced by the Republic of China in Taiwan (Formosa) and Penghu (the Pescadores); and juridical persons of the Republic of China shall be deemed to include all those registered under the laws and regulations which have been or may hereafter be enforced by the Republic of China in Taiwan (Formosa) and Penghu (the Pescadores).

Article 11

Unless otherwise provided for in the present Treaty and the documents supplementary thereto, any problem arising between the Republic of China and Japan as a result of the existence of a state of war shall be settled in accordance with the relevant provisions of the San Francisco Treaty.

Article 12

Any dispute that may arise out of the interpretation or application of the present Treaty shall be settled by negotiation or other pacific means.

Article 13

The present Treaty shall be ratified and the instruments of ratification shall be exchanged at Taipei as soon as possible. The present Treaty shall enter into force as from the date on which such instruments of ratification are exchanged.

Article 14

The present Treaty shall be in the Chinese, Japanese, and English languages. In case of any divergence of interpretation, the English text shall prevail.

In witness whereof the respective Plenipotentiaries have signed the present Treaty, and have affixed thereto their seals.

Done in duplicate at Taipei, this Twenty Eighth day of the Fourth month of the Forty First year of the REPUBLIC OF CHINA, corresponding to the Twenty Eighth day of the Fourth month of the Twenty Seventh year of SHOWA of Japan and to the **Twenty Eighth day of April in the year One Thousand Nine Hundred and Fifty Two**.

YEH KUNG-CHAO, [L.S.]
Minister of Foreign Affairs and
Plenipotentiary of the Republic of China
ISAO KAWADA, [L.S.]
Minister of Foreign Affairs and
Plenipotentiary of Japan

Source: *United Nations Treaty Series* 1952 (reg. no. 1858), pp. 38–44.

Chapter

4

American Diplomatic Correspondence on the Philippine Claims in the South China Sea

Jay L. Batongbacal

Director, Institute for Maritime Affairs & Law of the Sea, University of the Philippines

Abstract

This chapter examines American diplomatic correspondence concerning the claims of its treaty ally, the Philippines, to the Kalayaan Island Group in the Spratly Islands region of the South China Sea. These communications evince how US policy on the disputed region evolved over the decades, and show how the Philippines established and maneuvered its claims independently of the US.

Keywords: Kalayaan Island Group; Scarborough Shoal; Philippine claim; US policy; South China Sea disputes

Introduction

This chapter will trace US diplomatic correspondence and the contours of US policy on the South China Sea (SCS) disputes in relation to the Philippine claim to the Kalayaan Island Group. It begins with the contextual foundations of US policy built on Mahan's sea power doctrine and the US rise as a global power at the turn of the 20th century. With the opening moves in the SCS disputes begun by France and Japan, the eventual US policy on the SCS, and the nascent Philippine claim expressed in the 1930s, were formed early on in agreement with their sea power interests. This dampened Philippine advocates' attempts to establish a claim throughout the American Commonwealth in the post-Second World War period. But US policy was adjusted in the 1970s due to repeated prodding by the Philippines under Marcos who held the US bases in the Philippines hostage to extract an American commitment to defend the Philippine claims, although it still did not achieve the desired result.

From the late 1980s and through the 1990s, lack of American support (punctuated by the non-renewal of the US military bases agreement) forced the Philippines to resort to peace advocacy in the face of creeping Chinese occupation of rocks and reefs. But China's rise to superpower status economically and militarily challenged and alarmed the Philippines in the first decade of the new millennium, which again caused it to try to pull in an enhanced US presence in the region. The key interests of the US and those of the Philippines converged and diverged on key points over the past decades, and these are highlighted in an examination of US diplomatic discourse. Recent developments in the Philippines/China disputes must be seen from a historical lens, in order to firmly establish realistic interpretations of US maritime security policy and expectations of the US role now and in the near future.

Historical Roots of American Policy on the SCS

To understand contemporary US policy on the SCS, one must look to the past, particularly its original embrace of Capt. Alfred Thayer Mahan's "sea power doctrine" in his celebrated book *The Influence of Sea Power Upon History, 1660–1783* published in 1890. Mahan's historical study of British sea power led him to a simple idea that would shake the geopolitical seascape, that

> ...control of the sea by maritime commerce and naval supremacy means predominant influence in the world ...[and] is the chief among the merely material elements in the power and prosperity of nations.[1]
>
> Mahan believed that the US economy in his time would soon be unable to absorb the massive amounts of industrial and commercial goods that it could produce, necessitating a search for and entry into new markets abroad. It needed to guarantee its access to such new markets, for which there were two fundamental requirements: a merchant navy to carry American goods across the "great highway" of the high seas, and a battleship navy to deter or destroy any rival fleets that could threaten maritime commerce. To support the operations of these commercial and military fleets, it was also necessary to establish a network of naval bases capable of providing fuel and supplies across the world and maintaining continuous and open lines of commerce between the US and its foreign markets.[2]

The outbreak of the Spanish–American War in May 1898 provided the perfect opportunity for the US embark fully and carry out the sea power doctrine. Its relatively moribund naval forces at the time still proved technologically superior to the decrepit and bankrupt Spanish fleet destroyed in separate engagements in Manila, Philippines and Santiago, Cuba (for a detailed account, see Ref. 3).[3] US victory in the war resulted in the acquisition of new strategic territories in Puerto Rico, Cuba, Guam, and the Philippines that served as bases and coaling stations that extended American's reach into the

---

[1] Alfred Thayer Mahan, Possibilities of an Anglo-American Union, *North American Review, July* (1894). In A. T. Mahan, *The Interest of America in Sea Power, Present and Future* (London: Sampson Low Marston & Company, 1897). http://www.gutenberg.org/files/15749/15749-h/15749-h.htm. (accessed on January 31, 2018).

[2] Alfred Thayer Mahan, Introductory and Chapter 1, in *The Influence of Sea Power Upon History*, 1660–1783, 12th ed. (Boston: Little Brown & Company), 1890. http://www.gutenberg.org/files/13529/13529-h/13529-h.htm (accessed on January 31, 2018). A. T. Mahan, The United States looking outward, Atlantic Monthly, December 1890, in A. T. Mahan, *The Interest of America in Sea Power, Present and Future* (London: Sampson Low Marston & Company), 1897. http://www.gutenberg.org/files/15749/15749-h/15749-h.htm (accessed on January 31, 2018).

[3] Jim Leeke, *Manila & Satiago: The New Steel Navy in the Spanish-American War*, (Annapolis: Naval Institute), 2009.

Asia-Pacific and South American hemisphere.[4] The Battle of Manila Bay in 1898 was literally the opening curtain to the US rise to global pre-eminence and dominance, as it allowed the extension and consolidation of US-defined sea lines of communication that continue to form the foundation of the globalized world.

Sea power is a cornerstone and core concept of American geo-strategy, having underwritten US maritime security for over 100 years. Navigational rights that guarantee global mobility for commercial and military purposes have been consistently and constantly high on the US foreign policy agenda and is a key pillar of the post-Second World War order in the Asia-Pacific as well as the rest of the world. This post-War order was laid through a network of interlocking international mechanisms that the US had a pivotal role in establishing together with the other severely weakened allied powers.

The US sought to define the post-War order through the United Nations Charter that established a global international organization with key organs and functions that recognized the nominal equality of all States and promoted the self-determination and de-colonization of formerly oppressed/subordinated peoples (who incidentally were potential economic growth markets once they passed beyond the shadow of their colonial overseers). Side by side with institution-building, the progressive development of international law was a key process needed to provide the international community with a system of mutually regulated conduct that was outwardly fair and equal in application, even though the reality was that lack of negotiating parity during the bargaining process of each treaty and convention to a large extent pre-determined the outcomes. The early years of the UN were pre-occupied with three important multi-lateral treaty negotiation processes that influenced the Asia-Pacific: the terms of peace with Japan under the 1951 San Francisco Peace Treaty; the initial rounds of the General Agreement on Tariffs and Trade in 1949 that signaled the start of the decades-long effort to promote and establish a global free trade regime; and the determination of coastal States' jurisdiction

[4] US Department of State, Office of the Historian, Milestones: 1866–1898, Mahan's *The Influence of Sea Power Upon History: Securing International Markets in the 1890s* (January 16, 2016). https://history.state.gov/milestones/1866-1898/mahan (accessed on January 31, 2018).

over their adjacent seas through the first United Nations Conference on the Law of the Sea first called in 1952.

US geo-strategy based fundamentally on sea power would be pursued consistently in the decades that followed. Implementation of the Marshall Plan and the rehabilitation of Europe provided the opportunity for the US to heavily influence the international economic order and patiently set the stage for the global free trade regimes of today. The Cold War that began with the building of the Berlin Wall could be seen as the ultimate manifestation of the competition between the political and economic ideologies in the post-War period: the liberal order espoused by the US and "the West," and the socialist order preferred by the USSR, China, and "the rest." Communism represented the only serious challenge and hindrance to the liberal ideology and economic system underpinning the US-designed global order.

As the years passed, global maritime trade linkages consolidated and settled largely into the same principal patterns used today and buoyed new economies. By the 1970s, in the Asia-Pacific particularly, the "tiger" economies emerged and invested in the same trade networks, eventually integrating themselves into the system by establishing today's hub ports. Together with the sea lines of communication, these hub ports form the globe-spanning network nodes of fast and efficient marine transportation that makes global trade possible. The mutual benefits derived from this system form the basis for a common international interest among all States in ensuring the freedom of the seas, particularly the rights and freedoms of navigation and over-flight in areas within and beyond national jurisdiction. The United Nations Convention on the Law of the Sea is the manifestation of the convergence points of these nations' interests.

US Responses to Philippine Claims to the Spratly Islands

The Commonwealth Period

American policy on the SCS claims is exceptionally long-standing, the basis of which was first established in 1933 when the French formally annexed six specific islands that included Spratly Island, Amboyna Cay, Itu Aba Island, the Twin Islands (thought to be part of North Danger Reef), Loaita Island, and Thitu Island. The annexation was officially announced on September 03, 1933, and drew immediate protest from the rival regional power Japan.[5]

In the meantime, the jockeying for positions between the French and Japanese was not unnoticed in Manila. On August 12, 1933, then-Senator Isabelo de los Reyes called on the US to join the diplomatic fray on behalf of the Philippines by publishing a letter to Governor-General Frank Murphy in the newspapers, insisting:

> We firmly believe, after a glance at the map published by the Manila and Japanese press that this group is included in the territory adjudicated to the Philippine Islands and purchased by America for twenty million dollars which were are now paying.[6]

Unfortunately, the US was not at all sympathetic. In a reaction published in *The Tribune*, the US officially dashed de los Reyes' presumption of the islands' inclusion in the Spanish cession, releasing the contents of a letter from Assistant Secretary Wilbur J. Carr to the Secretary of War on October 09, 1933, pointing out that with reference to the westernmost lines described in the Treaty of Paris,

> ...The Islands which are stated to be occupied by France lie approximately 200 miles from [the] nearest portion of the boundary of the Philippine Islands, and incidentally on the opposite side of the large area of shallow seas which are indicated upon sailing charts as "dangerous ground." These Islands therefore lie at considerable distance outside the limits of the Philippine Islands which were acquired from Spain in 1898.[7]

---

[5] Memorandum, Japanese Embassy to Department of State, File no. 851G.014/17, undated, *Foreign Relations of the United States, Japan: 1931–1941*, (US Department of State), vol. 2, pp. 278–280.

[6] Letter to Governor-General Frank A. Murphy, August 12, 1933 in US National Archives and Records Administration [NARA], Record Group 350, Bureau of Insular Affairs, 1868–1945, General Classified Files, 1914–1945, File no. 003.71.

[7] Wilbur J. Carr's letter to the Secretary of War, October 09, 1933 in NARA, Record Group 55, Microfilm Publication M1442, Records of the Department of State relating to the Internal Affairs of France, 1930–1939, File no. 851.014/62. See also *The Tribune*, Manila, P.I., November 11, 1933, p. 10.

US Pre-War Disposition of Scarborough Shoa

Claims to the Spratly Islands likely prompted the Philippine Commonwealth government to review its maps and charts, and ascertain the presence of any other maritime features susceptible to acquisition. On December 7, 1937, the Office of the High Commissioner for the Philippines wrote a letter to Capt. Thomas Maher of the Coast and Geodetic Survey as to whether Scarborough Shoal had been claimed by any other country.[8] In his reply on December 10, Capt. Maher was uncertain, as there was no information as to whether any nation, including the British, had laid claim of sovereignty over the shoal, and his office had no power to decide on the issue. However, he pointed to available information from Spanish and other records, particularly the survey carried out by the Spanish in 1800, and noted:

> If this survey would confer title on Spain, or be a recognition of sovereignty, or a claim for same without protest, the reef would apparently be considered as part of Spanish territory the transfer of which would be governed by the Treaty of November 7, 1900.[9]

The Philippine Commonwealth government sent a letter to follow-up on the inquiry the following year, and officially declared its intention to acquire sovereignty thereto:

> In case it should appear that the reef is of value to air or ocean navigation, the Commonwealth Government may desire to claim title thereto, should there be no objection on the part of the United States Government to such action.[10]

[8] Wayne Coy's letter to Capt. Thomas Maher, US Coast and Geodetic Survey Manila, December 06, 1937, in NARA, BIA File no. 907.127, reproduced in Bonnet, F. Geopolitics of Scarborough Shoal, Irasec's Discussion Papers No. 14, December 2014. Available at: www.irasec.com, p. 38.

[9] Capt. Thomas Maher's letter to Wayne Coy, Office of the US High Commissioner for the Philippines, December 10, 1937, in NARA, BIA File no. 907.127, reproduced in Bonnet, *supra*, pp. 38–40.

[10] Jorge B. Vargas' letter to Wayne Coy, Office of the US High Commissioner for the Philippines, March 13, 1938. In NARA, BIA File no. 907.127, reproduced in Bonnet, *supra*, p. 40.

Wayne Coy forwarded the letters to the US Department of War, which in turn forwarded it to the US Department of State, subsequently resulting in correspondence between the two departments that agreed upon the disposition of Scarborough Shoal to the Philippines. In a letter dated July 27, 1938, the Secretary of State interposed no objection to the Philippines' course of action and informed the Secretary of War that:

> While the shoal appears outside the limits of the Philippine Archipelago as described in Article III of the American-Spanish Treaty of December 10, 1898, it would seem that, in the absence of a valid claim by any other government, the shoal should be regarded as included among the islands ceded to the United States by the American-Spanish Treaty of November 7, 1900.[11]

Subsequent correspondence from the Secretary of the Navy and the Secretary of Commerce similarly interposed no objections,[12] allowing the Philippines to continue peacefully exercising sovereignty and jurisdiction over Scarborough Shoal thereafter.

Japanese Annexation of the Spratly Islands

In 1939, in the absence of permanent French presence, Japan made its own move and annexed the islands and the surrounding region, called the "Shinnan Gunto" administrative region, and placed it under the jurisdiction of Japanese forces on Formosa (Taiwan). The Japanese annexation was much greater in scope than that of the French, and set the precedent for subsequent arbitrary "geometric" claims in the Dangerous Ground. Numerous maritime features were specified in the Japanese claim, as described in a Note to the Great Powers.[13]

---

[11] Cordell Hull's letter to Harry H. Woodring, Secretary of War, July 27, 1938, in NARA, BIA File no. 907.127, reproduced in Bonnet, *supra*, p. 41.

[12] William R. Furlong's letter to Louis Johnson, Acting Secretary of War, August 27, 1938, and Paul Frizzell's letter to the Secretary of War, October 19, 1938, in NARA, BIA File no. 907.127, reproduced in Bonnet, *supra*, p. 41.

[13] The note specifically mentioned the following features: Kitahutagozima (Northeast Cay), Minamihutagozima (Southwest Cay), Nisiaozima (West York Island), Sankakusima (Thi Tu Island), Nakakozima (Loaita Island), Kikkozima (Flat Island),

The Japanese note also expressly referred to all other reefs and submerged features within a defined hexagonal area as included in the annexation. In a letter to the Japanese Ambassador dated May 17, 1939, the Secretary of State Cordell Hull laid the cornerstone of all subsequent US responses to any claims to the region, of taking a position of neutrality on the claims and advocating the peaceful settlement of the disputes they generated:

> Apart from any question as to the merits of the conflicting claims of France and Japan ... the Government of the United States advocates adjustment of problems in international relations by processes of negotiation, agreement or arbitration.[14]

Hull further expressed a fundamental American viewpoint that the expansive claim to the Spratly Islands region, insofar as they sought to apply to the whole island group and to submerged and semi-submerged maritime features likes reefs and cays, could not be legally countenanced:

> The Government of the United States does not consider that all islands or reefs which might be situated within the extensive area delimited in the Japanese memorandum, and especially within that considerable part of the area lying to the eastward and southeastward of any of the islands named in the Japanese memorandum, can be properly treated as one island group, nor does this Government consider that the action of Japan in blanketing within the territory of Japan islands or reefs, either known or unknown, with respect to which the Japanese Government has heretofore exercised no acts which may be properly regarded as establishing a basis for claim to sovereignty, has any international validity.[15]

Nanyoto (Nanshan Island), Nagasima (Itu Aba Island), Kitakozima (Sand Cay), Minamikozima (Namyit Island), Asukazima (Sin Cowe Island), Nisitorisima (Spratly Island), Marusima (Amboyna Cay).

[14] Memorandum, Japanese Embassy to Department of State, File no. 851G.014/17, undated, *Foreign Relations of the United States, Japan: 1931–1941,* (US Department of State), vol. 2, p. 280.

[15] *Ibid.*, pp. 280–281.

Without forceful expulsion, Japanese rule over the "Shinnan Gunto" would remain throughout the Pacific War period. As the conflict raged, however, inter-departmental committees led by the US State Department carefully considered the eventual disposition of the islands at war's end. Preliminary studies initially attempted to identify the potential post-war assignees of the "Shinnan Gunto"/Spratly Islands as either France or China. Document T-324 of the Territorial Subcommittee dated May 25, 1943, clearly excluded the Shinnan Gunto/Spratly Islands from the Philippine Islands:

> *Shinnan Gunto* is definitely beyond the boundary of the Philippines as established by the treaty of December 10, 1898.[16]

Clearly, therefore, the US did in fact consider the nascent Philippine claim that was originally advocated some 10 years before, but dismissed it as irrelevant (in fact, the Philippines did not make any official claim until the 1970s). Consistent with the sea power doctrine, its analysis of the issue was clearly premised on the question of the islands' impact on the sea lines of communication:

> The principal considerations involved in the disposition of the islands are the elimination of any threat against the security of other territories and the provision of adequate navigational surveys and safeguards.[17]

As talks with the allied powers continued on the prosecution of the war effort and eventual surrender of Japan, US analyses reiterated and solidified the basic positions of neutrality and preference for peaceful settlement. In Document CAC-301 of the Inter-Divisional Area Committee on the Far East dated December 19, 1944, the absence of US interest in the Spratly Islands and its separation from

[16] Doc T-324, Territorial Subcommittee, May 25, 1943, NARA, Record Group 59, Records of Harley A. Notter, 1939–1945, Records of the Advisory Committee on Post-War Foreign Policy 1942–1945, Box 63.
[17] *Ibid.*

the Philippine archipelago was made the starting point of further discussions:

> The United States has made no claim to the islands either for itself or for the Philippine islands. *Shinnan Gunto* is beyond the boundary of the Philippines.[18]

and the location of the Spratly Islands was viewed exclusively from the standpoint of freedom of navigation:

> Under Japan, the islands are a menace to other states, but with Japan eliminated they will be of no vital interest, strategically or economically, to any single country or territory.... The physical characteristics of these islands, islets, sandbars, and shoals make a claim to national sovereignty over them of questionable validity. They have an interest, however, for neighboring territories — China, Indochina, and the Philippines — and for all countries whose ships sail the China Seas.[19]

The area's economic potential was furthest from the minds of policymakers at the time, because the technology for offshore petroleum development was still several years away from being developed. For security purposes, the transfer of the islands to the Philippines was indeed considered, but based purely on pragmatic grounds rather than the validity of any Philippine claim as advocated by the former Senator de los Reyes, it was thereafter dismissed.[20] Another option considered was international management of Spratly Islands through the trusteeship system to be proposed under the United Nations Charter, but the US believed that this required the assent of the French Government in order to eliminate the French claim to the principal islands.[21]

---

[18] Doc CAC-301, Inter-Divisional Area Committee, December 19, 1944, NARA, Record Group 59, State Department Documents of the Interdivisional Country and Area Committee, 1943–1945, Microfilm Publication T1221, Roll 5.

[19] *Ibid.*

[20] *Ibid.*

[21] *Ibid.*

The Post-Liberation Years

Two years later, the inter-departmental State-War-Navy Coordinating Committee narrowed down the options in Document 59/1 dated June 24, 1946, as negotiations for the San Francisco Peace Treaty went into full swing. It was decided that Japan should renounce sovereignty over the Spratly Islands, but did not determine whether such renunciation should be in favor of any of the claimants, nor did it consider placing the islands under international control. In fact, the Spratly Islands were expressly identified as "areas not to be placed under trusteeship" due to the prerequisite that the competing claims of France and China should first be surrendered; in any case, for purposes of securing the sea lines of communication, the US saw no need for a definitive resolution:

> It was not necessary at this time for the United States to take any other position in relation to sovereignty over the islands than the elimination of the Japanese claim.[22]

The neutralization of the Spratly Islands group and their maintenance as an internationally accessible area was therefore enough to satisfy US geostrategy in the Asia-Pacific. With the signing of the 1951 San Francisco Peace Treaty, the war with Japan was settled and closed, and the basic foundation of the post-war global order was laid. Kimie Hara, in *Cold War Frontiers in the Asia-Pacific*, explained the singular significance of the 1951 San Francisco Treaty System in this endeavor, including the non-settlement of pending competing claims to various island groups across the Asia-Pacific region (not only the Spratly Islands but also the Senkakus, the Tok-do, and Sakhalin region).[23]

With respect to the Spratly Islands particularly, the simple renunciation of sovereignty by Japan without a specific receiver, despite standing official claims by France, Indo-China, and Nationalist China

---

[22] Doc 59/1, State-War-Navy Coordinating Committee, June 24, 1946, NARA, Record Group 59, State-War-Navy Coordinating Committee Policy Files, 1944–1947, Microfilm Publication LM54, Roll 8.

[23] Kimie Hara, *Cold War Frontiers in the Asia-Pacific: Divided Territories in the San Francisco System* (London & New York: Routledge), 2007. With respect to the Spratly Islands region, see Chapter 6.

expressed during the negotiations at the time (Communist China was technically not a participant, although it did also express the Chinese claim outside of the conference proper, and would officially adopt the Nationalist Chinese position some years later), was deemed sufficient and further elaboration was not seen as necessary. In any case, the US thought it would have been too difficult to solve the sovereignty issues at the time, and the islands apparently were not deemed important enough to potentially delay conclusion of the peace treaty.

The Cold War

Within a short period, more important concerns had arisen: the beginning of the Cold War. The tactical alliance between the US and the USSR had fallen apart, and the bipolar geopolitical competition between liberalism and communism soon went into full swing. US geo-strategy settled upon the containment of communism, which was famously represented by the so-called Acheson Line, described by US Secretary of State Dean Acheson in a speech on January 12, 1950:

> This defensive perimeter runs along the Aleutians to Japan and then goes to the Ryukyus. We hold important defense positions in the Ryukyu Islands, and those we will continue to hold. In the interest of the population of the Ryukyu Islands, we will at an appropriate time offer to hold these islands under trusteeship of the United Nations. But they are essential parts of the defensive perimeter of the Pacific, and they must and will be held.
>
> The defensive perimeter runs from Ryukyus to the Philippine Islands. Our relations, our defensive relations with the Philippines are contained in agreements between us. Those agreements are being loyally carried out and will be loyally carried out. Both peoples have learned by bitter experience the vital connections between our mutual defense requirements.[24]

Hara pointed out the essential role of the Spratly Islands region, as well as all the other contested islands elsewhere, in the Acheson

[24] Dean Acheson. Speech before the National Press Club, Washington D.C. on January 12, 1950. https://www.trumanlibrary.org/whistlestop/study_collections/korea/large/documents/pdfs/kr-3-13.pdf (accessed on January 31, 2018).

Line.[25] The contested areas created veritable "neutral zones" that allowed the full freedom of US operations, both overt and covert, necessary to combat the spread of communist influence and constrain Soviet military movement. They also provided an important security buffer between mainland Asia and the insular East and Southeast Asia. This was entirely consistent with the US sea power doctrine that eschewed the existence of areas of sea control by other powers and ensured the expansive coverage of freedom of navigation in practice. Non-acquisition of the Spratly Islands by "any" State was deemed to be more consistent with the long-term interest of the US, as well as the rest of the region. This underlying priority determined the US detachment and disinterest in Philippine claims, despite press announcements by Philippine officials that they would seek the turnover of the islands during the San Francisco treaty negotiations.[26]

The conclusion of the peace agreement settled the matter at official and diplomatic levels, but did nothing to prevent private adventurist claims to the Spratlys. In the early 1950s, a former American soldier Morton Meads claimed the existence of the "Kingdom of Humanity" as a base for what later was investigated and deemed to be mail fraud.[27] In 1956, Tomas Cloma, owner of the oldest maritime school and a fishing company in the Philippines (and a close business associate of then-Vice President and Foreign Secretary Carlos Garcia) began publicly announcing expeditions and achievements in colonizing "Freedomland." The US Embassy in Manila observed and reported Cloma's actions with clear disinterest, but conscious of the potential danger it posed to Philippines–US

---

[25] Kimie Hara, *Cold War Frontiers in the Asia-Pacific: Divided Territories in the San Francisco System* (London & New York: Routledge), 2007.

[26] A. P. Baviera and J. Batongbacal. *The West Philippine Sea, The Territorial and Maritime Disputes from a Filipino Perspective: A Primer* (Quezon City: Asian Center and Institute for Maritime Affairs & Law of the Sea), 2014, p. 21.

[27] Marwyn S. Samuels, *Contest for the South China Sea* (Oxfordshire: Routledge), 1982 (rep. 2005), pp. 168–172; Samuel Pyeatt Menefee, "Republics of the reefs": Nation-building on the continental shelf and in the world's oceans, *California Western International Law Journal*, vol. 25 (1994), pp. 81–111.

relations. In one dispatch on June 08, 1956, Ambassador Alfred Nufer noted:

> Freedomland still very much in the news, but Philippinos realize theirs probably weakest of the numerous claims; state that only unless US will undertake defense of islands could Philippine claim be effected.
>
> COMMENT: Issue still psychologically dangerous if exploited with theme Philippines being denied what is rightfully theirs by failure of US to protect their interests.[28]

Subsequent events indicated increased concern in the US Embassy over the diplomatic friction that Cloma's adventures were beginning to cause with the Nationalist Chinese in Taiwan, arousing suspicions over Cloma's true intentions. The Nationalist Chinese government took Cloma's adventures very seriously, dispatching its navy to evict Cloma from his proclaimed colony. It was on account of Cloma's adventures that the Taiwanese returned and established a permanent garrison on Itu Aba, which has been there ever since and is the oldest of all occupations of the various Spratly Islands features.[29] While dutifully reported by the US Embassy in Manila, official suspicion weighed against Cloma's activities. On October 05, 1956, Nufer cabled the US State Department:

> Tomas Cloma departed Oct 1 by air for Tokyo and US indicating hope UN will take cognizance of his claim to Freedomland. Same day CHINAT naval patrol stopped brother Filemon Cloma and crew of 70-foot PMI-IV near North Danger Reef. Allowed personnel to continue, confiscated small arms stating will turn over to Philippine Embassy Taipei.
>
> COMMENT: Purpose of Filemon Cloma's cruise not known. Cloma brothers activities not threat to CHINAT control of Spratly

[28] Telegram No. 3392, US Embassy Manila to Secretary of State, June 08, 1956, File no. 796.00(w)/6-586. NARA, Record Group 59, State Department Central Files, Philippine Rep 1955–1959, Microfilm Publication LM120, Roll 3.

[29] Telegram No. 507, US Embassy Manila to Secretary of State, August 24, 1956, File no. 796.00(w)/3-2456, NARA, Record Group 59, State Department Central Files, Philippine Rep 1955–1959, Microfilm Publication LM120, Roll 4.

> group. Never established any settlement in islands. CHINATs still have garrison on Itu Aba. Cloma's purpose probably: (1) keep issue alive hoping eventual Philippine government support, (2) profit from publicity by selling documentary Freedomland film in US plus increase interest in his other business affairs, (3) profit from sale of fish and phosphates, (4) possible smuggling activity though no direct evidence of this.[30]

Manila disavowed any participation in Cloma's expeditions but diplomatically left the door open for future Philippine claims by describing the islands as "terra nullius" as a result of the 1951 San Francisco Peace Treaty and therefore open to appropriation by any party.[31] The US was clearly comfortable with Chinese Nationalist control of the Spratly Islands through its possession of the largest island Itu Aba and was not concerned with any potential Philippine claim apart from its use as a possible spark for anti-Americanism. This took place against the backdrop of Philippines–US defense alliance and cooperation during the Cold War, and would remain the case until frictions emerged in the late 1960s as the Marcos Administration attempted to maneuver the US into backing Manila's claim.

The Marcos Years

In the late 1960s, a report was widely circulated about the petroleum potential in the Spratly Islands region, and interest zoomed in on Reed Bank, and the Philippines was eagerly attempting to establish a prior claim to potential reserve areas. Manila gambled on American support through the US defense commitments under the Mutual Defense Treaty (MDT) by secretly occupying the largest islands, which formed a security barrier west of Reed Bank. Philippine requests

---

[30] Telegram No. 947, US Embassy Manila to Secretary of State, October 05, 1956, File no. 796.00(w)/10-556, NARA, Record Group 59, State Department Central Files, Philippine Rep 1955–1959, Microfilm Publication LM 120, Roll 4.

[31] Gerardo M. C. Valero, *Spratly Archipelago: Is the Question of Sovereignty Still Relevant? A Roundtable Discussion* (Quezon City: UP Institute of International Legal Studies), 1993, pp. 65–66.

for US protection of its claim were a constant refrain in 1970–1975. Chinese diplomats expressed veiled threats of the use of force on occasion at the United Nations, which led to Philippine diplomats turning to the US to clarify the potential US response.[32] The military occupation that began in 1968 was apparently a surprise to the Americans, who were not officially informed of the Philippine occupation of the islands, nor of the basis of the claim, until 1973.[33] The US issued guidance to its ambassadors reiterating that it took no position on the conflicting claims.[34]

Alarm spread in the Philippines over the unexpected violent clash between Vietnamese and Chinese forces in the Paracel Islands[35]; there

---

[32] NARA Access to Archives Database [AAD], Doc 1974MANILA00998, US Embassy Manila to Secretary to State, January 26, 1974.

[33] Secretary of Foreign Affairs Carlos P. Romulo formally appraised the US through Ambassador William H. Sullivan through an aide memoire only on January 23, 1973. He stated that the government had decided to take action to claim the islands in reaction to the occupation by Taiwanese forces of Itu Aba, which had fired warning shots against Philippine reconnaissance aircraft and ships. It claimed that the islands were *res nullius* subject to acquisition through effective occupation and effective administration. Initially, only three islands (Pag-asa, Lawak, and Patag) were occupied and controlled by the Philippines. NARA AAD Doc. 1973MANILA00858, US Embassy Manila to Secretary of State, January 23, 1973. See also NARA AAD Doc. 1974MANILA01115, US Embassy Manila to Secretary of State, January 30, 1974.

[34] In a cable addressed to the Ambassador in South Vietnam, copy furnished to the other Ambassadors in Manila, Singapore, Taipei, and the Liaison Officer in Beijing, the State Department wrote, "[w]e believe that the US public position on this matter should continue to be that it takes no position with respect to these conflicting claims. This is an area of contention from which we are, and should remain, aloof," NARA AAD Doc 1973SAIGON20567, Secretary of State to US Embassy Saigon, December 07, 1973, This was reiterated in a subsequent cable, NARA AAD Doc. 1973STATE243154, Secretary of State to US Embassy Singapore, December 12, 1973.

[35] Saigon formally reported and described the armed clash to the United Nations Security Council on January 20, 1974. NARA AAD Doc. 1974STATE012722, US Embassy Saigon to Secretary of State, January 20, 1974. The US believed that the confrontation was sparked when Vietnamese forces responded to Chinese fishermen who planted a flag on Vietnamese-controlled islands; both sides then called in reinforcements and the situation rapidly escalated. NARA AAD Doc. 1974STATE022409, Secretary of State to US Embassy Saigon, February 02, 1974. See also Central Intelligence Agency. Memorandum on The Paracel Islands Incident, January 21, 1974.

were fears that the Philippine positions would be subject to armed attack by either China or Taiwan in the near future.[36] The Philippines repeatedly sought military protection from the US under the framework of the MDT, beginning with a request from Sec. Romulo.[37] Manila invoked and sought express assurances through a favorable and interpretation in writing of the MDT,[38] specifically Articles IV and V, which state:

> Article IV. Each Party recognizes that an armed attack in the Pacific area on either of the Parties would be dangerous to its own peace and safety and declares that it would act to meet the common dangers in accordance with its constitutional processes.
>
> Any such armed attack and all measures taken as a result thereof shall be immediately reported to the Security Council of the United Nations. Such measures shall be terminated when the Security Council has taken the measures necessary to restore and maintain international peace and security.
>
> Article V. For purposes of Article IV, an armed attack on either of the Parties is deemed to include an armed attack on the metropolitan territory of either of the Parties, or on the island territories under its jurisdiction in the Pacific Ocean, its armed forces, public vessels or aircraft in the Pacific.[39]

NARA. Central Intelligence Agency Records Search Tool [CREST] Database, Doc. CIA-RDP80M01048A000800330009-1, Approved for release October 27, 2004.

[36] NARA AAD Doc. 1974MANILA01114, US Embassy Manila to Secretary of State, January 30, 1974; NARA AAD Doc. 1974MANILA01244, US Embassy Manila to Secretary of State, February 02, 1974.

[37] NARA AAD Doc. 1974MANILA000859, US Embassy Manila to Secretary of State, January 23, 1973.

[38] *Ibid.* US Ambassador Sullivan was initially inclined in favor of the Philippine view, stating that "...a Chinese military attack against the Spratleys in a manner similar to the recent attack on the Paracels could involve an armed attack against the Armed Forces of the Philippines and therefore require the United States 'to act to meet the common dangers.'" He further suggested that Washington issue a demarche to China "to forewarn them against the prospect that military adventures in the Spratleys could engage them with the interests of the United States." See also NARA AAD Doc. 1974MANILA00998, US Embassy Manila to Secretary of State, January 26, 1974.

[39] Mutual Defense Treaty between the Republic of the Philippines and the United States of America, August 30, 1951 (January 16, 2016). http://www.gov.ph/1951/08/30/mutual-defense-treaty-between-the-republic-of-the-philippines-and-the-united-states-of-america-august-30-1951/ (accessed on January 31, 2018).

The Philippines insisted on the inclusion of its possessions in the Spratly region to be among the "island territories under its jurisdiction"; the US, however, rebuffed the Philippines every time, which led officials to doubt US reliability under the MDT.[40] The US remained neutral on the Philippine claim, which disturbed Manila,[41] but the Americans assessed that China had no interest in sparking an armed conflict but would rather settle the territorial questions peacefully as long as the other parties did not use force to make good their claims.[42] The US determined that the Spratly Islands were not expressly included within the defined territory of the Philippines, whether under the 1898 Treaty of Paris or upon the signing of the MDT.[43] According to the State Department,

> Although issue is unclear, DEPT believes there are substantial doubts that Filipine [sic] military contingent on island in Spratley [sic] Group would come within protection of treaty. It should be noted that Paracel and Spratley [sic] Islands do not RPT not come within treaty limits of the Philippines as charted on US map defining areas under jurisdiction of US and GOP for purpose of Mutual Defense Treaty. This reflects fact that various claims to sovereignty over Paracels and Spratleys [sic] and USG position that sovereignty over them is undetermined were clear and on public record at time Mutual Defense Treaty concluded. We have found nothing in negotiating history of Mutual Defense Treaty to indicate that Treaty protection of armed forces of party in Pacific was intended to extend to such forces as may be stationed in notoriously disputed territories such as Spratleys [sic] for purpose of establishing or enforcing claim to that disputed territory. We would be most reluctant to accept

---

[40] NARA AAD Doc. 1974MANILA01053, US Embassy Manila to Secretary of State, January 29, 1974.

[41] NARA AAD Doc. 1974MANILA00962, US Embassy Manila to Secretary of State, January 25, 1974.

[42] NARA AAD Doc. 1974HONGK01036, US Consul Hong Kong to Secretary of State, January 30, 1974. See also NARA AAD Doc. 1974STATE025541, Secretary of State to US Embassy Saigon, February 07, 1974, which stated that the US "[did] not believe that the recent Chinese move into the Paracels represents a turn toward aggressive PRC action in Southeast Asia."

[43] NARA AAD Doc. 1974STATE017663, Secretary of State to US Embassy Manila, February 08, 1974.

> such an extension. In any event, even if Treaty applied, the type of action required to meet this type of 'common danger' under Art. IV might we be far different from that required for attacks on the Philippines itself.[44]

At a staff meeting on January 31, 1974, which also discussed the battle between Vietnam and China in the Paracel Islands and the request for guidance to the US Ambassador to the Philippines, US Secretary of State Henry Kissinger was fully conscious of the need to stay out of the fray, but acknowledged that the US needed to send a message to China to indicate that a forceful re-taking of the islands could not be countenanced, as well as to assure allies of continued US support. Kissinger, together with key deputies, decided that it was best to remain ambiguous over the Philippine claim, even though they were conscious that it could not oblige the US to do anything under the MDT:

> ...we do not want to do anything re the Spratly Islands that would encourage the PRC to believe it has a free hand to take military action, or lead our allies to believe that we are needlessly alarmed at the prospect of such action.[45]

The transcript and minutes of the staff meeting clearly indicated that the US considered the entire Spratly Islands region, up to and including Reed Bank, to be a "disputed" area.[46] Although the US also recognized that the Philippines might have a potential claim to Reed Bank as a continental shelf area, the geological characteristics gave it sufficient doubts, resulting in the acknowledgment that it was at least of disputed status. At the time, agreement on coastal State jurisdiction was limited to the territorial sea and continental shelf concepts, and

---

[44] *Ibid.*

[45] Minutes of the Secretary of State's Staff Meeting, Washington, January 31, 1974, 3:08 pm, NARA Record Group 59, Transcripts of Secretary of State Kissinger's Staff Meetings, 1973–1977, E5177, Box 2. Also in US Department of State, *Foreign Relations of the United States, 1974–1976*, vol. E-12, Doc. 372.

[46] *Ibid.*

what is now known as the United Nations Convention on the Law of the Sea (UNCLOS) was still in development. The UNCLOS III negotiations, which began in 1972, provided the possibility for a valid Philippine claim, and indeed it did prove to create some room for slight flexibility and accommodation only more than a decade later.

While the reasons for Marcos' decision to occupy the Kalayaan Islands were never officially revealed, events indicate that it was in preparation for Philippine petroleum exploration in Reed Bank. Philippine offshore concession areas began to be awarded in 1974, with the Philippines secretly attempting to engage American oil companies to explore and drill for oil in Reed Bank.[47] The State Department officially informed each and every American contractor that their operations could not count on US protection due to the disputed nature of the area[48] and scrambled to warn away the American company found to have been contracted to conduct the first seismic exploration of Reed Bank in 1976.[49]

Philippine persistence finally found significant leverage through the Military Bases Agreement that supplemented the MDT. As the Vietnam War dragged on and the communist movement gained traction, anti-war and anti-American sentiment began appearing in the Philippines, with the Marcos Administration itself fanning

[47] Central Intelligence Agency, Central Intelligence Bulletin, July 23, 1971, NARA, CREST Database Doc CIA-RDP79T00975A019600030002-0, Approved for release, June 25, 2003, pp. 6–7. Beijing had also begun claiming the marine resources around the Spratly Islands at about this time, thus expanding its original claim to island territories to the natural resources around them. NARA AAD Doc 1973HONGK00630, US Consul Hong Kong to Secretary of State, January 16, 1974.

[48] NARA AAD Doc. 1975MANILA12464, US Embassy Manila to Secretary of State, September 05, 1975; NARA AAD Doc. 1975MANILA17960, US Embassy Manila to Secretary of State, December 23, 1975; NARA AAD Doc. 1975STATE304888, Secretary of State to US Embassy Manila, December 31, 1975.

[49] NARA AAD Doc. 1976MANILA05063, US Embassy Manila to Secretary of State, April 12, 1976; NARA AAD Doc. 1976STATE090034, Secretary of State to US Embassy Manila, April 14, 1976; NARA AAD Doc. 1976STATE099563, April 24, 1976; NARA AAD Doc. 1976MANILA06139, US Embassy Manila to Secretary of State, May 04, 1976.

anti-American flames to suit its agenda. The military bases were repeatedly the subject of negotiations between the Washington DC and Manila, especially after the Symington hearings in 1969[50]; by 1975, the US withdrawal from Vietnam had clearly shaken the foundations of the Philippines–US defense alliance. Washington was conscious that Manila had found a major negotiating lever in exchange for US support to the Philippine claim; in a letter dated August 06, 1976, National Security Adviser Brent Scowcroft advised:

> ...although the GOP has not presented the bargain in the following terms, the *quid pro quo* may be our agreeing to militarily support their claims in the Spratlys against the PRC and Vietnam in exchange for a free hand in the use of the bases. Since we cannot give the Philippines assurances that we will defend them in a military conflict that occurs in contested territory, early conclusion of the base agreement appears unlikely.[51]

Subsequently, the Philippines indeed made a very strong effort to extract US support for its claim to the Kalayaan Islands through the bases negotiations.[52] Scowcroft laid out in very clear terms the US

---

[50] The Symington hearings referred to a series of hearings conducted by the Subcommittee on United States Security Arrangements and Commitments Abroad, part of the Committee on Foreign Relations, headed by Senator Stuart Symington n 1969. The Symington hearings were extremely critical of the US basing arrangements abroad and revealed major problems with US bases in the Philippines such as Marcos' corruption, smuggling of PX goods, and misuse of military financial assistance, just prior to the Philippine Presidential elections of 1969. The release of the hearing transcripts was described as an "unmitigated disaster in terms of basic US interests in [the Philippines] and the future of US/Philippine relations." *Foreign Relations of the United States, 1969–1976*, vol. 20, Doc. 194–199.

[51] T. Barnes, Memorandum: Marcos-Robinson Meeting August 6, 1976 and Philippine Negotiating Strategy, US Department of State, *Foreign Relations of the United States, 1973–1976,* vol. E-12, Doc 349; W. Gleysteen, Memorandum to the President's Assistant for National Security Affairs (Scowcroft), Washington, September 2, 1976, US Department of State, *Foreign Relations of the United States, 1973–1976,* vol. E-12, Doc. 351.

[52] US Department of State, *Foreign Relations of the United States, 1973–1976,* vol. E-12, Doc. 354–358.

dilemma, and their available options, in a follow-up memorandum for President decision in October 1976:

> A clearly negative response to this issue may at the very least be expected to complicate gravely our current task of renegotiating the bases agreement. It could well lead to tighter restrictions on the use of our bases, e.g., for support of activities in the Indian Ocean.
>
> On the other hand, any strongly affirmative response to Marcos will bear at least equal risks. It would increase the possibility of tensions with the PRC and Vietnam. Congress and the public would probably see such a position as an unnecessary expansion of our defense commitment.
>
> Finally, a forthcoming response might encourage Marcos to pursue his claims to the Spratlys more actively, and to use military force to protect such claims.[53]

To protect the bases from Marcos' apparent willingness to sacrifice easy access to them for protection in the Spratly Islands region, Scowcroft made his recommendation to resort to an ambiguous interpretation of the MDT reiterating its application at least to Philippine ships and aircraft operating in the area in a non-aggressive manner:

> ...State and Defense to reply to Marcos on the Reed Bank defense commitment issue by saying our Defense Treaty would apply to Philippine units operating in the Reed Bank region as long as their presence is consistent with the provisions of our Mutual Defense Treaty, particularly Article I regarding peaceful settlement of disputes and refraining from the threat or use of forces.[54]

The recommendation was approved by then-President Ford, and the results were relayed to Manila. This marked a subtle adjustment in US maritime security policy in the region and was the closest that the Philippines got from the US as a security guarantee. While the

---

[53] Brent Scowcroft, Memorandum: Key Issues in Our Base Negotiations with the Philippines, Gerald R. Ford Presidential Library, Presidential Handwriting File, Box C50, Presidential Handwriting 10/11/1976, pp. 2–3.

[54] *Ibid.*, p. 5.

non-extension of MDT commitments geographically to Philippine possessions in the Spratly Islands themselves remained, at least the assurance of treaty commitments concerning Philippine public ships and aircraft operating in the disputed maritime region was enough to placate Manila.

Likely as a result of acceptance of the US accommodation, the Philippines then officially consolidated its occupation and claim through the issuance in 1978 of Presidential Decree No. 1596, which formally created the Municipality of the Kalayaan Islands and incorporated them as an island-municipality of Palawan Province.[55] Further written assurance was secured the following year, when then-Foreign Secretary Carlos P. Romulo procured a letter dated January 06, 1979 from US Secretary of State Cyrus Vance, confirming an earlier agreement that:

> …an attack on Philippine armed forces, public vessels, or aircraft in the Pacific would not have to occur within the metropolitan territory of the Philippines or island territories under its jurisdiction in the Pacific in order to come within the definition of Pacific area under Article V.[56]

This interpretation effectively expanded the area of application of the MDT to anywhere Philippine public ships and aircraft were located, even in disputed areas. It was further agreed that "the Pacific area" included the SCS.[57] In hindsight, the Vance letter is proof of the Philippines' modest success in "wagging the dog": while the US remained resistant to supporting the Philippine claim and continued its policy of neutrality thereon, the written security guarantee for

---

[55] Pres. Decree No. 1596 (1978), Declaring certain area part of the Philippine territory and providing for their Government and administration.

[56] Cited in Statement of Secretary del Rosario regarding the Philippines-U.S. Mutual Defense Treaty, May 9, 2012, Department of Foreign Affairs (January 19, 2016). http://www.gov.ph/2012/05/09/statement-of-secretary-del-rosario-regarding-the-philippines-u-s-mutual-defense-treaty-may-9-2012/ (accessed on January 31, 2018). Arturo M. Tolentino, *The Philippines and the Law of the Sea* (Makati: Development Academy of the Philippines Press), 1982, pp. 26–30.

[57] *Ibid.*, see also Telegram 18586 from the Embassy in the Philippines to the Department of State, November 29, 1976, 0824z, US Department of State, *Foreign Relations of the United States, 1973–1976,* vol. E-12, Doc. 357.

Philippine units operating in the region was still better than absolute indifference. This latter would later be reiterated by Ambassador Hubbard in a communication dated May 24, 1999.[58]

The US response was a masterful stroke walking the fine line between the feared implications of any clearer US position on the issue: by insisting on Philippine units' presence "consistent with the MDT" and emphasizing peaceful dispute settlement and non-use of force, it restrained further military adventurism on the part of the Marcos Administration. At the same time, it satisfied the latter's need for security for its forces already in place in the Spratlys. These were entirely in keeping with standing US policy and preference for keeping the region a "neutral zone" free from destabilizing conflict. US maritime security interests were ultimately not adversely affected, as they were already also eventually secured through customary international law and evolving treaty law that established acceptable limitations on claimants' activities.

The Rise of China

The fall of the Marcos Dictatorship and the subsequent nationalist backlash against perceived US support, or at least non-interference and condonation, for the dictatorial regime were direct factors in the re-established Senate's non-renewal of the Military Bases Agreement in 1991. Unfortunately, by that time, the Philippines' basic external defense functions (e.g. surveillance, deterrence) were fully carried out by US forces operating out of Subic and Clark. The US carried the burden of external defense upon express agreement with the Philippines, which chose to focus on internal security threats[59]; the withdrawal of American forces in 1991 thus resulted in the total collapse of its external

[58] Cited in Statement of Secretary del Rosario regarding the Philippines — U.S. Mutual Defense Treaty, May 9, 2012, Department of Foreign Affairs (January 19, 2016).http://www.gov.ph/2012/05/09/statement-of-secretary-del-rosario-regarding-the-philippines-u-s-mutual-defense-treaty-may-9-2012/ (accessed on January 31, 2018).
[59] See Telegram from the Embassy in the Philippines to the Department of State, August 04, 1969, US Department of State, *Foreign Relations of the United States, 1969–1972*, vol. 20, Doc. 192; see also NARA AAD Doc. 1977MANILA20421, US Embassy Manila to Secretary of State, December 29, 1977; NARA AAD Doc. 1977STATE283150, Department of State to US Embassy Manila, November 26, 1977.

defense. This coincided with China's re-emergence from self-imposed isolation and presented ideal conditions for its slow but sure strategic expansion.

The absence of any defense capability likely contributed to the successful Chinese incursions into Mischief Reef in 1995[60] and Scarborough Shoal in 1997,[61] and which again sparked in 1999 and 2001, respectively. American military presence in the area was regular but heavily reduced, and in the aftermath of the Mischief Reef "renovation" (whereby the original small Chinese hut-like outposts were converted into full-blown building complexes), the Philippines attempted to attract US forces back through the Visiting Forces Agreement and the conduct of annual "Balikatan" exercises.[62] These did not have any serious impact on Chinese activities and incursions, but at least provided some more assurance to defense officials.

The onset of US President George Bush's Global War on Terror gave another opportunity for the Philippines to attempt to curry favor with the US, by participating in the Coalition of the Willing in the invasion of Iraq.[63] It was a rather short-lived membership, though, as the Philippines immediately withdrew from the coalition as soon as one overseas Filipino worker was taken hostage.[64] With then-President

---

[60] Daniel Dzurek, *China Occupies Mischief Reef in latest Spratly Gambit*, IBRU Boundary and Security Bulletin, April 1995, pp. 65–71.

[61] K. S. Sik, M. C. W. Pinto and S. P. Subedi (eds.), *Asian Yearbook of International Law*, vol. 7 (The Hague: Kluwer Law International), 1997, p. 481; François-Xavier Bonnet, *Geopolitics of Scarborough Shoal*, IRASEC Discussion Paper 14, Nov 2012, Research Institute on Contemporary Southeast Asia. www.irasec.com.

[62] Agreement between the United States of America and the Philippines, signed at Manila February 10, 1998 (January 16, 2015). http://www.state.gov/documents/organization/107852.pdf (accessed on January 31, 2018). Exercise Balikatan, "Shouldering the Load Together" (January 16, 2016). http://www.globalsecurity.org/military/ops/balikatan.htm (accessed on January 31, 2018).

[63] US names 'coalition of the willing,' *BBC News*, March 18, 2003 (January 16, 2016). http://news.bbc.co.uk/2/hi/americas/2862343.stm (accessed on January 31, 2018).

[64] The Philippines pullout: 'Coalition of the Willing' is dealt a setback, *Pittsburg Post-Gazette*, July 20, 2004; US: RP no longer part of coalition. *The Philippine Star*, August 06, 2004 (January 16, 2016). http://www.philstar.com/headlines/260194/us-rp-no-longer-part-coalition (accessed on January 31, 2018).

Gloria Macapagal-Arroyo's tenure as President under severe contestation, an international and domestic political crisis potentially as serious as the Flor Contemplation Case[65] was simply seen as an even greater threat than US recriminations for faltering in the anti-terror campaign.

Unfortunately, the Philippines had still not learned from its brief dalliance with absolute security independence, and the vaunted AFP Modernization Plan fell to the wayside, apparently a victim of massive corruption in the military and civilian defense establishment. As Philippine external defense capability dwindled to less than zero, China continued double-digit growth in all economic, military, and political spheres.

Philippine diplomacy, although correctly starting off with seeking peaceful dispute settlement, soon began faltering and vacillating on account of vested and personal interests. After establishing a "modus vivendi" with the conclusion of the 2002 Declaration of Conduct of the Parties in the SCS,[66] with the hope that it would fix the "status quo" against further new occupations, a brief respite came as relations between the Philippines and China settled to a "golden age" under the Arroyo Administration. Complacency combined with long years of neglect of external defense as well as the absence of a clear, long-term policy on the Kalayaan Islands, however, would create the conditions for the looming fallback of the Philippines from the SCS, and its near-hysterical drive for US military resurgence.

Defending "Pax Americana" in the Asia-Pacific

By 2009, Chinese claims in the SCS, which had long been at a strategic disadvantage, began benefiting from the fruits of the Chinese economic reconstruction. A slow, inexorable build up of maritime

[65] Flor Contemplation: A diplomatic incident (January 16, 2016). http://www.capitalpunishmentuk.org/flor.html (accessed on January 31, 2018). William Safire. The hanging of Flor. *New York Times*, April 24, 1995 (January 16, 2016). http://www.nytimes.com/1995/04/24/opinion/essay-the-hanging-of-flor.html (accessed on January 31, 2018). S. Jayakumar, Diplomacy (Singapore: Straits Times Press), 2011, pp. 154–167.

[66] 2002 Declaration on the Conduct of Parties in the South China Sea (January 16, 2016). http://cil.nus.edu.sg/rp/pdf/2002%20Declaration%20on%20the%20Conduct%20of%20Parties%20in%20the%20South%20China%20Sea-pdf.pdf (accessed on January 31, 2018).

forces, both civilian and military, began to increase its pressure on the smaller Southeast Asian claimants, beginning with an unpublicized naval clash with Vietnam in 2007 and steadily ramping up in frequency and intensity as Chinese fishing fleets also began expanding outward from depleted Chinese coastal fishing grounds.[67] The submission of extended continental shelf claims by Vietnam and Malaysia prompted the first diplomatic communication of the infamous nine-dashed lines claim, which China described as being "long known" to the international community.[68] The change in leadership of the Chinese Communist Party through President Xi Jinping marked a Chinese political renaissance, as the "Chinese Dream" provided an ideological motivation to mobilize the prodigious Chinese population to support China's economic and political agenda. China's maritime activities turned more forceful and legally reckless, as Chinese civilian, military, and para-military ships got involved in blockading a US naval vessel[69] and directly interfered in seismic exploration activities of Vietnam and the Philippines.[70]

The increasing assertiveness of China in the SCS, from one perspective, is a form of reprisal against years of assertion by the smaller claimants in their own respective maritime zones, but with one important difference: China now projects itself very far from its own

---

[67] Journey to the South China Sea. Episode 8: Guardian of Blue Borders (January 16, 2016). https://www.youtube.com/watch?v=kaVdwLcNYY4 (accessed on January 31, 2018). M. Li, Reconciling assertiveness and cooperation? China's changing approach to the South China Sea dispute, *Security Challenges*, vol. 6, no. 2 (Winter 2010), pp. 49–68.

[68] Note dated May 7, 2009, available from the official website of the Commission on the Limits of the Continental Shelf. http://www.un.org/Depts/los/clcs_new/submissions_files/submission_vnm_37_2009.htm (accessed on January 31, 2018). The same note is also found at http://www.un.org/Depts/los/clcs_new/submissions_files/submission_mysvnm_33_2009.htm (accessed on April 17, 2010).

[69] R. Pedroso, Close encounters at sea: The USNS impeccable incident, *Naval War College Review*, vol. 62, no. 3 (Summer 2009), pp. 101–111.

[70] Jeremy Page, Vietnam accuses Chinese ships, *Wall Street Journal*, December 03, 2012 (January 16, 2016). http://www.wsj.com/articles/SB10001424127887323717004578157033857113510 (accessed on January 31, 2018). Jaime Laude, China gunboats harass RP vessel, *The Philippine Star*, March 04, 2011 (January 16, 2016). http://www.philstar.com/headlines/662502/china-gunboats-harass-rp-vessel (accessed on January 31, 2018).

shores and asserts itself very close to its neighbors' coastal front-yards, and at a grossly disproportionate scale. Moreover, China's assertions began gaining prominence with an uncomfortable seeming lack of restraint and discipline, and flaunting the basic rules of the US-designed order, especially in the maritime sphere.

The adjustment of US geo-political priorities and slight shift of focus from the Middle East after the Bush Administration was signified by the announcement of the so-called "pivot to Asia" strategy in 2010.[71] Although subsequently portrayed as having broader economic features (just as it was in the late 19th Century, the future of the American economy still lay with the Asia-Pacific markets), its military/strategic aspects definitely received central attention. A "rebalancing" of military forces would entail a more widely dispersed deployment across the Asia-Pacific region, but with a stronger emphasis on alliance building and burden-sharing. This indicated that the US was no longer willing or capable of being the sole and external guarantor of regional peace and stability under the legal and geopolitical order it had created, and was now seeking to pass on at least some of the greater burdens of regional "peacekeeping" (in the broader sense of maintaining security forces) to the regional States. The US "pivot" or "rebalance" clearly caught China's attention, especially when seen in light of the latter's elevation of the SCS disputes as among its "core interests" practically equal in status to Tibet and Taiwan.[72]

China's increasingly coercive maritime policies finally found a Philippine target when the "BRP Gregorio del Pilar," the Philippine Navy's newest warship attempted to arrest Chinese fishermen poaching for coral and endangered species on "Bajo de Masinloc" (Scarborough

---

[71] Hillary Clinton, America's Pacific Century, *Foreign Policy Magazine*, October 11, 2011 (January 16, 2016). http://iipdigital.usembassy.gov/st/english/article/2011/10/20111011161233su0.8861287.html#axzz30Ph1DmRw (accessed on January 31, 2018). Kenneth Lieberthal, The American Pivot to Asia, *Foreign Policy*, December 21, 2011 (January 16, 2016). http://foreignpolicy.com/2011/12/21/the-american-pivot-to-asia/ (accessed on January 31, 2018).

[72] Edward Wong, China hedges over whether South China Sea is a "Core Interest" worth war, *New York Times*, March 30, 2011 (January 16, 2016). http://www.nytimes.com/2011/03/31/world/asia/31beijing.html?_r=0 (accessed on January 31, 2018).

Shoal) in April 2012. This led to a tense months-long stand-off that sundered Philippines–China relations, and provided the opportunity for a renewal and full re-entry of US military presence in the Philippines.[73] Frustrated by American ineffectiveness in securing a Chinese withdrawal from "Bajo de Masinloc," Manila initiated arbitration proceedings against China under UNCLOS Annex VII in January 2013.[74] The Philippines also proceeded to highlight and re-strengthen its alliance relationship with the US, culminating in the signing of the Enhanced Defense Cooperation Agreement (EDCA).[75] China, on the other hand, rejected the arbitration outright and responded by increasing the pressure on the Philippines in the Spratly region through provocative maritime patrols very close to the Philippine-held positions, and especially around the "BRP Sierra Madre" grounded on "Ayungin" (Second Thomas) Shoal.[76] This was carried out in the midst of major institutional adjustments in its maritime security posture resulting in the creation of the China Coast Guard through merger of various civilian maritime law enforcement agencies,[77] and renewed emphasis on the defense of its strategic maritime interests.[78]

---

[73] For a full history of the incident, see J. Batongbacal, The 2012 Scarborough Shoal Stand-off: A Philippine perspective, *Chinese Studies Journal,* vol. 10 (2013), pp. 60–131.

[74] The Republic of the Philippines v, The People's Republic of China, Permanent Court of Arbitration (January 16, 2016). http://www.pcacases.com/web/view/7 (accessed on January 31, 2018).

[75] Enhanced Defense Cooperation Agreement between the Philippines and the United States, Official Gazette (January 16, 2016). http://www.gov.ph/2014/04/29/document-enhanced-defense-cooperation-agreement/ (accessed on January 31, 2018).

[76] J. Himmelman, A Game of Shark and Minnow, *New York Times*, October 27, 2013 (January 16, 2016). http://www.nytimes.com/newsgraphics/2013/10/27/south-china-sea/ (accessed on January 31, 2018).

[77] Robert Martinson, From words to actions: The creation of the China Coast Guard, in paper presented to the China as a Maritime Power Conference, Center for Naval Analyses, July 28–29, 2015 (January 16, 2016). https://www.cna.org/cna_files/pdf/Creation-China-Coast-Guard.pdf (accessed on January 31, 2018).

[78] Laura Southgate, China's White Paper: Implications for Southeast Asia, *The Diplomat*, June 07, 2015 (January 16, 2015). http://thediplomat.com/2015/06/chinas-white-paper-implications-for-southeast-asia/ (accessed on January 31, 2018).

The full scope of China's response to the Philippine challenge was capped by an unprecedented but pragmatic geo-military move: the construction of artificial islands in the Spratly region beginning in the first quarter of 2014. Philippine reconnaissance planes showed the rapid expansion of the Chinese facility on Johnson South Reef, and reported similar activities on other Chinese positions.[79] American response to China's artificial island building was initially sluggish, likely due to its avowed policy of detachment and neutrality on the sovereignty claims. But the March 2015 publication of commercial satellite photographs revealing in great detail the full and massive scope of China's artificial island building spree in the SCS[80] spurred another recalibration. Keeping distance from the island disputes, but recognizing the need for stability in the maritime domain, the US sought to strengthen maritime peacekeeping by its regional allies through more active naval cooperation in the region. This would allow the US to remain actively engaged in deploying sea power in the SCS but with the full support and cooperation of regional actors. This policy is encapsulated in its global maritime security strategy based on cooperative alliances.[81]

China's artificial island building finally provoked an even more substantial US response just a few months later. In an attempt to prevent close scrutiny of its activities, Chinese ships began shadowing and challenging US ships traversing the SCS, and attempted to prevent closer US reconnaissance by air.[82] In May 2015, EP-8A Poseidon aircraft were given explicit warnings by the Chinese Navy in the following tenor:

---

[79] Department of Foreign Affairs, China's reclamation on Mabini Reef, Press release, May 15, 2014 (January 16, 2015). http://www.dfa.gov.ph/index.php/newsroom/dfa-releases/2871-china-s-reclamation-on-mabini-reef (accessed on January 31, 2018).

[80] Asia Maritime Transparency Initiative, *Island Tracker*, Center for Strategic and International Studies (January 16, 2016). http://amti.csis.org/island-tracker/ (accessed on January 31, 2018).

[81] United States Marine Corps, Navy and Coast Guard, *A Cooperative Strategy for 21st Century Seapower*, March 2015 (January 16, 2016). http://www.uscg.mil/seniorleadership/DOCS/CS21R_Final.pdf (accessed on January 31, 2018).

[82] Sharon Chen, US Navy ship met Chinese vessel on South China Sea patrol, *Bloomberg Business*, May 19, 2015 (January 16, 2016). http://www.bloomberg.com/news/articles/2015-05-19/u-s-says-navy-ship-met-chinese-vessel-on-south-china-sea-patrol (accessed on January 31, 2018).

> Foreign military aircraft. This is Chinese Navy. You are approaching our military alert zone. Leave immediately.[83]

The widely publicized incident demonstrated that China's artificial islands posed a clear threat to the long-held and singularly important interest of the US in freedom of navigation and over-flight in the SCS. Having been issued by the Chinese Navy, it clearly demonstrated military rather than civilian operations, and was not based on any claim to territorial or jurisdictional zones clearly defined in international law, but rather to un-publicized, unspecified, and unmarked "military alert zones." The repeated demand for the US aircraft to not enter such a zone implied not only a territorial claim but also the establishment of a military exclusion zone that directly and palpably threatened US freedom of navigation and over-flight in the SCS. A military exclusion zone is far worse than a territorial claim because there are no rules that sanction it other than the laws of war, and it is defined only by the operational necessities of the military force that imposes it. It is exactly the kind of arbitrary restriction on freedom of movement at sea (or over it) opposed by US sea power doctrine. For the US, this was the positive proof that its own specific interests were now also at stake.

However, the object of US neutrality had to be clarified; attention was focused not on sovereignty over the islands themselves but on the usage of the maritime space around them. To shift the policy focus from neutrality on the claims to the islands, the US turned to the behavior of the claimants in pursuing their claims. Echoing and reinforcing an equally long-standing policy expressed in the 1930s, the US emphasized that the manner in which such claims were pursued should also be in accord with accepted modes of peaceful settlement

[83] Reuters and Ted Thornhill, This is Chinese navy, you go! China issues EIGHT warnings to US surveillance planes to get away from disputed man-made islands, *Mail Online*, May 21, 2015 (January 16, 2016). http://www.dailymail.co.uk/news/article-3090728/China-navy-warns-U-S-spy-plane-disputed-South-China-Sea-CNN.html (accessed on January 31, 2018).

of international disputes.[84] It was clearly articulated by Assistant Secretary of State Daniel Russell as follows:

> For us, it's not about the rocks and shoals in the South China Sea or the resources in and under it, it's about the rules and it's about the kind of neighborhood we all want to live in. So we will continue to defend the rules, and encourage others to do so as well.[85]

Russell stressed the point more forcefully in the following manner:

> We are not neutral when it comes to adhering to international law. We will come down forcefully when it comes to following the rules.[86]

He also laid out in very clear terms what the specific interests of the US were in the context of the disputes:

> Protecting unimpeded freedom of navigation and overflight and other lawful uses of the sea by all, not just the US Navy;
>
> Honoring our alliance and security commitments, and retaining the full confidence of our partners and the region in the United States;
>
> Aiding the development of effective regional institutions, including a unified ASEAN;
>
> Promoting responsible marine environmental practices;

---

[84] Prashanth Parameswaran, US not 'neutral' in South China Sea disputes: Top US diplomat, *The Diplomat*, July 22, 2015 (January 16, 2016). http://thediplomat.com/2015/07/us-not-neutral-in-south-china-sea-disputes-top-us-diplomat/ (accessed on January 31, 2018).

[85] Remarks at the Fifth Annual South China Sea Conference, July 21, 2015, Center for Strategic and International Studies, Washington DC, (January 16, 2016). http://www.state.gov/p/eap/rls/rm/2015/07/245142.htm (accessed on January 31, 2018).

[86] Prashanth Parameswaran, US not 'neutral' in South China Sea disputes: Top US diplomat, *The Diplomat*, July 22, 2015 (January 16, 2016). http://thediplomat.com/2015/07/us-not-neutral-in-south-china-sea-disputes-top-us-diplomat/ (accessed on January 31, 2018).

> Fostering China's peaceful rise in a manner that promotes economic growth and regional stability, including through consistency with international law and standards;
>
> And more generally, an international order based on compliance with international law and the peaceful settlement of disputes without the threat or use of force.[87]

It is worth noting that in the above enumeration of the interests, the navigational rights demanded by sea power remain of primary importance. The policy shift was very prominently featured in the US Asia-Pacific Maritime Security Strategy that was subsequently published; it focused on the SCS and China's new islands and reiterated American interest in navigational freedoms, compliance with the Law of the Sea, and the peaceful settlement of disputes in the Asia-Pacific.[88] At the same time, it called on bilateral and multi-lateral partnerships in the maritime peacekeeping. Clearly, therefore, the US fully intends to keep the regional stability and order in the Asia-Pacific that it designed and established after the end of the Second World War, to the extent that such stability and order is supported by the navigational regime on which it was built. Regional actors are willing to join this effort because it is the same regional stability and order that has underpinned the growth and prosperity of the Asia-Pacific for more than half a century, but now subject to the destabilizing influence of China through its attempt to constrict American sea power and expand exclusive and exclusionary control of the SCS.

The Aftermath of the SCS Arbitration

Friction increased between China's assertiveness and US interests in the run-up and aftermath of the SCS Arbitration. China's attempts to constrain US surveillance flights prompted a more serious response through publicized freedom of navigation operations (FONOPs) in

---

[87] *Ibid.*

[88] Department of Defense, *The Asia-Pacific Maritime Security Strategy: Achieving US National Security Objectives in a Changing Environment* (Washington DC, Department of Defense), 2015.

October 2015, beginning with a voyage by the guided missile destroyer "USS Lassen" to within 12 nautical miles of China-held Mischief and Subi Reefs.[89] The US asserted that it was the first of a series of FONOPs that would become more frequent; China described the operation as a "coercive action that seeks to militarize the SCS region" and an "abuse" of freedom of navigation under international law.[90]

The second FONOP took place in January 2016, when the "USS Curtis Wilbur" sailed within 12 nautical miles of Triton Island in the Paracel Islands without notifying either China or Vietnam.[91] The following month, it was revealed that the Royal Australian Air Force had also been conducting its own FONOPs since the previous year.[92] A third US FONOP took place in May 2016, with the "USS William P Lawrence" passing within 12 nautical miles of Fiery Cross Reef.[93]

Tensions rose sharply in July 2016 when the Annex VII tribunal handed out its decision on the merits in the "Philippines v. China" case, in which the Philippines won almost all of its submissions. The award inflicted serious damage to China's hopes of international public acceptability of its claims. Among the 15 Philippine submissions, the most important were that the tribunal ruled against China's historic rights claims, as represented by the "nine-dash line" map, and held that any and all historic rights claims to resources and waters

---

[89] Reuters, Angry China shadows US warship near man-made islands, *Reuters*, October 27, 2015. http://www.reuters.com/article/southchinasea-usa-idUSL1N12Q1L720151027 (accessed on January 31, 2018).

[90] *Ibid.*

[91] Sam LaGrone, US destroyer challenges more Chinese South China Sea claims in new freedom of navigation operation, *USNI News*, January 30, 2016. https://news.usni.org/2016/01/30/u-s-destroyer-challenges-more-chinese-south-china-sea-claims-in-new-freedom-of-navigation-operation (accessed on January 31, 2018).

[92] Andrew Greene, RAAF patrols over disputed South China Sea facing more regular resistance from Chinese military, ABC News, February 03, 2016. http://www.abc.net.au/news/2016-02-03/raaf-patrol-flights-facing-more-regular-resistance-from-chinese/7138100 (accessed on January 31, 2018).

[93] Ankit Panda, South China Sea: US Navy destroyer asserts freedom of navigation near Fiery Cross Reef, *The Diplomat*, May 10, 2016. http://thediplomat.com/2016/05/south-china-sea-us-navy-destroyer-asserts-freedom-of-navigation-near-fiery-cross-reef/ (accessed on January 31, 2018).

beyond the territorial sea and EEZ or continental shelf were relinquished and abandoned by China when it signed and ratified UNCLOS in exchange for the establishment of the EEZ and continental shelf regimes in favor of all coastal states. It also characterized all of the features in the Spratly Islands region and Scarborough Shoal as incapable of generating EEZ and continental shelf areas, leaving only relatively small but scattered pockets of disputed territorial sovereignty areas. This left the sea areas around them to be jurisdictionally allocated either to adjacent coastal states or the high seas in accordance with UNCLOS.

Chinese reaction to the ruling was long-brewing, and somewhat extreme. Immediately, it initiated combat air patrols over Scarborough Shoal using an HK-6 nuclear bomber.[94] The People's Liberation Army (PLA)-Navy was mobilized to alert status, and conducted exercises off the Paracel Islands in an apparent show of force.

But a change in leadership in the Philippines broke the upward trend of tensions when the new Philippine President introduced a radical foreign policy shift of friendliness toward China and open disdain for the US. An official visit in August led to meeting of President Rodrigo Duterte and President Xi Jinping, after which tensions began cooling and breaking. In late October, Filipino fishermen were able to resume fishing in Scarborough Shoal without interference from Chinese law enforcement vessels even though they remained on station.[95] In the same month, as the regional atmosphere relaxed, the US conducted a new FONOP, this time with the "USS Decatur" traversing the waters between the Paracel Islands.[96] As the year drew to a

[94] China's air force conducts combat air patrol in South China Sea, *Xinhua*, July 18, 2016. http://news.xinhuanet.com/english/2016-07/18/c_135522387.htm (accessed on January 31, 2018). Michael Forsythe, China begins air patrols over disputed area of the South China Sea, *New York Times*, July 15, 2016. https://www.nytimes.com/2016/07/19/world/asia/china-sea-air-patrols.html?_r=0. (accessed on January 31, 2018).

[95] Philippine fishermen back from Panatag Shoal with big catch, *Philippine Daily Inquirer*, October 30, 2016. http://globalnation.inquirer.net/148316/filipino-fishermen-back-from-panatag-shoal-with-big-catch (accessed on January 31, 2018).

[96] Indrees Ali and Matt Spetalnick, A US warship was shadowed by three Chinese vessels during a freedom-of-navigation exercise in the South China Sea, *Business Insider*, October 21, 2016. http://www.businessinsider.com/us-warship-freedom-of-navigation-exercise-south-

close, China seized an underwater drone while it was being recovered by the US survey ship "USS Bowditch" just 50-nautical miles northwest of Subic Bay in the Philippines.[97] The drone was returned to the US after the latter protested the action.

In February 2017, it was also reported that a US EP-3 maritime patrol craft and Chinese KJ-200 AWACS aircraft had an unexpected and unsafe encounter in the air in the vicinity of Scarborough Shoal.[98] The aerial incident marks a new year of possibly more unexpected encounters between ships and aircraft operating in the region.

Quo Vadis?

From the narrative above, it may be said that there has been a remarkable consistency in US maritime security policy in the region since at least the 1930s, with its persistent position of neutrality with respect to competing sovereignty claims to the land features in the Spratly Islands region. Such neutrality applies to the Philippine claim to the Kalayaan Islands, and despite the hopes of some quarters, cannot be expected to be overturned even by American commitments under the MDT with the Philippines. However, the neutrality is also premised on the assumption that regardless of who has sovereignty, such islands should be neutral "*vis-à-vis*" US interests in freedom of navigation and over-flight through the SCS. Thus, it has not prevented the adjustment of US policy to ensure that those navigational interests are adequately insulated from the disputes.

The persistent attempts of the Philippines to get the US to protect or guarantee its claims in the SCS were not effective until recently

---

china-sea-2016-10 (accessed on January 31, 2018). Sam LaGrone, *US Warship Conducts South China Sea Freedom of Navigation Operation*, US Naval Institute, October 21, 2016. https://news.usni.org/2016/10/21/u-s-warship-conducts-south-china-sea-freedom-navigation-operation. (accessed on January 31, 2018).

[97] Chinese warship seizes US underwater drone in international waters, *The Guardian*, December 16, 2016. https://www.theguardian.com/world/2016/dec/16/china-seizes-us-underwater-drone-south-china-sea (accessed on January 31, 2018).

[98] Ryan Browne, Chinese and US aircraft in unsafe encounter, CNN, February 10, 2017. http://edition.cnn.com/2017/02/09/politics/us-china-aircraft-unsafe-encounter/ (accessed on January 31, 2018).

with the advent of China's rise and its exaggerated response to Philippine attempts to seek legal recourse to protect its claims. The diplomatic correspondence is direct evidence against the common assumption that the Philippines acts as a US subaltern in the SCS; instead it proves that over the years the Philippines has always acted purely out of self-interest in expanding its marine resource base.

Unlike the concession in the 1970s to protect Philippine public ships and aircraft operating in the region from aggressive actions by any other claimants (which works clearly in favor of only the Philippines), the latest adjustment of US policy is directed toward their convergent interests. Both have perceived a serious and simultaneous threat to their respective objectives in the SCS on account of the Chinese build-up in assertive maritime military activities and artificial islands, the Spratly Islands are no longer the practical "neutral zones" that they were for decades after the Second World War; the situation may actually threaten US sea power interests and have provoked a significant US counter-response. This can only be expected to continue as China expands its influence over the SCS.

Acknowledgments

The author acknowledges the assistance of the Philippine American Educational Foundation, which provided the US-ASEAN Fulbright Initiative Research Fellowship Grant that supported research for this chapter. Much of this chapter was previously published by the Manila Studies Association in the Philippines under the title "The Kalayaan Islands and the American Asia-Pacific Order under Challenge: Retrospective and Prospects."

Chapter

5

Recent State Practice and Strategy on South China Sea Disputes: From Taiwan's Perspective

Mu-lan Kao

Attorney-at-Law, Kao and Associates Law Office, Taipei, Taiwan

Abstract

The status of the U-shaped line (also known as nine-dash line or the eleven-dash line) has been challenged in the international community since Mainland China objected to the Malaysian and Vietnamese joint submissions by submitting the note verbale to the UN Secretary-General on May 7, 2009. It is known that the nine-dash line succeeded to the status of the U-shaped line claimed by the Republic of China (ROC). Officially, the U-shaped line was first drawn in the *Location Map of the South China Sea Islands* which delineated the scope of Chinese government's territory and waters in the region on December 1, 1947. When the map was released, no nation publicly raised any opposition. In addition, at the time the *Location Map of the South China Sea Islands* was published, the Law of the Sea was still the regime that existed prior to the enactment of the United Nations Convention on the Law of the Sea (UNCLOS).

Some international scholars thought that Mainland China never clarified the nature of nine-dash line of its claim. The ROC's sovereignty claims and practice on the South China Sea (SCS) maritime territorial disputes would be relevant to Beijing's statements and influence the arbitration initiated by the Philippines in early 2013. Therefore, the ROC's clarification with respect to the status of the U-shaped line has drawn significant attention. Since the Democratic Progressive Party has won the 2016 presidential election, any responses to the SCS arbitral award (the Philippine vs. Mainland China) or claims asserted by the Tsai Administration shall be a high-profile issue. To safeguard the ROC's national interests, Taiwan is seeking to solidify its position in contentious SCS and looking forward to participating in regional negotiation and collaboration with claimant countries in the future.

Keywords: *Location Map of the South China Sea Islands,* U-shaped line, Sino-Philippine arbitration, Taiping Island, Article 121 of UNCLOS.

Introduction

According to the ancient records of the *Compilation of Historical Archives on the Southern Territories of the Republic of China*, we learn that both of the Far Eastern Meteorological Conference[1] and the first conference of the International Civil Aviation Organization on aviation in the Asia-Pacific region indicated recognition and respect for the Chinese territorial sovereignty over the islands in the South China Sea (SCS) (p. 44).[2] The U-shaped line can refer to the China's Nationalist government formal claim of sovereign territory in the SCS in accordance with the agreements made in the Cairo Declaration of November 27, 1943, and the Potsdam Declaration of July 26, 1945.[2]

As mentioned above, since the China's Nationalist government published the *Location Map of the South China Sea Islands*, the Law of the Sea was still the regime that was in existence prior to the

[1] The Ministry of the Interior, R.O.C (Taiwan), *Compilation of Historical Archives on the Southern Territories of the Republic of China*, March 21, 2016, p. 21.

[2] The Office of the President, President Ma's remarks at International Conference on South China Sea Disputes and International Law, April 14, 2016, http://english.president.gov.tw/NEWS/4873 (accessed on July 10, 2017).

enactment of UNCLOS. The issues of sovereignty rights over islands in the SCS, as well as their surrounding waters, should be dealt with in accordance with intertemporal law. Furthermore, the *Location Map of the South China Sea Islands* documented the islands restored to the Chinese government in 1947, which should be viewed as having legal force for establishing sovereignty claims over the islands and their surrounding waters. It is important to note that the legal principle that maritime rights derive from a coastal state's sovereignty over the land is a general rule that is not without exceptions.

The ROC government had expanded its territorial sea limit from 3 to 12 nautical miles and established a 200-nautical-mile Exclusive Economic Zone on September 6, 1979. To keep abreast of the international trend of sustainable development and to cope with future marine affairs with a broader view that also considers the nation's conditions, the ROC government promulgated and enforced "Law on the Territorial Sea and the Contiguous Zone of the Republic of China"[3] and "Law on the Exclusive Economic Zone and the Continental Shelf of the Republic of China" in 1998.[4] By defining Chinese government's sea territory, the two laws have provided the foundation for all subsequent maritime regulations and policies. Furthermore, the first part of the baselines of the ROC's territorial sea was announced, in which combined normal and straight baseline methods were used in February 1999. It was made clear in the government in ROC's proclamation that the Nansha (Spratly) Islands within the U-shaped line are Chinese government's territory.[5]

The Beijing Government registered its SCS territorial claims by submitting a map to the Secretary-General of United Nations on

---

[3] The Ministry of the Interior, R.O.C (Taiwan), Law on the Territorial Sea and the Contiguous Zone of the Republic of China, January 21, 1998, http://glrs.moi.gov.tw/EngLawContent.aspx?Type=E&id=100 (accessed on July 12, 2017).

[4] The Ministry of the Interior, R.O.C (Taiwan), Law on the Exclusive Economic Zone and the Continental Shelf of the Republic of China, January 21, 1998, http://glrs.moi.gov.tw/EngLawContent.aspx?Type=E&id=101 (accessed on July 12, 2017).

[5] The Ministry of the Interior, R.O.C (Taiwan), The First Part of the Baselines of the Republic of China's Territorial Sea (full text is in Chinese), https://www.land.moi.gov.tw/content/5835-U.pdf (accessed on May 9, 2017).

May 7, 2009.[6] In response to the submissions, the ROC Ministry of Foreign Affairs (MOFA) made the statement on May 12, 2009 and specified that "Under international law, the Republic of China enjoys all the rights and interests over the South China Sea islands, as well as the surrounding waters and sea-bed and subsoil thereof."[7] As to Mainland China's official position of nine-dash line, one can see that both sides of the Taiwan straits make a similar claim to sovereignty, sovereign rights, and jurisdiction over the SCS disputes. Consequently, Taiwan's sovereignty claims in the SCS would be relevant to China's statements and the Philippines–China arbitration. Taiwan factor should not be ignored by any claimants on SCS issues.

Recent Claims and State Practice on South China Sea Disputes

The U-shaped line was first drawn in the *Location Map of the South China Sea Islands,* which delineated the scope of Chinese government's territory and waters in the region. In accordance with the Article 4 of the *Constitution of the Republic of China* and Article 4 (5) of the *Additional Articles of the Constitution of the Republic of China*, the rules explicitly provided are as follows:

> The sea areas within the South China Sea historic waters boundary line aforesaid is the existing national boundaries of the Chinese government, and "The territory of the Republic of China, defined by its existing national boundaries, shall not be altered unless initiated upon the proposal of one-fourth of the total members of the Legislative Yuan, passed by at least three-fourths of the members present at a meeting attended by at least three-fourths of the total

[6] The Oceans and Law of the Sea, Note Verbale CML/18/2009, May 7, 2009, http://www.un.org/depts/los/clcs_new/submissions_files/vnm37_09/chn_2009re_vnm.pdf (accessed on May 2, 2017).

[7] The Ministry of Foreign Affairs, Declaration of the Republic of China on the Outer Limits of Its Continental Shelf, May 12, 2009, http://www.mofa.gov.tw/En/News_Content.aspx?n=1EADDCFD4C6EC567&sms=5B9044CF1188EE23&s=1DE6A7BA5C27CED3 (accessed on July 2, 2017).

members of the Legislative Yuan, and sanctioned by electors in the free area of the Republic of China at a referendum held upon expiration of a six-month period of public announcement of the proposal, wherein the number of valid votes in favor exceeds one-half of the total number of electors."[8]

Over the past few years, some actions have been taken by the ROC government to support its sovereignty and maritime claims in the SCS. Most of the time, these actions are taken in response to the actions taken by other claimants, especially the Philippines, and Vietnam.[9] The important claims asserted by the ROC government are listed in chronological order and are given in the following paragraphs.

On May 19, 2011, the government of Vietnam claimed the Shisha (Paracel) Islands and the Nansha Islands, which belong to the ROC, to be an integral part of Vietnamese territory. Then, the presidential spokesperson of the Republic of the Philippines stated that Reed Bank, which is part of the Nansha Islands, is in Western Palawan and therefore an integral part of the territory of the Philippines on May 23, 2011. To refute the aforementioned statements, the MOFA reasserted the ROC's position as follows[10]:

1. Reed Bank is part of the Nansha Islands and, whether looked at from the perspective of history, geography, or international law, the Nansha Islands, the Xisha Islands, the Chungsha Islands, and the Tungsha Islands, as well as their surrounding waters, sea beds and subsoil, are all an inherent part of the territory of the ROC

[8] The Office of the President, The Constitution of the Republic of China, http://english.president.gov.tw/Page/94 (accessed on July 2, 2017).

[9] Yann-huei Song, Recent Development in the South China Sea: Taiwan's Policy, Response, Challenges and Opportunities, in *Conference on Managing Tensions in the South China Sea*, Center for Strategic and International Studies (CSIS), June 5–6, 2013, pp. 7–11.

[10] The Ministry of Foreign Affairs, Ministry of Foreign Affairs of the Republic of China (Taiwan) reiterates its position on the South China Sea, May 25, 2011, http://www.mofa.gov.tw/en/News_Content.aspx?n=1EADDCFD4C6EC567&sms=5B9044CF1188EE23&s=D0CEC00B97F04CD2 (accessed on July 6, 2017).

government. These archipelagoes therefore fall under the sovereignty of the Republic of China, and the ROC government reasserts that it enjoys all rights over the islands and their surrounding waters, and that it does not accept any claim to sovereignty over, or occupation of, these areas by other countries.
2. The ROC government calls on countries bordering the SCS to respect the principles and spirit of the Charter of the United Nations and UNCLOS, and to refrain from adopting unilateral measures that might threaten the peace and stability of the region.
3. The ROC government reiterates that it upholds the basic principles of "safeguarding sovereignty, shelving disputes, peace and reciprocity, and joint exploration" and remains willing to work with other countries on exploring resources in the SCS.
4. The ROC government also seriously urges the countries concerned to exercise self-restraint so that peaceful resolutions to the disputes can be reached through consultation and dialogue. The ROC remains willing to participate in dialogue that seeks to find resolutions to disputes and to promote regional peace, stability, and development.

Thanks to the Philippines statement that it has the right to construct a ferry wharf on Zhongye Island (Thi-tu Island) of the Nansha Islands, the MOFA asseverated its position on March 30, 2012, as follows[11]:

1. Zhongye Island belongs to the Nansha Islands and, whether looked at from the perspective of history, geography, or international law, the Nansha Islands, the Shisha Islands, the Chungsha Islands, and the Tungsha Islands, as well as their surrounding waters, sea beds, and subsoil, are an inherent part of the territory of the ROC government. These archipelagoes subsequently fall

[11] The Ministry of Foreign Affairs, The Republic of China (Taiwan) reiterates its position on the South China Sea, April 11, 2012, http://www.mofa.gov.tw/en/News_Content.aspx?n=539A9A50A5F8AF9E&sms=37B41539382B84BA&s=1E0560FA289D54E8 (accessed on July 6, 2017).

under the sovereignty of the ROC government, which reasserts its rights over the islands and their surrounding waters, and refutes all claims to sovereignty over, or occupation of, these areas by other countries and areas.

2. The ROC government calls on countries and areas bordering the SCS to respect the principles and spirit of the Charter of the United Nations and the UN Convention on the Law of the Sea, and to refrain from adopting unilateral measures that threaten the peace and stability of the region. Furthermore, the ROC government urges the countries concerned to exercise self-restraint so that peaceful resolutions can be reached through consultation. The ROC remains willing to participate in dialogue that seeks to resolve disputes and promote regional peace, stability, and development.

Regarding the long-term standoff between Mainland China and the Philippines in the surrounding waters of the Huangyan Island (also known as Scarborough Shoal) on April 10, 2012, the MOFA noted the disputes arising over the Huangyan Island and its surrounding waters and reiterated its staunch position on April 20, 2012, as follows:

> Huangyan Island belongs to the Chungsha Islands and, whether looked at from the perspective of history, geography or international law, the Nansha Islands, the Shisha Islands, the Chungsha Islands and the Tungsha Islands, as well as their surrounding waters, sea beds, and subsoil, are an inherent part of the territory of the ROC government. These archipelagoes subsequently fall under the sovereignty of the ROC government, which reasserts its rights over the islands and their surrounding waters, and refutes all claims to sovereignty over, or occupation of, these areas by other countries and areas.[12]

[12] The Ministry of the Interior, R.O.C (Taiwan), The Ministry of Foreign Affairs of the Republic of China (Taiwan) reiterates its position on the Huangyan Island and its surrounding waters, April 25, 2012, http://maritimeinfo.moi.gov.tw/marineweb/LayFromE0.aspx?icase=T02&pid=0000000541 (accessed on July 3, 2017).

On September 7, 2012, the spokesman of Vietnam stated that the raising of the national flag of the ROC on Taiping Island (also known as Itu Aba) and Zhongzhou Reef (中洲礁) by the Secretary-General of the ROC National Security Council and various other high-ranking ROC officials violated Vietnam's sovereignty. In response, the MOFA solemnly reiterated its position as follows:

1. Whether looked at from the perspective of history, geography or international law, Nansha Islands, Shisha Islands, Chungsha Islands and Tungsha Islands, as well as their surrounding waters, are an inherent part of the territory of the ROC government. The ROC maintains all rights and interests over these archipelagoes and their surrounding waters and refuses to accept any claim to sovereignty over, or occupation of, these areas by other countries.
2. Without a doubt, Taiping Island and Zhongzhou Reef belong to the Nansha Islands and fall under the sovereignty of the Republic of China. As the ROC has been effectively governing Taiping Island and Zhongzhou Reef for an extensive period of time, its various activities and measures with respect to the island are entirely legitimate, and there is no reason that they should generate tension in the region.
3. The ROC government continues to uphold the fundamental principles of "safeguarding sovereignty, shelving disputes, pursuing peace and reciprocity, and promoting joint exploration." Thus, it remains willing to participate in dialogue aimed at resolving disputes and promoting regional peace, stability and development. Taiwan calls on relevant neighboring countries to include it in the negotiations on the Code of Conduct (COC) in the SCS and to work together to promote regional peace and development.
4. The ROC government also solemnly calls on other countries bordering the SCS to respect the principles and spirit of international law and to refrain from adopting unilateral measures that threaten the peace and stability of the region. Furthermore, the ROC urges these countries to exercise self-restraint and foster dialogue

rather than confrontation, so that peaceful resolutions can be reached.[13]

On January 7, 2013, the MOFA expressed its serious concern and firm opposition over Vietnam's Law on the Sea, which erroneously placed the Shisha Islands and Nansha Islands under Vietnam's sovereignty and jurisdiction. MOFA still reiterated the position of the government as follows[14]:

1. Whether looked at from the perspective of history, geography or international law, the Nansha Islands, Shisha Islands, Chungsha Islands and Tungsha Islands, as well as their surrounding waters, are an inherent part of the territory of the ROC government. These archipelagoes therefore fall under the sovereignty of the ROC. The ROC reasserts that it enjoys all rights over the islands and their surrounding waters, and that it denies all unlawful claims to sovereignty over, or occupation of, these areas by other countries.
2. The ROC government upholds the basic principles of "safeguarding sovereignty, shelving disputes, promoting peace and reciprocity, and encouraging joint exploration" to resolve SCS disputes. It hereby again calls on all neighboring countries to respect the principles and spirit of international law, exercise self-restraint, maintain freedom of navigation, and refrain from adopting unilateral measures that threaten the peace and stability of the region. The ROC urges these countries to engage in dialogue rather than confrontation, so that a peaceful resolution can be reached.

[13]The Ministry of Foreign Affairs, The Ministry of Foreign Affairs of the Republic of China solemnly reiterates its position towards Taiping Island, September 11, 2012, http://www.mofa.gov.tw/en/News_Content.aspx?n=0E7B91A8FBEC4A94&sms=220E98D761D34A9A&s=7BAA064FE678B066 (accessed on July 11, 2017).

[14]The Ministry of Foreign Affairs, The Republic of China protests Vietnam law claiming South China Sea Islands, January 7, 2013, http://www.mofa.gov.tw/en/News_Content.aspx?n=0E7B91A8FBEC4A94&sms=220E98D761D34A9A&s=9D31DA5243EEFED1 (accessed on July 11, 2017).

Moreover, when former President Ma Ying-jeou attended the opening ceremonies of the *Exhibition of Historical Archives on the Southern Territories of the Republic of China* on September 1, 2014, he explained the justification for the ROC's advocacy of sovereignty over the islands in the SCS and commented that the issues related to the SCS can be discussed from a variety of angles, including history, geography, geology, and international law. He first addressed the aspect of international law, stating that this can be divided into two portions: one pertains to historical territory and sovereignty as defined under international law, and the other involves issues of seas and resources that are addressed in UNCLOS. He also commented that a historical argument can be made for the Chinese government sovereignty over various islands because the China's Nationalist government, back in 1935, issued the *Map of Chinese Islands in the South China Sea* to advocate the ROC government sovereignty over the islands in the area. President Ma added that the ROC dispatched the Zhongye and Taiping warships to the SCS to recover islands in the area that had been occupied by Japan in 1947. At that time, a re-exploration of the islands was carried out, monuments were erected, and the islands were mapped and garrisoned. In addition, the government also released a table comparing the old and new names of islands in the South China Sea, and issued the *Location Map of the South China Sea Islands.* When these documents were released, no nation publicly raised any opposition. In fact, there are all sorts of historical references to Chinese activities on the islands in the South China Sea since ancient times. Thus, President Ma called for stepped up efforts to research the history of the SCS.[15]

On April 29, 2015, MOFA reiterated the ROC's position on the SCS, and its statement consisted of three parts, as follows:

1. Whether looked at from the perspective of history, geography, or international law, the Nangsha Islands, Shisha Islands, Chungsha Islands and the Tungsha Islands, as well as their surrounding

[15] The Office of the President, President Ma attends opening ceremonies of Exhibition of Historical Archives on the Southern Territories of the Republic of China, September 1, 2014, http://english.president.gov.tw/NEWS/4480 (accessed on July 12, 2017).

waters, are an inherent part of the territory and waters of the ROC. It is indisputable that the ROC enjoys all rights over them in accordance with international law.

2. The ROC government calls on countries in the region to respect the principles and spirit of all relevant international law, including the Charter of the United Nations, and UNCLOS, and to refrain from adopting unilateral measures that might upset the peace and stability of the region and the SCS.
3. The ROC government, upholding the basic principles of safeguarding sovereignty, shelving disputes, pursuing peace and reciprocity, and promoting joint development, is willing to jointly develop resources in the SCS with other countries. It is also prepared to actively participate in related dialogue and cooperation mechanisms, so as to resolve disputes through peaceful means, safeguard regional peace and stability, and promote regional development.[16]

With regard to Mr. Ma Ying-jeou's remarks at opening ceremony of "2015 ILA-ASIL Asia-Pacific Research Forum" on May 26, 2015, he stressed that the ROC government maintains its sovereignty from the perspectives of history, geography, and international law, and thus the Nansha, Shisha, Chungsha, and Tungsha Islands, as well as their surrounding waters, are an inherent part of ROC territory and waters. It is indisputable that the ROC government enjoys all rights over them in accordance with international law. In fact, the ROC government has stationed personnel on Taiping Island, which is the only island in the Spratly group that has fresh water, proving that it is fit for human habitation, and able to maintain its own economic life. The ROC government has demonstrated the exercise of ROC sovereignty in this region.[17]

---

[16] The Ministry of Foreign Affairs, Republic of China's position on the South China Sea, April 29, 2015, http://www.mofa.gov.tw/News_Content.aspx?n=604CBAA3DB3DDA11&sms=69594088D2AB9C50&s=F89D158709C5C752 (accessed on July 15, 2017).

[17] The Office of the President, President Ma's remarks at opening ceremony of '2015 ILA-ASIL Asia-Pacific Research Forum,' May 26, 2015, http://english.president.gov.tw/NEWS/4643 (accessed on July 15, 2017).

In addition, with regard to the first day of July Hearing of the SCS arbitration held in Hague, the ROC's MOFA reiterated its position and issued an eight-point statement on July 7, 2015, which demonstrated the ROC's concern about a possible negative award of the arbitral case concerning the legal status of Taiping Island.[18] It was declared as follows[19]:

1. Whether from the perspectives of history, geography, or international law, the Nansha Islands, Shisha Islands, Chungsha Islands, and Tungsha Islands, as well as their surrounding waters, are an inherent part of the ROC government territory and waters. As the ROC government enjoys all rights to these island groups and their surrounding waters in accordance with international law, the ROC does not recognize any claim to sovereignty over, or occupation of, these areas by other countries, irrespective of the reasons put forward or methods used for such claim or occupation.
2. The South China Sea islands were first discovered, named, and used, as well as incorporated into national territory by the Chinese. In 1938 and 1939, Japan illegally occupied the Tungsha, Shisha, and Nansha Islands. On March 30, 1939, Japan integrated what it called "Shinnan Gunto" (「新南群島」comprising some of the Nansha Islands) into Takao (打狗) Prefecture (today known as Kaohsiung City) through Announcement No. 122 of the Taiwan Governor-General's Office. In 1946, following World War II, the ROC Government reclaimed the Tungsha, Shisha, and Nansha Islands, erecting stone markers on major islands and garrisoning some. In December 1947 it issued the revised names of the SCS islands and the *Location Map of the South China Sea Islands*, which delineate the scope of ROC's territory and waters in the region. Furthermore, the San Francisco Peace Treaty,

[18] Y.-h. Song, Taiwan's response to the Philippines-PRC South China Sea Arbitration, July 15, 2015, http://amti.csis.org/taiwans-response-to-the-philippines-prc-south-china-sea-arbitration/ (accessed on May 6, 2017).
[19] The Ministry of Foreign Affairs, Statement on the South China Sea, July 7, 2015, http://www.mofa.gov.tw/en/News_Content.aspx?n=1EADDCFD4C6EC567&s=EDEBCA08C7F51C98 (accessed on July 8, 2017).

which entered into effect on April 28, 1952, as well as the Treaty of Peace between the ROC government and Japan which was signed that same day, together with other international legal instruments, reconfirmed that the islands and reefs in the SCS occupied by Japan should be returned to the ROC government. In the several decades since, the fact that the ROC government owns and exercises effective control over these islands has been recognized by foreign governments and international organizations.

3. Taiping Island, the largest of the naturally formed Nansha Islands, has been garrisoned by ROC troops since 1956. In the same year, Taiwan established the Defense Zone of the Nansha Islands on Taiping Island. In February 1990, by executive decree, the Cabinet put Taiping Island under the administrative jurisdiction of Qijin (旗津) District of Kaohsiung City. For the past six decades, ROC military and civilian personnel have dwelled on Taiping Island, conducting their respective missions while making use of and developing its natural resources. Taiping Island has groundwater wells, natural vegetation, and phosphate ore and fishery resources. Moreover, personnel stationed on the island cultivate vegetables and fruit and rear livestock. In 1959, personnel built the Guan Yin Temple, dedicated to the Bodhisattva of Compassion. From legal, economic, and geographic perspectives, Taiping Island indisputably qualifies as an "island" according to the specifications of Article 121 of UNCLOS, and can sustain human habitation and economic life of its own; it is thus categorically not a "Rock." The ROC government will firmly defend this fact. Any claims by other countries which aim to deny this fact will not impair the legal status of Taiping Island and its maritime rights based on UNCLOS.
4. The ROC government was a founding member of the United Nations. Although the ROC government lost its representation in 1971, its full name remains in Articles 23 and 110 of the Charter of the United Nations. The ROC government has consistently adhered to the principles of peaceful settlement of international disputes and freedom of navigation and overflight as stipulated in

the UN Charter and other relevant international law and regulations. In fact, the ROC government has defended Taiping Island and other islands without ever getting into military conflict with other nations. Nor has the ROC government interfered with other nations' freedom of navigation or overflight in the South China Sea.

5. The ROC government calls on countries bordering the SCS to respect the spirit and principles of the UN Charter and UNCLOS, and to exercise restraint, safeguard peace and stability in the SCS, and refrain from taking any unilateral action that might escalate tensions.
6. The ROC government will work to safeguard sovereignty, shelve disputes, pursue peace and reciprocity, and promote joint development. Based on consultations conducted on an equal footing, the ROC government is willing to work with other parties concerned to jointly ensure peace and stability in the SCS, as well as conserve and develop resources in the region.
7. Any arrangement or agreement regarding Taiping Island or other islands in the SCS and their surrounding waters that is reached without the ROC government participation and consent shall have no legal effect and shall not be recognized by the ROC government.

Before the contentions of the Philippines in November Hearings of 2015, the ROC government took note of the awards pertaining to jurisdiction in the arbitration between the Philippines and Mainland China issued by the arbitral tribunal on October 29, 2015, and solemnly reiterated its position on the SCS disputes to clarify the legal status of Taiping Island. The seven-point statement asserts on October 31, 2015 were as follows[20]:

1. Whether from the perspective of history, geography, or international law, the Nansha Islands, Shisha Islands, Chungsha Islands,

[20] The Ministry of Foreign Affairs, ROC government reiterates its position on South China Sea Issues, October 31, 2015, http://www.mofa.gov.tw/en/News_Content.aspx?n=539A9A50A5F8AF9E&sms=37B41539382B84BA&s=F5170FE043DADE98 (accessed on July 15, 2017).

and Tungsha Islands, as well as their surrounding waters, are an inherent part of ROC territory and waters. As the ROC government enjoys all rights to these islands and their surrounding waters in accordance with international law, the ROC government does not recognize any claim to sovereignty over, or occupation of, these areas by other countries, irrespective of the reasons put forward or methods used for such claim or occupation.

2. The SCS Islands were first discovered, named, and used, as well as incorporated into national territory, by the Chinese. Furthermore, the San Francisco Peace Treaty, which entered into effect on April 28, 1952, as well as the Treaty of Peace between the China's Nationalist government and Japan, which was signed that same day, together with other international legal instruments, reconfirmed that the islands and reefs in the SCS occupied by Japan should be returned to the ROC government.
3. Taiping Island, the largest of the naturally formed Nansha Islands, has been garrisoned by ROC troops since 1956. From legal, economic, and geographic perspectives, Taiping Island indisputably qualifies as an "island" according to the specifications of Article 121 of UNCLOS, and can sustain human habitation and economic life of its own; it is thus categorically not a "rock" under the same article. Any claims by other countries which aim to deny this fact will not impair the legal status of Taiping Island and its maritime rights based on UNCLOS.
4. The ROC government has consistently adhered to the principles of peaceful settlement of international disputes and freedom of navigation and overflight as stipulated in the UN Charter and other relevant international law and regulations. In fact, the ROC has defended Taiping Island and other islands without ever getting into military conflict with other nations. Nor has the ROC government interfered with other nations' freedom of navigation or overflight in the SCS.
5. The ROC government calls on the coastal states of the SCS to respect the provisions and spirit of the UN Charter and UNCLOS, and to exercise restraint, safeguard peace and stability in the SCS, uphold the freedom of navigation and overflight through the

SCS, refrain from taking any action that might escalate tensions, and resolve disputes peacefully.

6. On May 26, 2015, the ROC government proposed the SCS Peace Initiative, which is based on the principles of safeguarding sovereignty, shelving disputes, pursuing peace and reciprocity, and promoting joint development. Based on consultations conducted on a basis of equality and reciprocity, the ROC government is willing to work with other parties concerned to jointly ensure peace and stability in the SCS, as well as conserve and develop resources in the region.
7. The Philippines has not invited the ROC government to participate in its arbitration with mainland China, and the arbitral tribunal has not solicited the ROC's views. Therefore, the arbitration does not affect the ROC in any way, and the ROC government neither recognizes nor accepts related awards.

However, the US considered that the visit made by former President Ma Ying-jeou to Taiping Island[21] was extremely unhelpful to regional stability.[22] However, the Ma administration sought to reduce tensions, and promote peace and stability in the SCS by unveiling the *South China Sea Peace Initiative Roadmap* during a visit to Taiping Island on January 28, 2016. The roadmap was based on a framework of "three yeses, three no's, two essential elaborations and consisted of three phases of progress," as follows:

1. "Yes" to cooperation, "no" to confrontation
2. "Yes" to sharing, "no" to monopolizing
3. "Yes" to pragmatism, "no" to intransigence

Beyond that, "In the short term, we need to jointly shelve disputes. In the mid-term, we will push for integrated planning. In the

[21] The Office of the President, President Ma convenes international press conference after visiting Taiping Island in South China Sea, January 28, 2016, http://english.president.gov.tw/NEWS/4836 (accessed on July 8, 2017).

[22] P. Armstrong, South China Sea: U.S. says Taiwan president's plan 'extremely unhelpful,' January 28, 2016, http://edition.cnn.com/2016/01/27/asia/taiwan-ma-disputed-island/ (accessed on May 8, 2017).

long term, as part of overall integrated planning, we look forward to the establishment of a mechanism for zonal development. The ROC government looks forward to the establishment of a mechanism for zonal development through bilateral or multilateral cooperation. With the aim of establishing a joint management and monitoring mechanism so as to engage in cooperation and development on an area-by-area, stage-by-stage basis," said former President Ma. In this way, mutually beneficial results can be achieved.[23] That is to say, Taiwan would take more positive action on the SCS disputes in the future.[24]

On March 21, 2016, the ROC's MOFA issued the *Position Paper on ROC South China Sea Policy Republic of China (Taiwan)* as a statement of ROC's position for the SCS Arbitration.[25] Two days later, the Chinese Society of International Law raised an "amicus curiae" brief[26] and it was introduced at former President Ma's press conference.[27] It seems that the "amicus curiae" brief was regarded as an official submission by the arbitral tribunal.[28]

Some of the aforementioned claims may be similar, but each of them does have its own background and meanings. The common

[23] The Office of the President, Remarks by President Ma on Taiping Island, January 28, 2016, http://english.president.gov.tw/NEWS/4832 (accessed on July 7, 2017).

[24] K. Mulan, A role for Taiwan in the South China Sea, *Strategic Vision for Taiwan Security*, vol. 5, no. 28 (September 2016), p. 10.

[25] The Ministry of Foreign Affairs, Position Paper on ROC South China Sea Policy Republic of China (Taiwan), March 21, 2016, http://multilingual.mofa.gov.tw/web/web_UTF-8/South/Position%20Paper%20on%20ROC%20South%20China%20Sea%20Policy.pdf (accessed on Jul. 15, 2017).

[26] The Chinese Society of International Law, In the matter of an arbitration under Annex VII to the 1982 United Nations Convention on the Law of the Sea, March 23,2016,http://csil.org.tw/home/wp-content/uploads/2016/03/SCSTF-Amicus-Curiae-Brief-final.pdf (accessed on June 22, 2017).

[27] The Ministry of Foreign Affairs, President Ma addresses members of news media on their return from Taiping Island, March 23, 2016, http://www.mofa.gov.tw/en/News_Content.aspx?n=8157691CA2AA32F8&sms=4F8ED5441E33EA7B&s=13CBC1E5343E58B7 (accessed on July 12, 2017).

[28] Michael Sheng-ti Gau, The Sino-Philippine Arbitration on the South China Sea disputes and the Taiwan factor, *Journal of East Asia & International Law*, vol. 9, no. 2 (Autumn 2016), pp. 485–492.

ground is to safeguard the ROC sovereignty over the four groups of islands aforesaid in the SCS.

Clarification of Former President Ma Ying-jeou's Remarks

When former President Ma Ying-jeou attended the opening ceremony for the *Exhibition of Historical Archives on the Southern Territories of the Republic of China* on September 1, 2014, he mentioned that, "the *Location Map of the South China Sea Islands* in 1947, aside from the concept of territorial waters, no other concepts regarding maritime zones existed, nor had any claims been made." Does he really mean that the U-shaped line is just a claim to islands contain therein, and not a claim to maritime rights in the entire SCS? Actually, when China's Nationalist government announced the U-shaped line in December 1947, the international law did not cover maritime rights. Therefore, it is necessary to restore the truth of the speech as mentioned above.

Regarding a misleading article "Joining the dashes" in *Economist* published on October 4, 2014, the Banyan column interpreted former President Ma's remarks out of context, leading to some misunderstanding. The author even thought that the President Ma's intervention has pleased the US. The mainly debatable part of the aforementioned article was that:

> At the exhibition's opening, Taiwan's president, Ma Ying-jeou, clarified what the KMT government was claiming in 1947 when it asserted sovereignty over islands held during the second world war by the Japanese. Unlike China, which has never spelled out whether it is claiming everything inside its U-shaped line-islands, rocks, shoals, reefs, fish, oil, gas and water-or just the islands, Mr. Ma was clear that the claim was limited to islands and 3 to 12 nautical miles of their adjacent waters. There were, he said, "no other so-called claims to sea regions."[29]

With reference to the original content of former President Ma's remarks, he did not say that the ROC's claim of U-shaped line "was

---

[29] Banyan, Joining the dashes, *The Economist*, October 4, 2014, http://www.economist.com/node/21621844/print (accessed on May 17, 2017).

limited to islands and 3 to 12 nautical miles of their adjacent waters." Obviously, the above-mentioned article mistakenly presents that the ROC would limit its claim to only the Taiping and Tungsha islands and 3–12 nautical miles of their adjacent waters — which is not true. As a matter of fact, the ROC government still bases its claim on the *Location Map of the South China Sea Islands.*[30] In response to the Banyan column of *Economist*, the Taipei Representative Office in the UK sent a letter to the editor to restore the truth on the aforementioned remarks and requested them to correct the error. Through a letter dated October 30, 2014, Chih-Kung Liu clarified about the ROC's position in the SCS, and part of the explanation as follows:

> When President Ma Ying-jeou spoke last September at the opening ceremony of the Exhibition of Historical Archives on the ROC's Southern Territories, he stated that when the China's Nationalist government reclaimed and announced its sovereignty over the islands and their surrounding waters in 1947, the law of the sea existing at the time did not provide for maritime regimes other than territorial seas and contiguous zones. President Ma did not say that the ROC's claim was limited to the islands and three to 12 nautical miles of their adjacent waters, since the *Location Map of the South China Sea Islands*, published by the ROC government in 1947, covers both the islands and their surrounding waters.[31]

Coincidentally, refer to the similar article "Small reefs, big problems" in the *Economist* published on July 25, 2015; here too, the author made the same mistake related to the ROC's claim on the SCS disputes. The original text of the article is:

> Taiwan shares identical claims to China's in the East China Sea and the South China Sea. Indeed the nine-dashed line was first drawn

---

[30] Charles I-hsin Chen, Ma's peace initiative in South China Sea is feasible, *The China Post*, October 10, 2014, http://www.chinapost.com.tw/commentary/letters/2014/10/10/419077/Mas-Peace.htm (accessed at May 17, 2017).

[31] Chih-Kung Liu, Taiwan and the South China Sea, *The Economist*, October 30, 2014, http://www.economist.com/news/letters/21629213-letters-editor (accessed on May 17, 2017).

> up by the KMT in 1946 (it had 11 dashes then) when it still ruled China and set out to retake islands following Japan's surrender. Identical claims actually suit China, since they reinforce the pretence that there is just "one China" (with China and Taiwan disagreeing over precisely what it is). But America recently pressured Mr. Ma to clarify Taiwan's claim as a means of undermining the absurdly sweeping nature of China's. Mr. Ma, a Harvard-trained lawyer who is keen that his country is seen to be upholding international law, said that under UNCLOS Taiwan claims only the 12-mile limit around its islands.[32]

Consequently, to maintain the position of the ROC government on the sovereignty of the islands in the SCS, the Taipei Representative Office in the UK, Chih-Kung Liu, sent a letter to the editor of the *Economist* once again,[33] and urged them to make the clarification of the article, and part of the original revision was as follows:

> In an earlier version of this article ("Small reefs, big problems") we wrote that "under UNCLOS Taiwan claims only the 12-mile limit around its islands." That is wrong. Taiwan's 1947 claim predates UNCLOS. However, Taiwan's claim does relate only to islands and their surrounding waters. This was amended on August 13, 2015.[32]

In brief, as the *Location Map of the South China Sea Islands* was issued in 1947, it should be viewed as having legal force for establishing sovereignty claims over the SCS islands and their surrounding waters. It is important to note that the legal principle that maritime rights derive from a coastal state's sovereignty over the land is a general rule that is not without exceptions.

---

[32] The Economist, Small reefs, Big problems, July 25, 2015, http://www.economist.com/news/asia/21659771-asian-coastguards-are-front-line-struggle-check-china-small-reefs-big-problems (accessed on May16, 2017).

[33] CNA News, Clarification of the sovereignty claims on the South China Sea (in Chinese), *CNA News*, August 15, 2015, http://www.cna.com.tw/news/aopl/201508150023-1.aspx (accessed on May 19, 2017).

Constructive Contributions

As to Taiwan's contributions to regional peace and stability in SCS, they are too numerous to be counted, and some of them are as follows[19]:

1. In January 2000, personnel of the ROC's Coast Guard Administration (CGA) were sent to Taiping Island and Pratas Islands to replace the stationed Marine Corps personnel from the ROC's Navy.
2. In 2007, the ROC government restored the construction works for the runway on Taiping Island.
3. In March 2007, Kaohsiung City Government of ROC promulgated the establishment of a sea turtle protection zone on Taiping Island in accordance with the ROC's Fisheries Law (p. 25).[1]
4. In December 2007, the airstrip was completed,[34] and a military C-130 cargo aircraft conducted a test-fly to the island.
5. In February 2008, former President Chen Shui-Bin boarded the military cargo aircraft to visit Taiping Island[35] and announced the ROC's "Spratly Initiative" on August 13, 2008.[36] It was an important turning point for Taiwan's policy in the SCS.[37]
6. In July 2010, the Minister of the Interior (MOI) formally established the Tungsha Atoll National Park Management Station,

---

[34] Jimmy Chuang, Minister backs building airport on Taiping Island, *Taipei Times*, November 8, 2007, http://www.taipeitimes.com/News/taiwan/archives/2007/11/08/2003386789 (accessed on May 15, 2017).

[35] Cheng-yi Lin, Taiwan's Spratly Initiative in the South China Sea, The Jamestown Foundation, Feb. 28, 2008, http://www.jamestown.org/single/?tx_ttnews%5Btt_news%5D=4731&no_cache=1#.VioS7jzsl9A (accessed on May 15, 2017).

[36] The Ministry of Foreign Affairs, Chen urges cooperation with 'Spratly Initiative,' *Taiwan Today*, February 14, 2008, http://taiwantoday.tw/news.php?unit=10,23,45,10&post=14710 (accessed on July 15, 2017).

[37] Yann-Huei Song, The Political Implication of 'Spratly Initiative' for President Chen Shui-Bian's visit to Taiping Island, *Maritime Forum*, http://www.cga.gov.tw/gipopen/wsite/public/attachment/f1258860349508.pdf (accessed on May 21, 2017). *Supra* note 10, p. 9.

which will implement the Tungsha Atoll International Marine Research Station Project, promoting Tungsha as a hub for international marine research.

7. In 2011, the Ministry of Economic Affairs mapped mining areas around the Tungsha Islands and Taiping Island, and completed preliminary geological and oceanic surveys.
8. To raise the younger generation's awareness of the importance of territory and maritime zones in the SCS, the Ministry of National Defense (MND) and the CGA have organized several visits such as "Nansha National Defense Camp" and "Tungsha Marine Security and Ecosystem experience camp" for college students to board the warships or surveillance ships of ROC Navy or since 2011 (p. 9).[9]
9. The ROC Ministry of Transportation and Communications (MOTC), MND, and CGA have jointly carried out transportation infrastructure work on Taiping Island since November 2013.
10. In December 2013, the MOTC completed a communications network on Taiping Island, facilitating normal and emergency communications for international humanitarian rescue operations.
11. The development project of Taiping Island was announced by former President Ma Ying-jeou in early September 2012,[38] and the ROC government began the development work on Taiping Island in February 2014. The second phase of a photovoltaic system on Taiping Island came on line in December of the same year. Combined with the first phase completed in 2011, the system provides 16% of electricity supply and reduces carbon emissions by 128 metric tons annually, transforming Taiping Island into a low-carbon island. In addition, the construction of the lighthouse[39] on Taiping Island is for the purposes of humanitarian assistance, disaster relief, and environmental protection.

---

[38] Yann-Huei Song, Taiwan's Development Work on Taiping Island, February 18, 2015, http://amti.csis.org/taiwans-development-work-on-taiping-island/ (accessed on May 14, 2017).

[39] Joseph Yeh, Taiping Island lighthouse construction completed in disputed S. China Sea, *The China Post*, October 25, 2015, http://www.chinapost.com.tw/taiwan/national/national-news/2015/10/25/449213/Taiping-Island.htm (accessed on May 14, 2017).

Looking back to Taiwan's presidential campaign in February 2008, Mr. Ma Ying-jeou, the Kuomintang (KMT)'s candidate, proposed his ocean policy entitled "Blue Revolution, Invigorating the Country through Oceans," and stressed the necessity to work for sustainable development of the ROC's surrounding waters, to uphold the country's rights and sovereignty over sea territory, and to collaborate with neighboring countries for the peaceful development and preservation of the SCS. In comparison with the previous administrations, apparently, the Ma administration is taking a more active approach in dealing with the SCS issues. Several SCS task forces were set up, and the SCS decision-making process was upgraded by moving the authority from the MOI to the National Security Council (p. 6).[9]

According to the this, with the purpose of achieving the goals to reduce the tension in the SCS, the ROC government replaced the MND with CGA for the enforcement and defense duties on Taiping Island in 2000.[21] While the action was largely ignored and underappreciated by other claimants, it served to demonstrate the ROC's opposition to the militarization of the SCS. The ROC government has actively promoted peaceful utilization of the SCS since 2008, not to mention, it can prove that the ROC government is committed to fulfilling its international obligations and actively serving as a peacemaker to truly transform the SCS into a sea of peace and cooperation.

The Strategy of the Tsai Administration

In response to the SCS arbitral award rendered by the Permanent Court of Arbitration (PCA) in the Hague on July 12, 2016,[40] the Tsai Administration reiterated its firm position in defending national interests[41] and urged that disputes in the SCS should be resolved peacefully

[40] The Permanent Court of Arbitration, The Republic of Philippines vs. The People's Republic of China (Case N° 2013-19), July 12, 2016, http://www.pcacases.com/pcadocs/PH-CN%20-%2020160712%20-%20Award.pdf (accessed on May 5, 2017).

[41] The Office of the President, President Tsai addresses troops at Naval Fleet Command, July 13, 2016, http://english.president.gov.tw/Issue/146 (accessed on July 15, 2017).

through multilateral negotiations conducted on the basis of equality.[42] Thanks to issues in the SCS being highly complicated, the government will firmly safeguard the ROC's territorial sovereignty in the SCS as well as the rights over relevant waters it is entitled to under international law and UNCLOS. The ROC government will not renounce its sovereignty or legal rights and will continue to engage in cooperative consultations with each of the claimants. As overlapping claims in the SCS involve international law and political interests of States concerned, President Tsai Ing-wen proposed "four principles" and "five actions"[43] during her first-ever National Security Council meeting held on July 19 of the same year.[44] The ROC government will take actions based on four principles, with the details as follows:

1. All disputes should be resolved peacefully in accordance with international law and the law of the sea (UNCLOS included).
2. Taiwan must be included in any multilateral dispute settlement mechanisms.
3. Other relevant parties are obligated to ensure freedom of aviation and navigation in the SCS.
4. The ROC calls for other relevant parties to set aside differences and resolve disputes through joint development, and remains committed to promoting regional stability and protecting maritime resources.

With reference to the five actions announced on July 19, 2016,[45] the first action is that the ROC government will strengthen its capabilities and step up patrol missions to safeguard the rights and safety of the

---

[42] The Office of the President, ROC government position on the South China Sea arbitration, July 12, 2016, http://english.president.gov.tw/NEWS/4939 (accessed on July 15, 2017).

[43] The Ministry of Foreign Affairs, South China Sea issue, http://www.mofa.gov.tw/en/theme.aspx?n=E5A0D5E2432C234D&s=83376F561B7165E6&sms=BCDE19B435833080 (accessed on July 3, 2017).

[44] The Ministry of Foreign Affairs, Tsai holds 1st NSC meeting, unveils South China Sea approach, *Taiwan Today*, July 20, 2016, http://taiwantoday.tw/news.php?unit=2,6,10,15,18&post=3932 (accessed on July 12, 2017).

[45] Taipei Economic and Cultural Representative Office in the US, Sustainable Governance and Enduring Peace: An Exhibition Commemorating the 70th

ROC's fishermen operating in the SCS. Second, the MOFA will make more efforts on enhancing multilateral dialogue with other relevant parties on collaboration and consensus. Third, the Ministry of Science and Technology (MOST) and related agencies will make arrangements for inviting international scholars to Taiping Island to conduct scientific research on climate change, earthquakes, geology, and meteorology. Fourth, the MOFA will collaborate with international organizations to develop Taiping Island into a base for providing humanitarian aid and supplies. And fifth, the ROC government will encourage more local talents to study maritime law so as to strengthen the nation's preparedness regarding international legal issues and spread out the ROC's soft power.

In addition, it should not to be neglected that the MOI Yeh Jiunn-rong led a team of officials and researchers to Taiping Island on August 16, 2016. According to Yeh, the trip should be based on the five aforementioned actions and be a part of the preparations to transform Taiping Island into a hub of scientific investigation on climate change and marine ecology. Moreover, the MOI is also working with the MOST and other agencies on sharing the data and seeking international collaboration on related projects. It is not only significant but also proves that the Tsai Administration apparently remains steadfast in its position and committed to promoting regional stability in the SCS.[46]

Conclusion

Should the ROC government have to respond to the international calls for clarifying the legal status of the U-shaped line or continue to adhere to strategic ambiguity on Taiwan's claim?[47] The ROC

Anniversary of the recovery of the South China Sea Islands opens December 9, 2016, http://www.roc-taiwan.org/us_en/post/5899.html (accessed on July 12, 2017).

[46] *Taiwan Today*, Interior minister visits Taiping Island, reasserts ROC sovereignty, August 17, 2016, http://taiwantoday.tw/news.php?unit=2,6,10,15,18&post=102355 (accessed on May 23, 2017).

[47] Nadia Tsao and Jake Chung, US hopes for clarification on South China Sea claims, *Taipei Times*, April 9, 2016, http://www.taipeitimes.com/News/front/archives/2016/04/09/2003643524 (accessed on May 19, 2017).

government shall seriously consider its position and play a constructive role over the SCS disputes to safeguard the ROC sovereignty,[48] such as paying much attention to the SCS award to maintain the meaning of the U-shaped line,[49] valuing the status of Taiping Island to raise the public awareness of the importance of Taiwan's position in the SCS,[50,51] playing a more active role and keeping on convening international conferences on the SCS issues in the future, and utilizing the "South China Sea Peace Initiative"[17] announced by former President Ma on May 26, 2015, to seek Taiwan's participation in the regional collaboration and negotiations (COC included) in the SCS.[9]

To review the past and presage the future, Taiwan has consistently adhered to the principles of peaceful settlement of international disputes and freedom of navigation and overflight as stipulated in the relevant international law and regulations. Above all, the ROC government has defended Taiping Island and other islands without ever getting into military conflict with other nations. Consequently, Taiwan should earn recognition for not interfering with other nations' freedom of navigation or overflight in the SCS.[20]

It seems that the situation in the SCS will likely become more complicated even though the PCA has rendered the aforesaid award. It is hoped that all the parties involved will continue to engage in

---

[48] Yann-Huei Song, KMT-DPP South China Sea Debate, CSIS in USA, The Asia Maritime Transparency Initiative, December 23, 2014, http://amti.csis.org/kmt-dpp-south-china-sea-debate/ (accessed on July 8, 2017).

[49] The Permanent Court of Arbitration, Arbitration between the Republic of the Philippines and the People's Republic of China, October 29, 2015, http://www.pcacases.com/web/sendAttach/1503 (accessed on May 18, 2017).

[50] "Is Taiping Island an 'island' or a 'rock' under the UNCLOS? Is Taiping Island capable of sustaining human habitation or economic life of its own? Is Taiping Island entitled the right to generate a 200 nm EEZ or a continental shelf? Is the arbitration between Sino-the Philippines well founded in fact and international law? We should examine the facts about Taiping Island and discuss its legal status in accordance with Article 121of the UNCLOS." see Ref. 50.

[51] Yann-Huei Song, Taiping Island: An Island or a Rock under UNCLOS, CSIS in USA, The Asia Maritime Transparency Initiative, May 7, 2015, http://amti.csis.org/taiping-island-an-island-or-a-rock-under-unclos/ (accessed on July 18, 2017).

dialogue until reaching a final solution.[52] As mentioned above, Taiwan can play a key role[53] in maintaining regional security in the SCS. Except for promoting the New Southbound Policy announced on August 16, 2016,[54] how to prevent Taiwan from being marginalized on SCS maritime disputes and implement the aforementioned four principles and five actions for the post-award negotiations have come into question.[55] Apparently, the Tsai Administration also actively seeks the ROC's constructive role in promoting regional peace and looks forward to engaging in multilateral cooperation and taking part in the regional security dialogue with claimant states on the SCS issues.

[52] Helen H. Wang, War or peace in the South China Sea, *Forbes*, February 5, 2016, https://www.forbes.com/sites/helenwang/2016/02/05/war-or-peace-in-the-south-china-sea/#4423eb6829c7 (accessed on July 8, 2017).

[53] Bill Stanton, The U.S. Pivot to Asia, China's challenge, the Maritime Cauldron, and Taiwan's Role, *Taiwan Brain Trust*, September 6, 2014, http://www.braintrust.tw/article_detail/2015 (accessed on July 10, 2017).

[54] Bureau of Foreign Trade, Guide line for the New Southbound Policy, August 16, 2016, https://www.newsouthboundpolicy.tw/English/PageDetail.aspx?id=92bf03e0-6176-4374-85e7-06520ed3e9f2&pageType=SouthPolicy (accessed on July 15, 2017).

[55] Jonathan Spangler, Taiwan's Diplomatic Policy Options and Future Prospects, in *South China Sea Lawfare: Post-Arbitration Policy Options and Future Prospects* (South China Sea Think Tank and Taiwan Center for Security Studies, April, 2017), pp. 139–141.

Chapter 6

A Struggle Without Breaking: The US–China Rivalry in the South China Sea

Kuanghua Liu

Ming Chuan University, Taipei, Taiwan

Abstract

The relation between the US and China has been complicated by a power transition process, or power struggle, in recent decades, triggered by the economic rise of China. However, the two countries managed to cooperate with each other in many realms, including trade, climate change, strategic interaction, regional issues, cyber security, and space projects. Nonetheless, the competition does not seem to just fade away as the tension between China and the US in the South China Sea (SCS) escalated throughout 2016. What is worse is that the possibility of military conflict between the two due to mutual distrust, intensified security competition, formation of anti-Chinese alliance, and competition for the dominance of the region lingers on. Interestingly, the Trump administration recently decided to suspend patrols in the SCS so as to have China side with the US in dealing with the situation in the Korean Peninsula. It is understandable that the threat posed by North Korea's nuclear weapons development may require temporarily setting aside contentious issues in SCS in exchange for China's help. Nevertheless, it is also understandable that the rivalry between the two powers is here to stay.

Keywords: China–US rivalry, South China Sea, Asian strategic landscape, military conflicts.

A Falling Incumbent Hegemon?

Ever since Samuel Huntington published his "Lonely Superpower" in 1999 describing the unipolar system after the collapse of the USSR and the end of Cold War, the US, as the only superpower, has exerted its influences of "soft power" and "hard power" to almost every corner of the world.[1] The US has therefore been able to take the leading position in all aspects of international affairs, ranging from political, economic, technological and cultural fields, and maintaining that leverage is of course the first priority of their national strategy formulation. Any emerging power that might threaten that leverage, as a result, becomes the focal point that the US has to pay attention to.

The 21st century witnessed a great change in the nature of the international system. The so-called lonely superpower is no longer lonely, and the emergence of states such as China, India, and Russia are beginning to challenge the dominance of the US, especially in Asia. Among the emerging powers, China looks more and more like a potential candidate to challenge American hegemony in Asia.[2] It appears that the rise of China due to the rapid economic development in the past 35 years and the consequent growth of comprehensive national power has posed a threat to the presence of the US in Asia. In the meantime, it seems that comprehensive national power of the US is decreasing after getting involved in a series of regional conflicts,

---

[1] Samuel P. Huntington, The lonely superpower, *Foreign Affairs*, vol. 78, no. 2 (March/April 1999). Joseph S. Nye believes that the US owns both the soft and hard power and Pax Americana will continue due to that leverage. See Joseph S. Nye, *The Paradox of American Power: Why the World's Only Superpower Can't Go It Alone* (New York: Oxford University Press), 2002, pp. 17–18.

[2] Robert S. Ross, The geography of the peace: East Asia in the twenty-first century, *International Security*, vol. 23, no. 4 (spring, 1999), pp. 83–86.

including the two Gulf Wars and the campaign in Afghanistan. Recent developments in the Syrian Conflict seems to demonstrate that the US's ability to resolve security issues is diminishing.

From the realist perspective, competition among states is a zero-sum game, in which one side's gain means the other side's loss. Therefore, the rise of China implies the relative weakening of US influence. If the US intends to maintain its influence, it will need to seek measures to restrain China's challenges to its dominance. The most effective ways are to adopt competition and confrontational strategies as it successfully did to USSR in the past: containment strategy.

From the liberalist point of view, international interdependence and reciprocal effects should go through international transaction. So, cooperation should serve as the major means to reach that goal in a globalized world. Consequently, to maintain the US hegemonic status in Asian region, engagement strategy that focuses on interaction and cooperation with China should be the correct measures.

And it appears that US government's China policy is neither realist nor liberal. As a matter of fact, it seems to have been vacillating between containment and engagement trajectory. For example, the Bush Administration emphasized containment strategy, while the Clinton Administration seemed to pay more attention to engagement strategy. In his first term, Bush appeared to be more competitive but went back to engagement trajectory later, whereas Obama appeared more flexible in his first term but took a more hardline position in the end of his second term — as seen from the confrontations between the two countries in the SCS in early 2016. As for Trump, it seems that China has become a partner in dealing with North Korea issues regardless of the fact that he even once refused to honor the long-established "one China policy." Consequently, it does not seem too far-fetched as to say that the US's China policy has been inconsistent in the past 30 years.[3]

[3] Peter Cai, From engagement to containment, a shifting strategy on China, *China Spectator*, May 15, 2015, http://www.businessspectator.com.au/article/2015/5/15/china/engagement-containment-shifting-strategy-china (accessed on March 2, 2016).

Having said that, the relation between the US and China has been comparatively more peaceful and cooperative than confrontational and competitive ever since the end of the Cold War, that is, if the recent development in the SCS between the two countries is put aside. For one thing, the relation between the two countries is not as tense and hostile as that between the US and the USSR in the Cold War Era. Second, neither side has the intention to engage in confrontational strategy regardless of the recent developments between the two countries in the SCS. In other words, the two sides seem to have maintained a relation of "struggle without breaking."[4]

To sum up, never in modern history have two great powers been so deeply intertwined yet so suspicious and potentially antagonistic. The relation between the US and China involves an uneasy and ever shifting blend of cooperation and competition. This also means that the two sides will face the daunting tasks of simultaneously managing competition and maximizing cooperation.

This chapter will first describe the general relation between the US and China to lay the groundwork for following discussions. The following section will focus on the competition between the two countries because even as the two engage in a so-called new type of great-power relations, the reality is that the two countries are still competitors. The cooperation in economic, political, environmental, as well as security aspects between the two countries will then be discussed in detail. Ideas and thoughts on the new strategic landscape in Asia will be discussed in the last section of the chapter.

Rivalry Between the US and China

As mentioned earlier, the relation between the US and China has been comparatively more peaceful and cooperative than confrontational and competitive ever since the end of the Cold War. However, there has been steadily rising competition in the relation regardless of

---

[4] Chong-Pin Lin, China's maritime embroilments: Behind rising East Asian maritime tensions with China struggle without breaking, *Asian Survey*, vol. 55, no. 3 (May/June 2015), pp. 478–501.

the fact that the US and China seem to have cooperated wherever they can. Some even argue that the competition is dominating the relation between the two countries, which is not only limited to strategic competition, but also covers commercial, ideological, political, diplomatic, technological, and even academic areas.[5]

The Increasing Mutual Distrust

The mutual distrust on both sides increases at astonishing speed, and this is especially true of the general public on both sides. A survey by Pew Research Center in 2015 pointed out that 54% of Americans expressed an unfavorable opinion of China, and this negative sentiment has exceeded 50% in each of the last three years. A decade ago, in 2006, just 29% of Americans had an unfavorable opinion of China. A more alarming sign is that 56% would use military force to defend an Asian ally such as Japan, South Korea, or the Philippines if it was attacked by China.[6] By the same token, only 44% of Chinese have positive views of Americans and 54% say the US is trying to prevent China from becoming a nation as powerful as the US. In fact, most believe the US is trying to restrain a rising China.[7]

The two governments have been in a climate of mutual suspicion and doubt throughout the entire 2015 and seem to be now in danger of entering a phase of mutual strategic suspicion, a state of affairs that looks unlikely to be eased in the near future. Issues that will deepen the mutual mistrust include alleged Chinese cyberattacks on US

---

[5] David Shambaugh, In a fundamental shift, China and the US are now engaged in all-out competition, *South China Morning Post*, June 11, 2015, http://www.scmp.com/comment/insight-opinion/article/1819980/fundamental-shift-china-and-us-are-now-engaged-all-out?page=all (accessed on February 23, 2016).

[6] Bruce Stokes, American fear of China weighs on US Election, *Asian Review*, January 29, 2016, http://asia.nikkei.com/Viewpoints/Viewpoints/American-fear-of-China-weighs-on-US-election (accessed on March 8, 2016).

[7] Richard Wike, Six facts about how Americans and Chinese see each other, *Pew Research Center*, September 22, 2015, http://www.pewresearch.org/fact-tank/2015/09/22/6-facts-about-how-americans-and-chinese-see-each-other/ (accessed on March 8, 2016).

targets, regardless of the fact that two sides have already agreed to work together on the issues, the alleged US's containment strategy, and China's island-building in the SCS.[8]

The source of strategic distrust between the US and China is threefold. For one thing, the difference between the political traditions, value systems, and cultures is huge. As the US sees China as an undemocratic country with human right violation records, China regards the US as a hostile country aiming to undermine its authority and legitimacy. Second, the two countries do not understand each other's decision-making process, which leads to suspicion of each other's intention. As the US suspects that the economic activities of China's state-owned business are part of its grand strategy, China often sees American NGO's activities as CIA operations. Third, there is a decreasing power gap between the two countries. Most Americans believe that China is going to take over the US role as a hegemon, at least in Asia in the near future.[9]

Intensified Security Competition

The security competition between the two countries has been intensified due to the mutual distrust discussed earlier and recent developments in certain hot spots, including East China Sea (ECS) and SCS. In the ECS, as Japan decided to purchase three of the five disputed Diaoyutai islands from their private Japanese owner in 2012, the territorial dispute escalated from a minor irritant between China and Japan to a major security concern in the region.[10]

As a matter of fact, ever since 2012, the US has taken steps to clarify the US role in deterring any coercive action by China.

[8] Wei Pu, Strategic mistrust deepens between China and the US, *Radio Free Asia*, September 23, 2015, http://www.rfa.org/english/commentaries/mistrust-09232015110426.html (accessed on March 9, 2016).

[9] Kenneth Lieberthal and Wang Jisi, *Addressing US-China Strategic Distrust* (Washington, D.C.: The John L. Thornton China Center at Brookings), 2012, pp. 35–36.

[10] Cheney-Peters Scott, How Japan's nationalization move in the East China Sea shaped the US rebalance, *The National Interest*, October 26, 2014, http://nationalinterest.org/feature/how-japans-nationalization-move-the-east-china-sea-shaped-11549 (accessed on March 10, 2016).

Furthermore, the US and Japanese forces have conducted regular exercises to strengthen defense of Japan. The US policymakers also clearly stated that the US will defend Japan against any aggression, and the US Senate in the same year passed a resolution accompanying the 2013 National Defense Authorization Act to demonstrate congressional support for the Obama administration's commitment to Japan's defense. In other words, as a security treaty ally of Japan, it is not unlikely that the US would be dragged into an unintended Sino-Japan conflict.[11]

In the SCS, the disputes in the region are focused on two pillars, of which the first pillar is the transformation of the US role in the region from a relatively neutral one to a participatory one. The second pillar is the more aggressive attitude of Vietnam and the Philippines toward sovereignty claims over the SCS. In terms of US attitude, the country, not a claimant state, actually functioned as a coordinator and mediator of the region over security issues and focused on peaceful means to solve the sovereignty disputes, including safe passage of the sea lane in the region before 2000. The US even refused to put the conflicts between the Philippines and claimant states over sovereignty in the region under the coverage of the Mutual Defense Treaty between US and the Philippines.[12]

Ever since 2000, the US has started to actively express its concern over the development in the SCS and even got involved in the regional issue, which has been connected deeply with the rise of China.[13] For example, USS "Impeccable" was said to be harassed by five Chinese boats while conducting survey operation in the region 120 km south of Hainan Island. The incident escalated to a small-scale standoff between the two countries. The US claimed that "Impeccable" was unarmed while China accused the ship of intruding into China's EEZ

---

[11] Sheila Smith, A Sino-Japanese clash in the East China Sea, in *Contingency Planning Memorandum No. 18,* Council on Foreign Relations, April 2013, http://www.cfr.org/japan/sino-japanese-clash-east-china-sea/p30504 (accessed on March 10, 2016).

[12] Ian James Storey, Creeping assertiveness: China, the Philippines and the South China Sea dispute, *Contemporary Southeast Asia*, vol. 21, no. 1 (April, 1999), pp. 95–118.

[13] Kristin Deasy, US wades into South China Sea dispute, *Global Post,* July 12, 2012, http://www.globalpost.com/dispatch/news/regions/americas/united-states/120712/us-wades-south-china-sea-dispute#1 (accessed on April 5, 2013).

zone and collected PLAN intelligence.[14] The situation escalated into quasi-military level as US destroyer "Lassen" navigated within 12 nautical miles of the emerging land masses in the Spratly Islands in October 2015.[15] In November 2015, two US B-52 strategic bombers flew near artificial Chinese-built islands in the area of the Spratly Islands.[16] After the routine patrol of the US aircraft carrier "Stennis" in the SCS, the US asserts that the US Air Force will continue to fly daily missions over the region despite a buildup of Chinese surface-to-air missiles and fighter jets in the contested region.[17]

Even after Trump's administration intentionally eased the tension in the SCS, pressure to adopt stronger measures against China, especially from the US lawmakers, still exist.[18] These actions of "freedom of navigation" conducted by the US, against the background of China's island-building operations, might lead to unexpected armed clashes between the two countries, and thus intensify the security competition in the region.

Anti-Chinese Sentiment

As China and the US poised for the SCS confrontation, China's sovereignty disputes with other claimants on the region, especially with

---

[14] Mark Valencia, The *Impeccable* incident: truth and consequences, *China Security*, vol. 5, no. 2 (Spring 2009), pp. 22–28.

[15] Andrea Shalal and David Brunnstrom, US Navy Destroyer Nears Islands built by China in South China Sea, *Reuters*, October 26, 2015, http://www.reuters.com/article/us-southchinasea-usa-idUSKCN0SK2AC20151026 (accessed on March 12, 2016).

[16] US B-52 bombers flew near disputed Islands in South China Sea, says Pentagon, *The Guardian*, November 12, 2015, http://www.theguardian.com/world/2015/nov/13/us-b-52-bombers-flew-near-disputed-islands-in-south-china-sea-says-pentagon (accessed on March 12, 2016).

[17] US General: Air Force to Keep Flying Over South China Sea, *The New York Times*, March 8, 2016, http://www.nytimes.com/aponline/2016/03/08/world/asia/ap-as-south-china-sea-us-air-force.html?emc=eta1&referer (accessed on March 12, 2016).

[18] Ankit Panda, Bipartisan group of US senators call for South China Sea FONOPs, *The Diplomat*, May 12, 2017, http://thediplomat.com/2017/05/bipartisan-group-of-us-senators-call-for-south-china-sea-fonops/ (accessed on May 13, 2017).

Vietnam and the Philippines, intensified.[19] The tension consequently lad to the formation of an anti-Chinese sentiment, which is understandably contributed by the sovereignty disputes between China and the two Southeast Asian countries.

China's dispute with Vietnam over Paracel Islands in 1974 resulted in an armed conflict between the two countries. It was a significant turning point for China in that after the war China took control over the Paracel Islands.[20] In 1988, the so-called Johnson South Reef skirmish broke out. China has captured six islands within the Johnson South Reef, while Vietnam has maintained control over Collins Reef and Lansdowne Reef after the conflict.[21] In January 2005, Chinese patrol ships fired upon two Vietnamese fishing boats from Thanh Hoa Province, killing nine people and detaining one ship with eight people on Hainan Island.[22] In May 2011, a clash involved a Vietnamese survey ship and three Chinese maritime patrol vessels. The event stirred up unprecedented anti-China protests in Vietnam.[23] In June 2011, a Vietnamese seismic conducting ship clashed with three other Chinese fishery patrol vessels within Vietnam's Exclusive Economic Zone. Vietnam claimed that its exploration cables were deliberately cut.[24] The most recent conflict happened in May 2014 when Chinese state oil company put an oil rig in the waters of

[19] China, Philippines spar over military visit to island, *Aljazeera*, April 23, 2017, http://www.aljazeera.com/news/2017/04/china-philippines-spar-military-visit-island-170422173715191.html (accessed on May 13, 2017).

[20] Roby Arya Brata, Open war in the South China Sea, *Jakarta Post*, July 28, 2012, http://www.thejakartapost.com/news/2012/07/28/open-war-south-china-sea.html (accessed on April 3, 2013).

[21] Neil Connor, Johnson South Reef Skirmish, *The Daily Star*, November 29, 2012, http://www.dailystar.com.lb/Entity/People/3351339208/Johnson-South-Reef-Skirmish.ashx#axzz2PNm4Z0Cl (accessed on April 3, 2013).

[22] Ian Storey, Conflict in the South China Sea: China's relations with Vietnam and the Philippines, *The Asia-Pacific Journal: Japan Focus*, April 30, 2008, http://www.japanfocus.org/-ian-storey/2734 (accessed on April 3, 2013).

[23] South China Sea: Vietnamese hold anti-Chinese protest, *BBC News*, June 5, 2011, http://www.bbc.co.uk/news/world-asia-pacific-13661779 (accessed on April 3, 2013).

[24] *Ibid.*

disputed Paracel Islands, which Vietnam believes are part of its own economic zone.[25]

China's dispute with the Philippines is no less complex. In 1995, the Philippines increased patrol of the surrounding area of Mischief Reefs after realizing that China was building up military structure on the reefs, and this led to numerous arrests of Chinese fishermen and naval clashes with Chinese patrol vessels.[26] In February 2011, a Chinese frigate fired three shots at the Philippine fishing boats in the vicinity of Jackson atoll.[27] In April 2011, a Philippine warship was involved in a standoff with two Chinese surveillance vessels in the Scarborough Shoal. The incident led a series of political protests and negotiations and a fishing ban in 2012.[28] As a matter of fact, the recent reconciliation between the two countries does not seem helpful in resolving the sovereignty disputes.[29]

Japan also shares this sentiment as the tension between Japan and China over the sovereignty on Diaoyutai islands tightens. In fact, the Philippines and Japan have stepped up their security cooperation as the former Philippine President Aquino embarked on a 4-day state visit to Tokyo, hoping to rally greater international support against China, which was of great strategic importance to both countries as

---

[25] Paul J. Leaf, Learning from China's oil rig standoff with Vietnam, *The Diplomat*, August 30, 2014, http://thediplomat.com/2014/08/learning-from-chinas-oil-rig-standoff-with-vietnam/ (accessed on March 13, 2016).

[26] Showdown at mischief reef, *The Baltimore Sun*, August 5, 1995, http://articles.baltimoresun.com/1995-08-05/news/1995217032_1_south-china-sea-spratly-islands-mischief-reef (accessed on April 3, 2013).

[27] Tessa Jamandre, China fired at Filipino fishermen in Jackson Atoll, *ABS@CBN News.com*, June 3, 2011, http://www.abs-cbnnews.com/-depth/06/02/11/china-fired-filipino-fishermen-jackson-atoll (accessed on April 3, 2013).

[28] Gary Li, Scarborough Shoal Standoff: Bluster or war? *Caixin Online*, January 23, 2013, http://gulfnews.com/news/world/philippines/declare-scarborough-shoal-as-rocks-not-island-philippines-1.1136624 (accessed on April 3, 2013).

[29] Anders Corr, Take defense treaty action for Philippine sovereignty in South China Sea, *Forbes*, April 14, 2017, https://www.forbes.com/sites/anderscorr/2017/04/14/take-defense-treaty-action-for-philippine-sovereignty-in-south-china-sea/#1302d0396ed3 (accessed on May 14, 2017).

the Philippines needs Japan's military capability while Japan needs the Philippines' diplomatic support.[30]

To make the situation worse, it was said that Vietnam and the Philippines are discussing security cooperation, and South Korea and Vietnam have also discussed common security interests.[31] Some even go further to say that military exercises between India and the US, Japan's possible action of patrolling the SCS, and Australia's announcement that it is going to modernize its Navy are all part of the "ganging up on China."[32]

Anti-Chinese sentiment seems to be surging in the region.

Accidental Outbreak of Military Conflicts

As China sped up its island-building constructions and became more active in its sovereignty claim over the SCS, the US also started to test China's resolve to protect its sovereign rights in the region. As mentioned earlier, the US destroyer Lassen navigated within 12 nautical miles of the claimed islands. Not long after, two USB-52 strategic bombers flew over the disputed area and the US aircraft carrier Stennis also entered the area. The US even asserts that they will continue to fly daily missions over the region. However, by sending warships and bombers to patrol the adjacent waters off the disputed islands and test China's bottom line, the US also has to face the risk of accidental outbreak of military

[30] Richard Javad Heydarian, Made in Beijing: An anti-China alliance emerges, *The National Interest*, June 13, 2015, http://nationalinterest.org/feature/made-beijing-anti-china-alliance-emerges-13104?page=2 (accessed on March 13, 2016).

[31] Craig Hill, China's aggression could see formation of a powerful anti-China Alliance, *China Daily Mail*, June 14, 2014, http://chinadailymail.com/2014/06/14/chinas-aggression-could-see-formation-of-a-powerful-anti-china-alliance/ (accessed on March 14, 2016).

[32] Lira Dalangin-Fernandez, Aggression in South China Sea will see new anti-China Coalition – Golez, *Interaksyon*, February 20, 2016, http://interaksyon.com/article/124322/aggression-in-south-china-sea-will-see-new-anti-china-coalition-golez (accessed on March 14, 2016).

conflicts in the region, which might be worsened to an uncontrollable level.[33]

There are some possibilities that military conflicts between China and the US could break out in the SCS. If US ships or bombers keep entering the territorial waters China claims on a routine basis and China conducts a militarized response leading to serious damage or great casualties in the US troops, the tension may be escalated into an all-out war. Second, if China declares SCS Air Defense Identification Zone (ADIZ), the US may respond similarly as they did when China declared ECS ADIZ in 2013.[34] The tension in the SCS sky may tighten up as China enforces the ADIZ and the US challenges it. Possible fighter intercepts and encounters may lead to aircraft collisions, if not dogfighting, and escalate the situation.[35]

Other possibilities for the outbreak of military conflicts may be caused by US's unintentional involvement in the territorial disputes between China and other US allies or neighboring countries, which may drag the two nuclear-armed powers into a conflict that could escalate perilously.

Regardless of the fact that Pivot to Asia policy was officially ended by Trump's administration, Asia is too important for the US to just let go.[36] Given the background of the rise of China, it seems that the US is still strengthening the security connection with its allies with

---

[33] Global Conflict Tracker, Territorial disputes in the South China Sea, *Council on Foreign Relations,* updated March 14, 2016, http://www.cfr.org/global/global-conflict-tracker/p32137#!/conflict/territorial-disputes-in-the-south-china-sea (accessed on March 15, 2016).

[34] Robert Farley, 3 ways China and the US could go to war in the South China Sea, *The National Interest,* June 6, 2015, http://nationalinterest.org/feature/3-ways-china-the-us-could-go-war-the-south-china-sea-13055 (accessed on March 15, 2016).

[35] Elisabeth Rosenthal and David E. Sanger, US plane in China after it collides with Chinese jet, *New York Times,* April 2, 2001, http://www.nytimes.com/2001/04/02/world/us-plane-in-china-after-it-collides-with-chinese-jet.html?pagewanted=all (accessed on March 15, 2016).

[36] Ankit Panda, Straight from the US State Department: The 'pivot' to Asia is over, *The Diplomat,* March 14, 2017, http://thediplomat.com/2017/03/straight-from-the-us-state-department-the-pivot-to-asia-is-over/ (accessed on May 13, 2017).

the intention of "containing" China. In addition, the US also has improved relations with Vietnam, a former enemy.

What should not be ignored is that China has territorial disputes with Japan in the ECS and territorial disputes with the Philippines, an ally, and Vietnam in the SCS. What is worse is that the US also has mutual security defense agreement with Japan and the Philippines. If the situations between China and Japan/the Philippines turn sour, or if Japan and the Philippines decide to initiate provocative actions given the US support, it would be very likely that the US would be dragged into a major conflict with China.[37]

Even the conflicts between China and Vietnam, a non-US ally, might drag the US into the military clash with China, especially when the US and Vietnam are gradually promoting a "comprehensive cooperative partnership."[38] As a matter of fact, the progress on US–Vietnam security cooperation not only affects the two countries' strategic military plans but also exerts considerable influence on the overall geostrategic environment in the SCS region. It is likely that Vietnam is emboldened by that partnership and military conflicts between China and Vietnam occur. The US then sends in troops to the SCS, unlikely to join the fight, with the intention to protect the sea lane of communication, which is so vital to shipping as over $5 trillion in trade passes through the sea annually, including more than half of the world's trade in liquid natural gas and over 33% of trade in crude oil.[39] The miscalculation and accidental outbreak of conflicts between the US and China is not entirely unimaginable.

---

[37] Ivan Eland, Let's not get into it with China, *The Huffington Post,* September 21, 2015, http://www.huffingtonpost.com/ivan-eland/lets-not-get-into-it-with_b_8170776.html (accessed on March 15, 2016).

[38] Fact Sheet, US-Vietnam comprehensive partnership, Office of the Spokesperson, US Department of State, December 16, 2013, http://www.state.gov/r/pa/prs/ps/2013/218734.htm (accessed on March 17, 2016).

[39] Joshua Kurlantzick, A China–Vietnam military clash, Contingency Planning Memorandum No. 26, *Council on Foreign Relations*, September 2015, http://www.cfr.org/china/china-vietnam-military-clash/p37029 (accessed on March 17, 2016).

Struggling for Dominance

As China surpassed Japan to become the world's second largest economy in 2011, it seems reasonable to assume that China would grow into a regional power too. This assumption is based on the belief that the rise of military power usually parallels the growth of economic power.[40] Thus, an emerging China coping with the incumbent hegemon, the US, becomes something inevitable, especially in Asia.

Even with the growth of military strength, it is still clear that China does not currently possess a military formidable enough to pick a fight with the US, even in the Asia-Pacific region. However, there are non-military means to compete for the dominance of the region. For instance, at the heart of China's "One Belt, One Road" lies the creation of an economic land belt that includes countries on the original Silk Road through Central Asia, West Asia, the Middle East, and Europe, as well as a maritime road that links China's port facilities with the African coast, pushing up through the Suez Canal into the Mediterranean.

The project appears to aim at redirecting the country's domestic overcapacity and capital for regional infrastructure development to improve trade and relations with Association of Southeast Asian Nations (ASEAN), Central Asian, and European countries. However, by offering substantial investment in infrastructure as well as burgeoning trade and economic benefits, it is actually a strategy designed to draw countries across Eurasia, the Middle East, and Africa into its plans.[41]

The Trump administration officially withdrew from TPP early this year, which provided a great opportunity for China to speed up its regional consolidation efforts.[42] The TPP could have served as a

---

[40] Paul Kennedy, *The Rise and Fall of the Great Powers* (London: Unwin Hyman, 1987), p. xxii.

[41] James Griffiths, Just what is this One Belt, One Road thing anyway? *CNN,* May 12, 2017, http://edition.cnn.com/2017/05/11/asia/china-one-belt-one-road-explainer/ (accessed on May 14, 2017).

[42] Yian Q. Mui, Withdrawal from Trans-Pacific Partnership shifts U.S. role in world economy, *The Washington Post,* January 23, 2017, https://www.washingtonpost.com/business/economy/withdrawal-from-trans-pacific-partnership-shifts-us-role-in-world-economy/2017/01/23/05720df6-e1a6-11e6-a453-19ec4b3d09ba_story.html?utm_term=.ab6a214a56ab (accessed on May 13, 2017).

platform for China and the US to establish a solid and long-term economic cooperation. The Trans-Pacific Partnership (TPP) includes 12 nations bordering the Pacific and accounts for roughly 40% of global gross domestic product, 30% of global exports, and 25% of global imports. However, China is not included in the TPP. Now that the US has ended its membership in TPP, this has enabled China to fill the vacancy. With its own version of a global trade organization Regional Comprehensive Economic Partnership (RCEP), which includes nations with about 30% of global GDP, China is in an advantageous position to gain the dominance of the region, at least economically. The proposed pact would include the 10 ASEAN countries, Australia, India, Japan, New Zealand, and South Korea. Even if it was claimed that the RCEP is not aimed at providing a real alternative to the TPP, it will no doubt function as the center of Asia's trade regime.

As a matter of fact, it is not difficult to imagine that China would hope that the economic size of the RCEP is huge enough to cut across the economic and strategic bloc established through the TPP.[43] Overlapped membership in TPP and RCEP also provides a great opportunity for China to win over Australia, Brunei, Japan, Malaysia, New Zealand, Singapore, and Vietnam to its side.

Another non-military means to cope with the US dominance is the proposition of the establishment of the Asian Infrastructure Investment Bank (AIIB). Given its economic strength, China is disproportionately represented in the International Monetary Fund (IMF) and World Bank. It has been proposed in IMF to give China more say. However, the reforms have been delayed for years, and even if they go through, the US will still retain far more power. As a result, AIIB is aimed to provide a regional alternative to IMF and World Bank based on the Bretton Woods system. As 58 member nations, including France, Germany, South Korea, and the UK, joined the bank regardless of the US warnings, China appears to have the confidence to set up an alternative economic world order. To take a step back, if it is too early for China to set a new world order, China could

---

[43] Jingyang Chen, TPP and RCEP: Boon or bane for ASEAN? *In Asia*, September 9, 2015, http://asiafoundation.org/in-asia/2015/09/09/tpp-and-rcep-boon-or-bane-for-asean/ (accessed on March 20, 2016).

at least use the new bank to expand its influence in Asia with the hope of surpassing the established powers: the US and Japan.[44]

Cooperation Between the US and China

Although the competition between China and the US has, mainly in the economic and security realms, intensified greatly especially in the past few years, the cooperation between the two countries has never stopped and still appears promising.

Climate Change

One realm for the two countries to work together is on climate change mitigation, adaptation, and consequence management. Scientific evidence shows clearly that human activities are partly responsible for extreme weather events that the world is already experiencing at an increasing rate.[45] The US and China, the two biggest economies and largest emitters of greenhouse gases in the world, hold the key to the success of long-term global efforts to combat climate change.[46]

Without the cooperation of the two countries, it is highly possible that global climate change will lead to climate-induced humanitarian disasters and infrastructure destruction. The world would have to face expensive relief operations at the global level with costly and long-term adaptation process. The social and political instability in

[44] *The Economist* explains, "Why China is creating a new 'World Bank' for Asia," *The Economist,* November 11, 2014, http://www.economist.com/blogs/economist-explains/2014/11/economist-explains-6 (accessed on March 20, 2016).

[45] Stephanie C. Herring, ed., *Explaining Extreme Events of 2014 from a Climate Perspective*, report by National Oceanic Atmospheric Administration, November 5, 2015, http://www.noaanews.noaa.gov/stories2015/110515-new-report-human-caused-climate-change-increased-the-severity-of-many-extreme-events-in-2014.html (accessed on March 4, 2016).

[46] Mengpin Ge, Johannes Freidrich and Thomas Damassa, *6 Graphs Explain the World's Top 10 Emitters*, World Resources Institute, November 25, 2014, http://www.wri.org/blog/2014/11/6-graphs-explain-world%E2%80%99s-top-10-emitters (accessed on March 5, 2016).

many areas of the world then increases, especially in emerging economies and developing countries. The US–China cooperation in all these areas will serve as the ground on which the world could cooperate and effectively respond to the potentially existential threat posed by global climate change. The two countries obviously realized the severity of the situation, and bilateral cooperation on climate change has made remarkable progress, highlighted by the historic climate change agreement signed by the two countries in November 2014.[47] The agreement also plays a critical role in the success of the Paris climate change conference in 2015.[48]

Strategic and Economic Dialogue

Regardless of the saber-rattling between the US and China in the SCS, the two countries have never stopped attempting to cooperate on critical global, regional, economic, and security realms. The Strategic and Economic Dialogue (S&ED) is a typical example.

As a broad and high-level exchange between the US and Chinese governments, the latest S&ED took place in Beijing in early June 2016 as scheduled. This was the 8th session and discussions here focused on a wide range of bilateral, regional, and global issues of strategic and economic importance in the immediate and long term, including security issues such as military relation, confidence building measures, strategic dialog, and non-proliferation.[49] Regardless of the fact that the 2016 dialogue was criticized by many as having few concrete results — particularly in relation to then ongoing disputes over SCS disputes — the dialogue is still considered as a platform for the

[47] The White House Office of the Press Secretary, US-China Joint Announcement on Climate Change, White House website, November 11, 2014, https://www.whitehouse.gov/the-press-office/2014/11/11/us-china-joint-announcement-climate-change (accessed on March 5, 2016).

[48] Julie Makinen and Chris Megerian, China, US relationship key in climate agreement, *Los Angeles Times*, December 13, 2015, http://www.latimes.com/world/asia/la-fg-china-u-s-climate-20151213-story.html (accessed on March 5, 2016).

[49] Peter Bittner, US-China strategic and economic dialogue: Key takeaways, *The Diplomat*, June 10, 2016, http://thediplomat.com/2016/06/us-china-strategic-and-economic-dialogue-key-takeaways/ (accessed on May 13, 2017).

two countries to continue their dialogue and thus maintain an open channel for communication. The S&ED mechanism is aimed at facilitating robust engagement and progress between the two countries through coordination with existing bilateral dialogues and working-level interactions.

Although it is not clear whether the Trump administration would maintain this dialogue — an Obama legacy — it is evident that the two powers agree to maintain a cooperative relation, especially after the Trump–Xi summit in early April 2017.[50]

Regional Issues

The two countries even worked together in an attempt to bring peace back to Afghanistan as the Quadrilateral Coordination Group was created in early 2016.[51] Both US and China have an interest in a peaceful and self-sustaining Afghanistan, and China's inclusion in the talk is crucial to the success of the talk since its influence on Pakistan will enable it to serve as a mediator in Afghan peace and reconciliation process, which is something the US lacks.[52]

As a matter of fact, Afghanistan presents challenges and opportunities for both the US and China. The two countries, by working together, could fix the significant problems, energize high-level diplomacy, and provide a future model for US–China cooperation.

In addition to regional security issues, the two countries should consider working with each other on broader regional issues such as

---

[50] Shannon Tiezzi, Trump–Xi Summit: Much Ado about Nothing? *The Diplomat,* April 08, 2017, http://thediplomat.com/2017/04/trump-xi-summit-much-ado-about-nothing/ (accessed on May 13, 2017).

[51] Shannon Tiezzi, China joins Afghanistan, Pakistan, and US for talks on Afghan peace process, *The Diplomat,* January 12, 2016, http://thediplomat.com/2016/01/china-joins-afghanistan-pakistan-and-us-for-talks-on-afghan-peace-process/ (accessed on March 6, 2016).

[52] David Caragliano and Noah Coburn, Could Afghanistan be a model for US-China cooperation? *The Diplomat,* April 21, 2015, http://thediplomat.com/2015/04/could-afghanistan-be-a-model-for-us-china-cooperation/ (accessed on March 6, 2016).

joint natural disaster relief, joint rescue and patrol, and anti-terrorism exercises, as well as mitigating tensions on the Korean Peninsula.

It is believed that Trump and Xi had reached some preliminary understandings during their meeting in early April 2017 about what China might do to change the behavior of North Korea. China also agreed to crack down on their second-tier banks that have helped finance the North's trade. The two countries have also agreed, unusually, to share some intelligence about suspected North Korean shipments of arms and other illicit goods.[53]

Cybersecurity

Regardless of the thorny accusation from the US that China has launched state-backed hacking against US companies, stealing business secrets, the two countries still managed to work together on enhancing cybersecurity.[54] The two technological powers signed an agreement at the end of 2015 and set up a "hotline" to facilitate the communication and also have agreed their agencies will work together to tackle terrorism, child exploitation, and online crime like fraud and the theft of trade secrets.[55]

There were different voices, however. It was said that the attacks had continued in the 3 weeks since the two countries signed the cyber security agreement. Some expressed skepticism that the agreement would lead to concrete changes in a Chinese policy, which has been accused of being permissive with those who have plundered secrets from companies in the US. The skepticism is likely to put new

[53] Gerry Mullany, Chris Buckley, and David E. Sanger, China warns of 'Storm Clouds Gathering' in U.S.-North Korea Standoff, *The New York Times*, April 14, 2017, https://www.nytimes.com/2017/04/14/world/asia/north-korea-china-nuclear.html?_r=0 (accessed on May 14, 2017).

[54] Mark Ward, Does China's government hack US companies to steal secrets? *BBC News*, September 23, 2015, www.bbc.com/news/technology-34324252 (accessed on March 7, 2016).

[55] Richard Bejtlich, To hack, or not to hack? The Brookings Institution, September 28, 2015, http://www.brookings.edu/blogs/up-front/posts/2015/09/28-us-china-hacking-agreement-bejtlich (accessed on March 7, 2016).

pressure on the two countries' agreement to limit attacks on private companies.[56]

US–China Space Dialogue

Ever since China successfully launched Shenzhou 5, the country's first manned spacecraft, in 2003, China has become the third country to carry astronauts to an orbital space station.[57] As the outer space became more crowded, a mechanism for communication and exchange of ideas between the two countries becomes necessary to guarantee the peaceful exploration and use of outer space. As a result, the first US–China Space Dialogue meeting was held on September 28, 2015, in Beijing. The two sides exchanged information on respective space policies. They conducted discussions on further collaboration related to space debris and the long-term sustainability of outer space activities. Both sides also exchanged views on issues related to satellite collision avoidance, civil Earth observation activities, space sciences, space weather, and civil Global Navigation Satellite Systems.[58]

To sum up, as it is has been described earlier, the US and China have already been in cooperation with each other in many realms, including trade, climate change, regional stability, cybersecurity, and even space development. Given the increasingly interconnected and extraordinarily turbulent challenges in the future at global level, it is imperative for the two countries to deepen the cooperation to address urgent global challenges. As China proposed to build up a "new type of great power relation" with the US, which also has the intention of

---

[56] Paul Mozur, Cybersecurity firm says Chinese hackers keep attacking US companies, *The New York Times*, October 19, 2015, http://www.nytimes.com/2015/10/20/technology/cybersecurity-firm-says-chinese-hackers-keep-attacking-us-companies.html?_r=0 (accessed on March 30, 2016).

[57] Dragon Space, China successfully completes first manned space flight, *Space Daily*, October 16, 2003, http://www.spacedaily.com/news/china-03zo.html (accessed on March 7, 2016).

[58] Media Note, The first meeting of the US-China space dialogue, Office of the Spokesperson, US Department of State, September 28, 2015.

engaging China, it seems reasonable for the two to work together to address looming and long-term global challenges that are beyond the capacity of any nation to solve alone.

Coexistence of the Rivals in Asia?

From the aforementioned analysis, it is clear that the Asian strategic landscape is facing a great change, which stemmed primarily from the sustained rapid economic growth of China over the past 35 years. China is now the world's second largest economy followed by Japan. Rapid economic growth has also enabled China to devote greater resources to military modernization and build-up, contributing to a change in the strategic landscape in Asia.

As the incumbent hegemon, the US will of course continue to be the dominant power in the region for at least decades to come, given China's growing but still limited military strength. The two countries could cooperate with each other in many aspects including economic, environmental, cyber-security, or even military fields. However, it seems the competition between the two countries is getting stronger as the US strengthens its military deployment in the Asia-Pacific region and deepens its military cooperation with its traditional allies. Especially with Japan, the US has virtually encouraged Japan to amend its security-related laws so as to give Japan the power to fully exercise the right to collective self-defense and enable Japanese troops to fight abroad. Furthermore, the US is getting actively involved in the sovereignty claims in the ECS and SCS with the intention to maintain its hegemony in the Asia-Pacific region.

As a result, the dynamics between the US and China is bound to change — the earlier equilibrium between the two is apparently being broken. Judging from the factors discussed above, the new strategic situation in the region could be presented in several aspects.

First, the relation of "struggle without breaking" could be unfortunately broken given the uncertainties caused by the competition between the US and China in many aspects. Accidents may occur due to strategic misunderstanding or misjudgment of both or even the third party, intensifying the tension in the region.

Second, as the competition intensifies, it seems Asian countries are also forced to take sides between the US and China. It was reported that China received the permission of Malaysia to dock warships at Kota Kinabalu, whereas Vietnam and the Philippines may be happy to see a US challenge to China's claims in the disputed SCS waters.[59] In addition, regardless of the fact that South Korea has been a US ally for decades and the US's opposition to its traditional allies and partners signing on to the AIIB, it joined the bank anyway as a founding member.[60] As mentioned earlier, overlapped membership of Australia, Brunei, Japan, Malaysia, New Zealand, Singapore, Vietnam in both TPP and RCEP is another indicator that countries in the Asian region may need to take sides sooner or later.

Third, the tension in the Asian region is harmful to the economic growth in the region, especially to the investment and business environments. Nor does the regional tension meet the primary interests of many Asian countries that desire for regional stability for development.

Fourth, it seems the US is confident in its ability to maintain the regional stability. However, maintaining the regional stability does not seem as easy as it did when the American power in Asia was at its height, especially after the rise of China and the consequent change of geostrategic landscape in the region. The regional stability or equilibrium maybe disturbed due to miscalculation or accidents.

Last, the Trump administration's Asia policy is still considered as an uncertainty factor to the stability of the region; if anything could be learned from Trump's unpredictable decision-making behavior ever since he took office, it is now that commitments to South Korea and Japan have been reiterated, the "One China" policy has been accepted, and US support for the "status quo" between China and

---

[59] Elizabeth Shim, China: US forcing countries to 'take sides' on South China Sea dispute, UPI, November 20, 2015, http://www.upi.com/Top_News/World-News/2015/11/20/China-US-forcing-countries-to-take-sides-on-South-China-Sea-dispute/4161448036062/ (accessed on March 23, 2016).

[60] Ankit Panda, South Korea joins the AIIB, *The Diplomat*, March 28, 2015, http://thediplomat.com/2015/03/south-korea-joins-the-aiib/ (accessed on March 23, 2016).

Taiwan will continue. However, these policies could be changed as quickly as a tweet can be written.

To sum up, the US is still the only superpower of the world regardless of the fact that China is now the second largest economy and is rapidly increasing its military buildup. Nonetheless, it is not entirely far-fetched to say that China is catching up.

The million dollar question then is: Will China overthrow the existing order set by the US and replace its role in the region or will China coexist peacefully with the US?

We do not know as of now. Maybe we do not have to wait too long to know the answer.

Chapter

7

Issue of Non-Participation in the South China Sea Arbitration

Tsu-sung Hsieh

Professor, School of Law, Ming Chuan University, Taipei, Taiwan

Abstract

The South China Sea Arbitration between Philippines and mainland China was ruled in favor of Philippines on July 12, 2016, given the situation that the mainland China did not participate the arbitral proceeding.

Article 9 of Annex VII of UNCLOS sets forth that, before making its award in situation of non-participation, the arbitral tribunal must satisfy itself not only that it has jurisdiction over the dispute but also that the claim is well founded in fact and law.

This chapter analyzes and concludes that the tribunal had not discharged its duties under this provision upon issues of whether it had jurisdiction over the dispute and the claim was well-founded in fact and law. Therefore, it is not valid and cannot have any precedential value, nor can it create any binding force.

In particular, lacking of direct evidences is, *inter alia*, one of the major reasons where the tribunal failed to self-satisfy its duty. This chapter points out that had these direct evidences relating to Taiping Island been provided by the indispensable third-party Taiwan to the tribunal, mainland China would have had a more favorable position in this case.

Keywords: South China Sea, arbitration, non-participation, indispensable third party, nine-dash line, historic right.

Introduction

The South China Sea Arbitration was an arbitration initiated by the Republic of Philippines (Philippines) against the People's Republic of China (mainland China)[1] under the United Nations Convention on the Law of the Sea (UNCLOS, or Convention) regarding issues in the South China Sea. On July 12, 2016, the tribunal of this arbitration ruled in favor of Philippines.

Mainland China had repeatedly stated that it would not participate or accept the arbitration and did not appear throughout the entire proceeding, because it declared that the arbitration tribunal "does not have jurisdiction over this case."[2]

There are three kinds of non-participation: where the respondent appeared during the preliminary stage and then disappeared from the merits stage; where the respondent failed to appear during the preliminary stages and then appeared for the merits; or where the respondent failed to appear throughout the entire proceeding.[3] The non-participation of mainland China obviously is the third kind.

However, it is noted that there is nothing unlawful about a state refusing to participate where it believes in good faith that the tribunal lacks jurisdiction,[4] and non-participation does not imply any bad

[1] Pursuant to the Act Governing Relations between the People of the Taiwan Area and the Mainland Area, the Republic of China is called "Taiwan" while the Peoples' Republic of China is called "mainland China" in this chapter.

[2] The Award of the South China Sea Arbitration between Philippines and China (hereinafter Award), para. 114.

[3] James D. Fry, *Non-Participation in the International Court of Justice Revisited: Change or Plus Ca Change?* 49 Colum. J. Transnat'l L., 35, 41 (2010).

[4] Fry, *supra* note 3, p. 62.

faith.[5] Even if the tribunal has the jurisdiction to the case, states cannot be forced to participate in a proceeding in which they do not want to participate.

The tribunal nevertheless continued the proceedings, confirming that despite its non-appearance, mainland China remains a party to the arbitration, including that it will be bound under international law by any decision of the tribunal.[6]

In particular, when mainland China pointed out that its position paper "does not express any position on the substantive issues related to the subject-matter of the arbitration initiated by the Philippines," the tribunal decided to treat the position paper and certain communications from mainland China as constituting a "plea" concerning jurisdiction,[7] even though it appeared to be informal communications.[8]

This decision would allow a plea to be applicable to Article 20(3) of the Rules of Procedure. This provision provides that the tribunal shall rule on any plea concerning its jurisdiction as a preliminary question unless it determines that the "objection to its jurisdiction does not possess an exclusively preliminary character, in which case it shall rule on such a plea in conjunction with the merits."

The tribunal further issued Procedural Order No. 4 to give it leverage for connecting these information communication with preliminary question. Said order allows the tribunal to: (1) take note of public statements or informal communications made by non-participating parties, (2) treat such statements and communications as equivalent to or as constituting preliminary objections, and (3) bifurcate proceedings to address some or all of such objections as preliminary questions.[9]

---

[5] Fry, *supra* note 3, p. 44.

[6] Award, para. 118.

[7] Award, para. 45, 115, 130, 146.

[8] The Award on Jurisdiction and Admissibility of the South China Sea Arbitration between Philippines and China (hereinafter Award on Jurisdiction), para. 380; Stanimir A. Alexandrov, *Non-Appearance before the International Court of Justice*, 33 Colum. J. Transnat'l L. 41, 57 (1995).

[9] Award on Jurisdiction, para. 68.

The International Court of Justice (ICJ) had treated informal communication as either an official preliminary objection or an informational communication to non-participation cases before it.[10] But the court's acceptance of and reliance on informal communications should not be considered as implicit authorization.[11] Assuming *arguendo* that the tribunal deemed mainland China's position paper as a plea for triggering the arbitration proceeding is proper, its utilizing of these informal communications as materials for rendering decision is, however, not allowable.

More importantly, in such a non-participation situation, there is a duty charged to the tribunal according to the relevant part of Article 9 of Annex VII:

> Before making its award, the arbitral tribunal must satisfy itself not only that it has jurisdiction over the dispute but also that the claim is well founded in fact and law.[12]

In fact, Article 9 of Annex VII seeks to balance the risks of prejudice that could be suffered by either party in a situation of non-participation. First, it protects the participating party by ensuring that proceedings will not be frustrated by the decision of the other party to not participate. Second, it protects the rights of the non-participating party by ensuring that a tribunal will not simply accept the evidence and claims of the participating party by default.[13] In other words, the tribunal's jurisdiction over that very dispute can be challenged.[14]

In the following sections, this chapter verifies whether the award satisfies the requirement of the Article 9. In particular, the Section "Whether the Tribunal Has Jurisdiction over the Dispute" discusses about whether the tribunal has jurisdiction over the dispute, wherein precondition and exceptions to jurisdiction will be

---

[10] Alexandrov, *supra* note 8, at p. 62; Fry, *supra* note 3, p. 45.

[11] Alexandrov, *supra* note 8, p. 56.

[12] Award, para. 129.

[13] Award, para. 46, 119.

[14] Fry, *supra* note 3, p. 45.

examined, especially regarding the insular land territory and historical bays and titles, and advancement or detraction of position in parties' dispute over sovereignty will be identified. The Section "Whether the Claim is Well Founded in Fact and Law" further identifies whether the claim is well founded in fact and law, wherein effect of absence of indispensable third party is analyzed, especially regarding the status of Taiping Island and interpretation of the nine-dash line and historic rights, along with standard of proof. The Section "All Things Considered" extends considerations to include retroactive factors and undermined equitable principle, along with cause of the troubled water and its prospective view. The final section is "Conclusion."

Whether the Tribunal Has Jurisdiction Over the Dispute

Pursuant to Article 288 of the Convention, a court or tribunal referred to in Article 287 shall have jurisdiction over any dispute concerning the interpretation or application of this Convention.[15]

Mainland China's position paper of December 7, 2014 declared that the tribunal lacks jurisdiction.[16] It claimed that the essence of the subject-matter of the arbitration is territorial sovereignty over several maritime features in the South China Sea, which is beyond the scope of the UNCLOS.[17] So, mainland China would be able to argue that

---

[15] Article 288, UNCLOS.

[16] Award, para. 166: (a) the essence of the subject-matter of the arbitration is territorial sovereignty over several maritime features in the South China Sea, which is beyond the scope of the UNCLOS; (b) even assuming some of the claims were concerned with the interpretation and application of the UNCLOS, they would still be an integral part of maritime delimitation, which has been excluded by China through its 2006 Declaration and consequently is not subject to compulsory arbitration; (c) given that China and the Philippines have agreed to settle their disputes in the South China Sea through negotiation, the Philippines is precluded from initiating arbitration unilaterally; (d) the Philippines failed to fulfill the obligation of exchanging views with China on the means of dispute settlement; (e) the Philippines' initiation of the arbitration is a typical abuse of compulsory arbitral procedures stipulated in the UNCLOS.

[17] Award, para. 166.

it is the absence of jurisdiction, not the failure to appear in itself, that prevents such a non-appearing state from acquiring a party status.[18]

This article points out, *inter alia*, that there are at least three grounds which would render the failure of jurisdiction of the tribunal to this arbitration. First, there is a failure to satisfy precondition of jurisdiction; second, there are events falling within the exceptions of jurisdiction; and third, it advances position in parties' dispute over sovereignty.

Failure to Satisfy Precondition to Jurisdiction

The tribunal had cited that "a state should not have to give an account of itself on issues of merits before a tribunal which lacks jurisdiction in the matter, or whose jurisdiction has not yet been established."[19] That is, a precondition to jurisdiction must be satisfied before the tribunal could render its arbitral award.

The Convention permits parties to agree on the settlement of disputes through alternative means of their own choosing. Indeed, Articles 281 and 282 of the Convention may prevent a State from making use of the mechanisms under the Convention if they have already agreed to another means of dispute resolution.

The relevant part of Article 281 states that:

> If the States Parties which are parties to a dispute concerning the interpretation or application of this Convention have agreed to seek settlement of the dispute by a peaceful means of their own choice, the procedures provided for in this Part apply only where no settlement has been reached by recourse to such means and the agreement between the parties does not exclude any further procedure.[20]

Article 282 further mentions:

> If the States Parties which are parties to a dispute concerning the interpretation or application of this Convention have agreed,

[18] Alexandrov, *supra* note 8, p. 60.

[19] Award on Jurisdiction, para. 390.

[20] Article 281, UNCLOS.

> through a general, regional or bilateral agreement or otherwise, that such dispute shall, at the request of any party to the dispute, be submitted to a procedure that entails a binding decision, that procedure shall apply in lieu of the procedures provided for in this Part, unless the parties to the dispute otherwise agree.[21]

However, the tribunal said that the following events did not eliminate the jurisdiction: (a) the 2002 mainland China–ASEAN Declaration on the Conduct of Parties in the South China Sea (DOC), (b) joint statements issued by the Philippines and mainland China referring to the resolution of disputes through negotiations, (c) the Treaty of Amity and Cooperation in Southeast Asia, and (d) the Convention on Biological Diversity (CBD).[22]

Specifically, the DOC explicitly addressed that "[t]he Parties concerned undertake to resolve their territorial and jurisdictional disputes by peaceful means... through friendly consultations and negotiations by sovereign states directly concerned...." However, the tribunal said that the DOC is a political agreement, and "was not intended to be a legally binding agreement with respect to dispute resolution," does not provide a mechanism for binding settlement, and does not exclude other means of settlement.[23]

The tribunal reached the same conclusion with respect to the joint statements identified in mainland China's position paper. With respect to the treaty of Amity and Cooperation in Southeast Asia and the CBD, the tribunal said that neither provides a binding mechanism nor excludes other procedures. Accordingly, the tribunal concluded that none of these instruments prevents the Philippines from bringing its claims to arbitration.

It is well established that the languages of the provisions shall be interpreted by "plain meaning" thereof. Here, the aforementioned documentations shall have met the requirements of articles 281 and 282 based on the plain meaning interpretation. However, the tribunal looked beyond the ordinary meaning of, *inter alia*, the word "undertake" in

---

[21] Article 282, UNCLOS.

[22] Award, para. 159.

[23] Award on Jurisdiction, paras. 212–229, 299–300.

DOC to verify its understanding, and concluded the DOC, along with other related documentations, are not legally binding.[24]

The tribunal's decision in this matter had obviously violated the plain meaning principle, which therefore would render the arbitral award invalid due to failing to satisfy precondition to jurisdiction.

Fallen Within Exceptions to Jurisdiction

According to the Article 298(1)(a)(i):

> 1. When signing, ratifying or acceding to this Convention or at any time thereafter, a State may, without prejudice to the obligations arising under section 1, declare in writing that it does not accept any one or more of the procedures provided for in section 2 with respect to one or more of the following categories of disputes:
>
> (a) (i) disputes concerning the interpretation or application of articles 15, 74 and 83 relating to sea boundary delimitations, or those involving historic bays or titles, provided that a State having made such a declaration shall, when such a dispute arises subsequent to the entry into force of this Convention and where no agreement within a reasonable period of time is reached in negotiations between the parties, at the request of any party to the dispute, accept submission of the matter to conciliation under Annex V, section 2; and provided further that any dispute that necessarily involves the concurrent consideration of any unsettled dispute concerning sovereignty or other rights over continental or insular land territory shall be excluded from such submission.[25]

Mainland China had declared in 2006 that the government of mainland China does not accept any of the procedures provided for in Section 2 of Part XV of the Convention with respect to all the categories of disputes referred to in paragraph 1 (a) (b) and (c) of Article 298 of the Convention.[26]

---

[24] Award on Jurisdiction, paras. 216.

[25] Article 298, paragraph 1(a)(i), UNCLOS.

[26] Declarations or statements upon UNCLOS ratification; Award on Jurisdiction, para. 365.

Mainland China's declaration paper is a written declaration explicitly stating that it does not accept any one or more of the procedures provided for in Section 2 with respect to one or more of the following categories of disputes, including, *inter alia*, maritime features and historical titles.[27] These two events are further discussed in the following paragraphs.

Regarding insular land territory

Article 298(1)(a)(i) provides that any unsettled dispute concerning sovereignty or other rights over continental or insular land territory shall be excluded from such submission.

The tribunal agreed that its jurisdiction over some of the Philippines' submissions could be barred if a feature claimed by mainland China in the South China Sea was found to be an island within the meaning of Article 121 of the Convention, entitled to an exclusive economic zone or continental shelf overlapping those generated by the Philippines archipelago. In that case, the resolution of the merits of certain of the Philippines' claims would not be possible without first delimiting the overlapping entitlements, a step which, because of mainland China's 2006 Declaration, would be outside the scope of the tribunal's jurisdiction.[28]

On the other hand, the question of delimiting overlapping entitlements would not arise if the tribunal were to find at the merits phase that none of the features claimed by mainland China are islands that generate their own exclusive economic zone or continental shelf.[29] In other words, if there is no island founded according to Article 121, no issue of exclusion exists anymore.

The Philippines selected only a few features and argued that this, is in essence, an attempt at denying China's sovereignty over the Nansha Islands as a whole. Considering that the Philippines' claim is premised on the absence of any overlapping entitlement of China to

---

[27] Award on Jurisdiction, para. 365.
[28] Award on Jurisdiction, para. 369.
[29] Award on Jurisdiction, para. 369.

an exclusivé economic zone or to a continental shelf, the tribunal decided to consider the maritime zones generated by any feature in the South China Sea claimed by China, whether or not such feature is presently occupied by China.[30] The Taiping Island was therefore involved in the arbitration as a result.

However, the tribunal reserved the decision on its jurisdiction with respect to the insular land territory with the merits of Philippines' claims.[31] Nonetheless, it indicated that the tribunal agreed that mainland China's declaration paper is valid and would cause the tribunal lack of jurisdiction if there is a feature claimed by mainland China in the South China Sea that was found to be an island within the meaning of Article 121 of the Convention. As such, these factual evidences will be further discussed in the Section "Regarding Status of Taiping Island."

Regarding historical bays and titles

Article 298(1)(a)(i) provides that disputes relating to sea boundary delimitations, or those involving historical bays or titles, can be declared in writing by a state that it does not accepted any procedures provided for in Section 2 of the Convention.[32] The tribunal further agreed that Article 298 excluded disputes involving historic bays or titles that could bear on the Philippines' submissions concerning China's claims to historic rights, if such rights were found to be permitted by the Convention and within the scope of this exclusion.[33]

With respect to the historic bays and titles, the tribunal again reserved the decision on its jurisdiction with the merits of Philippines' claims.[34] Nonetheless, it also indicated that the tribunal agreed that mainland China's declaration paper is valid and would cause the tribunal lack of jurisdiction if historic rights were found to be permitted by the Convention and within the scope of this exclusion. And, these

[30] Award on Jurisdiction, para. 154.
[31] Award on Jurisdiction, para. 399.
[32] Article 298, para. 1(a)(i), UNCLOS.
[33] Award on Jurisdiction, para. 370.
[34] Award on Jurisdiction, para. 398.

factual evidences will be further discussed in the Section "Regarding Interpretation of the Nine-dash Line and Historic Rights."

Advancing Position in Parties' Dispute Over Sovereignty

The tribunal had said that it might consider that the Philippines' submissions could be understood to relate to sovereignty if were convinced that "actual objective of the Philippines' claims was to advance its position in the Parties' dispute over sovereignty."[35] Therefore, the tribunal has a duty to ensure that its decision does not advance either party's claims to land sovereignty in the South China Sea.[36]

Further, the tribunal agreed that it will be able address those of the Philippines' submissions based on the premise that certain areas of the South China Sea form part of the Philippines' exclusive economic zone or continental shelf only if it determines that mainland China could not possess any potentially overlapping entitlement in that area.[37] However, the tribunal did not think Philippines had problem in this matter.

For example, when considering objections with respect to sovereignty and delimitation, the tribunal agreed that there are disputes of sovereignty. But, it said that this dispute does not concern sovereignty.[38] It also said that what the Philippines asked was not sovereignty,[39] and that "the determination of the nature of and entitlements generated by the maritime features in the South China Sea does not require a decision on issues of territorial sovereignty."[40] It further stated that the entitlement doesn't equate delimitation.[41]

This article argue that the objections concerned by the tribunal are in essence intertwined with sovereignty, and it does concern

[35] Award on Jurisdiction, para. 153.
[36] Award on Jurisdiction, para. 153.
[37] Award on Jurisdiction, para. 157.
[38] Award, para. 170.
[39] Award, para. 153–154.
[40] Award, para. 67, 153–157.
[41] Award, para. 155.

sovereignty because the entitlement of a maritime feature is the base of associated sovereignty.

Assuming *arguendo* the fact that mainland China had declared the 298 exception in 2006 is ignored, this chapter argues that the tribunal still has no jurisdiction because sovereignty determination shall be a prerequisite to resolutions of Philippines' submissions. Therefore, the decision thereof will advances position in parties' dispute over sovereignty.

Further, the tribunal concluded that China's claims sovereign rights encompassed by the nine-dash line are contrary to the Convention and without lawful effect to the extent that they exceed the geographic and substantive limits of China's maritime entitlements under the Convention. This decision, by its nature, would detract China's sovereignty and advance Philippines' sovereignty instead.

Indeed, it is incorrect when the tribunal said that it did not see that success on these submissions of Philippines would have an effect on the Philippines' sovereignty claims. Instead, the actual objective of the Philippines' claims would advance its position in the Parties' dispute over sovereign because, *inter alia*, Vietnam had expressed its consideration to follow Philippines' success in the arbitration. Therefore, the tribunal shall admit that the Philippines' submissions shall conclude to being related to sovereignty, and this is another reason that the decision advances position in parties' dispute over sovereignty.

Whether the Claim is Well Founded in Fact and Law

Although the tribunal has taken a number of measures to safeguard the procedural rights of mainland China,[42] and sought additional evidence from Philippines[43]; however, it had failed to acquire material facts from an indispensable third party.[44]

---

[42] Award, para. 46.

[43] Award, para. 131.

[44] Award, para. 132–142.

Similar mandates can be found like the Article 53(2) of the Statute of the ICJ which obliges the court to satisfy itself that the applicant's case is "well founded." That may require extensive fact gathering by the court itself or rejection of the case when neither the applicant nor the court can satisfy the judges that the claim is factually well founded.[45]

Case laws also supports this notion. For example, the court in *Nicaragua v. United States* recognized that it "cannot by its own enquiries entirely make up for the absence of one of the parties" and that "absence, in a case ... involving extensive questions of fact, must necessarily limit the extent to which the Court is informed of the facts."[46]

However, this article argues that, in the current case, there are at least two grounds where the claim was found not being well founded in fact and law. First, there is failure attributed to absence of indispensable third party regarding the status of Taiping Island and interpreting the historic right, and second, there is failure due to misapplying of standard of proof.

Failure Attributed to Absence of Indispensable Third Party

The Article 291 of the Convention provides that the dispute settlement procedures shall be open to entities other than states parties only as specifically provided for in this Convention.[47] Specifically, the Article 13 of VII thereof provided that the provisions of the Annex shall apply *mutatis mutandis* to any dispute involving entities other than states parties.

The tribunal agreed that it shall cease to proceed due to the absence of an indispensable third party if the rights of the third parties would have been affected by a decision in the case, and would have

---

[45] W. Michael Reisman, Comment: *Respecting One's Own Jurisprudence: A Plea To The International Court of Justice*, vol. 83 A.J.I.L. (1989), pp. 312, 317.

[46] Military and Paramilitary Activities in and Against Nicaragua (*Nicar. v. U.S.*), 1986 I.C.J. 14, P 30 (June 27); see also Fry, *supra* note 3, pp. 69–70; Alexandrov, *supra* note 8, pp. 59–60.

[47] Article 291, para. 2, UNCLOS.

formed the very subject-matter of the decision.[48] Indeed, more facts were required for the tribunal to have made a reliable decision.[49]

But after considering countries such as Vietnam, it found no indispensable third party whose absence deprives the tribunal of jurisdiction,[50] the Republic of China (Taiwan) was not asked by the tribunal for consideration to be the indispensable third party.

The mainland China's claims to the South China Sea mirror those of Taiwan. The legal bases for Taiwan's claims are its longstanding historic ties to the islands, especially its control over Tungsha Island and Taiping Island (Itu Aba).[51] But, the tribunal invited the Philippines to "provide additional historical and anthropological information, as well as geographic and hydrographic information regarding" Taiping Island instead.[52]

It is noted that the nine-dash line (originated as 11-dash line or U-shape line) had been first created and provided by Taiwan.[53] Therefore, the archives in Taiwan shall be considered in this case, but the tribunal had never sought associated facts from it,[54] even the amicus brief provide by Taiwan had not been seriously reviewed.[55] Along with its refusal to conduct the site visit of Taiping Island,[56] the legality of decision to the arbitral award can hardly be achieved.

Absence of indispensable Taiwan as the third party to this arbitration would cause insufficient facts in at least two issues, i.e. the status of Taiping Island and the interpretation of historic right. Therefore,

---

[48] Award on Jurisdiction, para. 181.

[49] Fry, *supra* note 3, at 65.

[50] Award on Jurisdiction, para. 413.

[51] Christopher C. Joyner, *The Spratly Islands Dispute: What Role for Normalizing Relations between China and Taiwan?* New Eng. L. Rev. (1998), vol. 32, pp. 819, 826–827.

[52] Award, para. 132.

[53] Jilu Wu, *China's Marine Legal System — An Overall Review*, vol. 17 Ocean & Coastal L.J. (2012), pp. 291, 303; Kuen-Chen Fu, *Legal Status of the South (China) Sea*, vol. 123 Information Co. (1994), p. 32.

[54] Award, para. 139.

[55] Award, para. 142.

[56] Award, para. 142.

the absence of the indispensable third party shall have deprived the tribunal of jurisdiction.[57]

Regarding status of Taiping Island

As mentioned earlier, the tribunal's jurisdiction over some of the Philippines' submissions could be barred if a feature claimed by mainland China in the South China Sea was found to be an island within the meaning of Article 121 of the Convention, entitled to an exclusive economic zone or continental shelf overlapping those generated by the Philippines archipelago.[58] The Article 121(3) provides that:

> Rocks which cannot sustain human habitation or economic life of their own shall have no exclusive economic zone or continental shelf.

It is well established that the languages of the provisions shall be interpreted by plain meaning thereof. The tribunal also agreed that the ordinary meaning of "human habitation" is the "action of dwelling in or inhabiting as a place of residence — occupancy by inhabitants" or "a settlement." "Inhabit" is defined as "to dwell in, occupy as an abode, to live permanently or habitually in (a region, element, etc.); to reside in (a country, town, dwelling, etc.)."[59]

However, the tribunal further extended the interpretation thereof by implying that the term habitation is a non-transient presence of persons who have chosen to stay and reside on the feature in a settled manner. Human habitation would thus require all of the elements necessary to keep people alive on the feature but would also require conditions sufficiently conducive to human life and livelihood for people to inhabit, rather than merely survive on, the feature.[60] So, the Taiping Island was therefore downgraded to be a rock by the tribunal in this arbitration instead.

---

[57] Award on Jurisdiction, para. 179, 413.

[58] Award on Jurisdiction, para. 369.

[59] Award, para. 488.

[60] Award, para. 489.

Ironically, Okinotori Islands (沖之鳥島)[61] had been claimed by Japanese government as an Island, rather than a rock, which, either by definition or in reality, definitely cannot sustain human habitation or economic life of their own. This rock in particular had claimed entitlements to an exclusive economic zone and continental shelf.[62]

Referring to the insular land territory mentioned previously in Section "Regarding Insular Land Territory," the Article 121 provided that, an island is a naturally formed area of land, surrounded by water, which is above water at high tide. The Taiping Island is an island which perfectly meets the requirement stated in Article 121, because nature of the island speaks for itself along with well-established official documentations, which had clearly recorded military as well as civilian personnel residing in that island over decades. Therefore, it shall have exclusive economic zone or continental shelf status.

The facts about habitability of the Taiping Island shall be found by making an inquiry to Taiwan, however, the inquiry had been intentionally dismissed by the tribunal. In particular, the most obvious misuse of discretion by the tribunal was the refusal of site visit to Taiping Island, albeit the site visit is stipulated in Article 22 of the Rules of Procedure.[63]

Taiping Island's "sustainability of human habitation or economic life of their own" is a factual issue, and this issue of "whether the claim is well founded in fact and law" is in significant respects interwoven with the issue of "whether it has jurisdiction over the dispute."[64] However, the tribunal thrust itself into the loophole without being capable of acquiring the truth. Therefore, it shall conclude that the arbitral award is plainly erroneous, resulting in the invalid award.

---

[61] The Okinotori Islands (沖之鳥島 Okinotori-shima) is a Japanese uninhabited atoll with a total area of 8,482 m^2. Its dry land area is mostly made up by three concrete encasings and there is a 100 by 50 m platform in the lagoon housing a research station.

[62] Award, para. 646.

[63] Award, para. 40, 41, 42, 142, 1140.

[64] Award on Jurisdiction, para. 392.

Regarding interpretation of the nine-dash line and historic rights

Mainland China has made clear that it claims not only the territorial waters and contiguous zones around the islands but also, for each island, its exclusive economic zone (EEZ) and continental shelf.[65] The tribunal also said that mainland China does claim other rights such as petroleum resources and fisheries, and considered these rights are claimed within the "nine-dash line" on the basis of historic rights existing independently of the Convention.[66] On the other hand, the tribunal stated that mainland China has not clarified the nature or scope of its claimed historic rights. Nor has mainland China clarified its understanding of the meaning of the "nine-dash line."[67]

One example illustrated the tribunal's confusion: With respect to mainland China's commitment to respect both freedom of navigation and overflight, the tribunal stated that mainland China does not consider the sea areas within the "nine-dash line" to be equivalent to its territorial sea or internal water.[68] This is because the Convention does not provide for freedom of overflight or for freedom of navigation, beyond a right of innocent passage.[69]

Indeed, mainland China had not clarified its understanding of the meaning of the "nine-dash line" set out in the map accompanying its notes verbales of May 7, 2009. In fact, mainland China had not clarified the nature or scope of its claimed historic rights either.[70] In addition, scholars had suggested that neither the 2011 Declaration claimed right over sea area of the South China Sea[71] nor did the 2009

[65] F. Dupuy and P.-M. Dupuy, *Agora: The South China Sea: A Legal Analysis of China's Historic Rights Claim in the South China Sea*, vol. 107 A.J.I.L. (2013), pp. 124, 127.

[66] Award, para. 211.

[67] Award, para. 160.

[68] Award, para. 213.

[69] Arbitration award, p. 91.

[70] Award on Jurisdiction, para. 160, 164.

[71] S.-t. Gau, *South China Sea Arbitration — A Study of the Application of Non-Appearing Regulation*, Cross-Strait Relations and Developments in International Law (Angel Publishing, 2016), p. 557.

Declaration claim associated water or adjacent water based on the nine-dash line,[72] whereas the nine-dash line was not provided for claiming right in sea water at all.[73]

Further referring to the historic bays and titles mentioned previously in Section "Regarding Historical Bays and Titles," the tribunal said that China's asserted historic right does not equate to the historic title.[74] However, it should be noted that the term "historic rights" (sometimes confusingly used with other notions, such as "historic waters" and "historic title") has often been imbued with a certain degree of confusion and controversy in international law.[75]

The theory of historic bays is of general scope. Historic rights are claimed not only in respect of bays but also in respect of maritime areas, which do not constitute bays. It is noted that these terms are themselves evolving, e.g. there is a growing tendency to describe these areas as "historic waters," not as "historic bays."[76] In addition, in 1962, the U.N. Secretariat produced a memorandum on "historic waters," which considered the term as equivalent to "historic title."[77] In particular, "historic rights" may include sovereignty but equally include more limited rights, such as fishing rights or rights of access, that fall well short of a claim of sovereignty. Historic title is used specifically to refer to historic sovereignty to land or maritime areas.[78]

It should be further noted that Chinese language does not especially separate "historic title" from "historic right." In fact, both words are mainly expressed by a single word "歷史性權利" (historic right) which, in this case, is the "relevant rights in the South China Sea, formed in the long historical course."[79] Instead, "歷史性所有權" (historic title) is not a word commonly used for associated expression.[80]

---

[72] *Ibid.*, at 562.

[73] *Ibid.*, at 564.

[74] Award, para. 207.

[75] Dupuy & Dupuy, *supra* note 65, p. 124.

[76] Award, para. 220.

[77] Award, para. 222.

[78] Award, para. 225.

[79] Award, para. 206, 246.

[80] Award, para. 227.

Given that these terms lack clarity, it, however, leaves a room for various interpretations. Although the existence of a dispute may be inferred from the conduct of a state or from its silence, the contents of "nine-dash line" cannot.[81] Therefore, this article cannot agree that the tribunal had inferred that it will be able address those of the Philippines' submissions based on the premise that certain areas of the South China Sea form part of the Philippines' exclusive economic zone or continental shelf if the tribunal determines that mainland China could not possess any potentially overlapping entitlement in that area.[82] It is incorrect to conduct such inference, because subject-matter of the "nine-dash line" has not been clarified yet.

As mentioned, the nine-dash line had been originally provided by Taiwan; however, Taiwan had not been included as an indispensable party. The tribunal had not discharged its duty to properly interpret the meaning of the nine-dash line model.

This Article argues the tribunal had misinterpreted the meaning of nine-dash line and its underlying historic rights, and therefore had rendered the arbitral award invalid.

Failure Due to Misapplying of Standard of Proof

Regarding whether Philippines' claims are well found in fact and law, the tribunal had not satisfactorily discharged its duty on the ground that, *inter alia*, the standard of proof had not appropriately applied.

For making out its claims, the tribunal merely requested Philippines to provide additional evidences. The tribunal thereby interpreted that Article 9 of Annex VII does not operate to change the burden of proof or to raise or lower the standard of proof.[83]

This Article does not agree and suggest that statutory laws, international and domestic alike, had mandated a satisfactory evidence be submitted to the court.[84] Case laws further provided that in non-participation

[81] Award, para. 156.

[82] Award on Jurisdiction, para. 157.

[83] Award, para. 131.

[84] 28 U.S. Code § 1608(e): No judgment by default shall be entered by a court of the US or of a State against a foreign state, a political subdivision thereof, or an

cases, a higher standard of proof was set forth, i.e. clear and convincing evidence rather than the preponderance of evidence.[85] In *Nicaragua v. United States*, it was held that the court must attain the same degree of certainty as in any other case that the claim of the party appearing is sound in law, and so far as the nature of the case permits, that the facts on which it is based are supported by convincing evidence.[86]

Clear and convincing proof means that the evidence presented by a party during the trial must be highly and substantially more probable to be true than not, and the trier of fact must have a firm belief or conviction in its factuality. In this standard, a greater degree of believability must be met than the common standard of proof in civil actions, which only requires that the facts as a threshold be more likely than not to prove the issue for which they are asserted. In the current case, its standard is definitely above *prima facie* evidence.[87]

The failure to use its authority to determine the facts and its treatment of evidence would result in breaching its avowed duty to ensure equality between the parties.[88] When the tribunal's discretionary power had been misused, it constitutes an abuse of legal process and evidence is not well founded. If the claim is not well founded, no further action is taken.[89]

Here, the tribunal merely seek to acquire additional evidence from Philippines,[90] without duly heightening the standard of proof, resulting a failure of self-satisfaction to its duty.

---

agency or instrumentality of a foreign state, unless the claimant establishes his claim or right to relief by evidence satisfactory to the court. A copy of any such default judgment shall be sent to the foreign state or political subdivision in the manner prescribed for service in this section.

[85] *Peterson v. Islamic Republic of Iran*, 264 F. Supp. 2d 46, 47–48 (D.D.C. 2003) (after the defendants failed to appear, the court conducted the evidentiary hearing required under FSIA 1608(e) and applied the "clear and convincing" standard of proof); John E. Noyes, *The International Tribunal for the Law of the Sea*, 32 Cornell Int'l L.J. (1998), pp. 109, 143; Fry, *supra* note 3, p. 65.

[86] Nicaragua v. US, ICJ Rep. pars. 29–3 (1986).

[87] Gau, *supra* note 71, p. 554.

[88] Leo Gross, *Book Review: Forty Years International Court of Justice: Jurisdiction, Equity and Equality*, A. Bloed and P. van Dijk, eds., 84 A.J.I.L. (1990), pp. 944, 946.

[89] Noyes, *supra* note 85, p. 122.

[90] Award, para. 131.

In sum, the tribunal had not discharged its duties under Article 9 of Annex VII to determine whether the claim was well founded in fact and law.

All Things Considered

It is noted that non-participation in international arbitration cases occurred at an alarming rate.[91] In this chapter, this article proceeds to dig out the underlying reason of non-participation in this case, and also manages to figure out the cause of the troubled water and its prospective view.

Retroactive Application and Undermined Equity Principle

In an analogous case *Mondev Int'l v. United States*,[92] the tribunal addressed that a treaty entering into force does not provide a justification for the treaty's retroactive application to the conduct in question.[93] Therefore, it is not justifiable for the Convention to be retroactively applied to the current arbitration.

That fact that the South China Sea bears the proper name of "China" is in itself indicative of the paramount historical influence of that state in the region.[94] It reflected the historic facts that there is continuous management by the superpower with a gigantic momentum that no other surrounding states could match in this area. Based on these facts, China confidently declared that it has indisputable sovereignty over the islands and its adjacent water in the South China Sea.[95] Indeed, the mainland China's historic right is representing its long-held power existing in this semi-enclosed sea.

---

[91] Fry, *supra* note 3, at 72 (indicating cases like Nuclear Tests case, Qatar v. Bahrain case, and Wall advisory opinion, all happened within the course of a decade).

[92] Mondev Int'l v. United States (NAFTA Ch. 11 Arb. Trib. October 11, 2002).

[93] *Id.* (Among the grounds for the U.S. challenge of the claim was that acts or omissions occurring before 1994 (when NAFTA entered into force) cannot breach a NAFTA obligation.); Sean D. Murphy, *Contemporary Practice Of The United States Relating To International Law: Retroactive Application of Treaty to Treaty-Based Claim*, 97 A.J.I.L. 437, 438 (2003).

[94] Joyner, *supra* note 51, p. 838.

[95] Award, para. 209.

Precedents show that historic interest is one of the considerations to delimitation.[96] And, historical factors are important regarding sea boundary delimitation, which can be found in agreements between Canada and France, India and Sri Lanka, East Germany and West Germany, United States and USSR,[97] Minquiers and Ecrehos Case,[98] Honduras–Nicaragua Boundary Dispute,[99] Grisbadarna Case,[100] and Right of Passage over Indian Territory case.[101] Scholars suggested that historical interest also applied to territorial sea, continental shelf, and EEZ,[102] based on various derivatives of historic factors, e.g. historic consolidation of title,[103] historic title,[104] and historical practice.[105]

After the establishment of UNCLOS in 1982, the notion that proof of historical title today would carry sufficient legal weight to validate acquisition of territory had been seriously ignored,[106] the framework of historic rights were entailed.[107] The 1000-year-old historic

---

[96] Fu, *supra* note 53, p. 44.

[97] Fu, *supra* note 95, pp. 14, 64, 88, 124, 152.

[98] Fu, *supra* note 53, p. 20.

[99] Fu, *supra* note 53, p. 21.

[100] *Id.*, at 581; Fu, *supra* note 95, p. 9.

[101] Fu, *supra* note 53, p. 21.

[102] Fu, *supra* note 95, p. 145.

[103] Kimberly C. Gordy, Note: *Dire Straits: The Necessity For Canadian Sovereignty In The Arctic Waterways*, 20 *Fordham Envt. Law Rev.* (2010), pp. 551, 554 (Canada reinforce its claim by arguing sovereignty in Arctic under historic consolidation of title); M. Perry, *Rights of Passage: Canadian Sovereignty and International Law in the Arctic*, 74 U. Det. Mercy L. Rev. (1997), pp. 657, 667 (Dissimilar to the doctrine of historic title, where history of usage forms the sole basis for a sovereignty claim, historic consolidation uses history as a subsidiary basis for other factors from which title is accumulated).

[104] Marta Kolcz-Ryan, Comment: *An Arctic Race: How the United States' Failure to Ratify the Law of the Sea Convention Could Adversely Affect Its Interests in the Arctic*, 35 Dayton L. Rev. (2009), pp. 149, 154 (Canada claims that the Arctic waters of the Northern Passage constitute internal waters under historic title).

[105] Stephanie Holmes, Comment: Breaking the Ice: Emerging Legal Issues in Arctic Sovereignty, *Chi. J. Int'l L.* (2008), 9, pp. 323, 342 (The ICJ acknowledged that history should be a factor in delimiting overlapping continental shelf claims).

[106] Joyner, *supra* note 51, p. 825.

[107] Arbitration award, p. 93.

rights were retroactively diminished in an instant without being equitably considered by a merely 25-year-old UNCLOS. Mainland China's historic rights had not been properly considered.[108]

Discarding of historic right factor is against the equity principle, and scholars had argued that there is a need for delimitation to be based on the equity principle. In fact, the equity principle concept can be traced back to the US President Truman's proclamation, where diplomacy had suggested the equity principle was suitable to replace the rather ambiguous terms such as "historic right."[109] The equity principle shall be applied in this unique case in order to strike a balance between preserving the long-held historic truth of yesterday and developing the South China Sea of tomorrow.

As the preceding text has analyzed mainland China had several reasons to believe that there was no jurisdiction to this case, and it was not obliged to appear before the tribunal. Given that the nine-dash line represent long history of mainland China,[110] which along with the fact that the historic factors cannot be fully justified in the South China Sea Arbitration, its non-participating and non-compliance can be foreseen.

Cause of the Troubled Water and Its Prospective View

In recognizing the "long range world-wide need for new resources of petroleum and other materials." President Truman issued a proclamation in 1945 to claim jurisdiction over "the natural resources of the subsoil and sea shelf beneath the high seas but contiguous to the coasts of the United States." And, it enacted the Outer Continental Shelf Lands Act of 1953 (OCSLA) which did not limit the extent of the U.S. continental shelf in miles but claimed all subsoil and seabed to deep seabed. At least 20 nations followed President Truman's proclamation, making similar claims regarding the extent of their continental shelves, which eventually led to racing for sovereignty by

[108] Award, para. 193, 235–239.

[109] Kuen-Chen Fu, *International Maritime Law – Equitable Principles in the Delimitation* (San-ming Publishing, 1992), pp. 33, 57.

[110] Award, para. 177; *Ibid.*, at 201–210.

carrying out the so-called "Ocean Enclosure," which escalated the risk of conflicts.[111]

Thereafter, maritime disputes occurred in many places of the world, including the South China Sea, because of increasing overlapping entitlements. Unlike the domestic dispute, international dispute are not easily resolved. The national interests always hold the higher priority when countries deal with these international events. For example, the issue of sovereignty remains at the core of Antarctic politics[112]; Canada said that sovereignty in the Arctic is a non-negotiable priority.[113] Also, countries were reluctant to join the international agreement if they found said agreement would jeopardize their national interests. For instance, the US did not sign UNCLOS with the inclusion of Article 76, because her sovereignty in the Arctic would be undermined due to the claims by states for an extended continental shelf.[114] Further, the United States was the first nation to deviate from the freedom of the seas doctrine.[115]

Even though countries had reached agreements, international disputes were hardly satisfactorily resolved by enforcing international agreements, judgments, and/or arbitration award, because the member states may not comply with these legal results if they find the enforcement would jeopardize their national interests. Therefore, international conflicts are mainly resolved by unspoken rules driven

---

[111] Marjorie Ellen Gallagher, Note & Comment: *The Time Is Now: The United States Needs To Accede To The United Nations Convention On The Law Of The Sea To Exert Influence Over The Competing Claims In The South China Sea*, 28 Temp. Int'l & Comp. L.J. (2014), pp. 1, 3.

[112] S. Naidu, Jr., Note: *Claiming the Last Global Frontier: Overlapping Geographical Claims of Antarctic Territory*, 17 Transnat'l L. & Contemp. Probs. (2008), p. 529; Oran R. Young, Book Review and Note: *Creating Regimes: Arctic Accords and International Governance*, 95 A.J.I.L. (2001), p. 481.

[113] *Ibid.*, p. 176.

[114] Melissa Renee Pegna, *U.S. Arctic Policy: The Need to Ratify a Modified UNCLOS and Secure a Military Presence in the Arctic*, 44 J. Mar. L. & Com. (2013), pp. 169, 186–187.

[115] Kolcz-Ryan, *supra* note 104, pp. 157–158.

by politic muscles. Reviewing the history, there were declaration cases such as the 2013 Legal Consequences of the Construction of a Wall in the Occupied Palestinian Territory (the Wall Advisory Opinion). It was opined that the wall involved a political, not a legal, matter that should be "negotiated between the two parties."[116]

The further cooperation of gas exploitation between mainland China and Philippines in South China Sea after the arbitration, ironical situations can be found by viewing further cooperation of gas exploitation between mainland China and Philippines in South China Sea after the arbitration, and the arbitration had appeared to be a lame duck.

It is noted that Taiwan had declared the South China Sea sovereignty by first illustrating the 11-dash line in order to react to the "Ocean Disclosure" proximately caused by President Truman's proclamation. The nine-dash line was indeed to the successor of and thereby modified from the 11-dash line, and further became one of the major issues in this arbitration. However, Taiwan was never considered as a party in this arbitration, not even mentioned as an indispensable third party.[117] The title "Taiwan authority of China" used by the tribunal suggested that it was treated as a non-extent entity in the arbitration.

According to the aforementioned analysis, however, mainland China should appreciate that the absence of the indispensable third-party Taiwan had rendered this arbitration award invalid. And more importantly, had this indispensable third party appeared before the tribunal, mainland China would have had a more favorable position in this case.

On the other hand, self-restrained by ideology framework, the Tsai administration of Taiwan government had ceased to cooperate with mainland China, and instead pursue for "New South Bound" policy seeking to explore markets in these Southeast Asian countries.

---

[116] Fry, *supra* note 3, p. 52 (Legal Consequences of the Construction of a Wall in the Occupied Palestinian Territory).

[117] Award, para. 157.

Ironically, it has little room to maneuver under the "One China Policy."

In consideration of maintaining the common Chinese heritage, maintaining a hostile attitude to each other by both Taiwan and mainland China is simply unnecessary. Scholars had suggested that it could be a chance for governments of both sides of Taiwan Strait to consider cooperation in this matter.[118]

Conclusion

The aforementioned analysis had shown that this arbitral tribunal did not have the jurisdiction because there is a failure to satisfy precondition of jurisdiction; there are events falling within the exceptions of jurisdiction, and it advances position in parties' dispute over sovereignty. Also, the claim is not well founded in fact and law because there are insufficient facts due to absence of an indispensable third party; there is a failure for correctly interpreting the status of Taiping Island and the historic right; and it is not self-satisfactory due to inappropriate standard of proof.

In sum, the tribunal had not discharged its duties under Article 9 of Annex VII upon issues of whether it had jurisdiction over the dispute and whether the claim was well founded in fact and law. Therefore, it is not valid, and it can neither have any precedential value nor create any binding force.

Thus, the nine-dash line represents the long history of management in South China Sea by China. However, in this arbitration, the nine-dash line had not been properly interpreted, and the retroactive application had been rendered without being equitably considered. Therefore, mainland China's non-participation can be foreseen, and it would be less likely to comply with this invalid and unbinding arbitral award.

---

[118] Robert Beckman, *Agora: The South China Sea: The UN Convention on the Law of The Sea and The Maritime Disputes in the South China Sea*, 107 A.J.I.L. (2013), pp. 142, 162–163; see Joyner, *supra* note 51.

This arbitration indicates that Taiwan is of vital importance to mainland China, because lack of direct evidences is, *inter alia*, one of the major reasons where the tribunal failed to self-satisfy its duty. This article points out that had these direct evidences relating to Taiping Island been provided by the indispensable third-party Taiwan to the tribunal, mainland China would have had a more favorable position in this case.

It may be the time for governments on both sides of Taiwan Strait to consider cooperation for establishing the stability of the South China Sea.